Pearl Harbor Survivors

Pearl Harbor Survivors

An Oral History of 24 Servicemen

HARRY SPILLER

McFarland & Company, Inc., Publishers
Jefferson, North Carolina, and London

ALSO BY HARRY SPILLER
FROM MCFARLAND

American POWs in Korea:
Sixteen Personal Accounts (1998)

Prisoners of Nazis: Accounts by American
POWs in World War II (1998)

Frontispiece: The capsized USS *Utah,* and the USS *Raleigh* in the background, after the Japanese attack on Pearl Harbor, December 7, 1941.

Library of Congress Cataloguing-in-Publication Data

Spiller, Harry, 1945–
    Pearl Harbor survivors : an oral history of 24 servicemen / Harry Spiller.
      p.   cm.
    Includes index.

    ISBN-13: 978-0-7864-1179-5
    (softcover binding : 50# alkaline paper)

    1. Pearl Harbor (Hawaii), Attack on, 1941— Personal narratives.
2. World War, 1939–1945 — Personal narratives, American.   3. United
States— Armed Forces— Biography.   4. Oral history — United States.
I. Title.
D767.92.S65   2002
940.54'26 — dc21   2001051315

British Library cataloguing data are available

Cover photograph: ©2001 Corbis Images

Manufactured in the United States of America

McFarland & Company, Inc., Publishers
  Box 611, Jefferson, North Carolina 28640
  www.mcfarlandpub.com

To all of those who
were on Oahu, Hawaii,
on December 7, 1941,
and their families.

Contents

Contents

Introduction

At 7:55 on Sunday morning, December 7, 1941, a date that will live in infamy, the Japanese naval and air forces suddenly attacked United States military installations of the Marines, the Army, the Navy, the Coast Guard and the U.S. Pacific Fleet at Pearl Harbor.

The attack lasted nearly two hours with two separate waves of planes. By the time it was over, approximately 2,400 men were killed and another 1,500 wounded.

The Japanese concentrated their attack on the seventh fleet at Pearl, and because of this the action is most often referred to as the Pearl Harbor attack. This designation has sometimes overshadowed the fact that all stations suffered casualties and severe damage; there was great anguish among the soldiers of the forts and the airmen of the Army, Navy, and Marine Corps, many of whom committed acts of heroism during the sweeping Japanese assault.

Those who were there that day will never forget. Others will remember the news and the shock and disbelief that they experienced when they received the news.

To get a true picture of what it was like to be suddenly running for your life in a rain of .50 caliber rounds from a Japanese Zero, to watch helplessly as battleships were sunk, airfields destroyed, barracks levelled, to be trapped inside a dark ship that was slowly capsizing, or to swim through burning oil — one needs to walk in the footsteps of men who lived through the attack on Oahu.

Aerial shot of fleet anchored in Pearl Harbor, altitude 4,000', looking northwest.

This book contains 24 personal accounts of men who on Sunday morning, December 7, 1941, suffered the attack by the Japanese forces. The stories run the gamut from men at Kaneohe Air Station and Hickam Field, to an officer, one of only a handful of men, who escaped the USS *Oklahoma* after she capsized, and to men of the USS *Nevada*, the only battleship which got underway during the attack to Schofield barracks. It should be understood that there are accounts of experiences and the scenes of action witnessed and reported from more than one point — naturally, these are different versions of the same events. The credibility of the persons reporting and the facts reported has been found unimpeachable. I chose these stories because they are original reflections from survivors of the Pearl Harbor attack.

I was born in 1945, just before the end of the war, and grew up hearing stories and watching movies about World War II. This era has continued to fascinate me and is the inspiration for writing this book. The information for it came from interviews with Pearl Harbor survivors, personal documents of Pearl Harbor survivors, military records from the National Archives in Washington, D.C., the National Headquarters of the

Pearl Harbor Association, the U.S. Department of the Navy in Washington, D.C., and from another book on Pearl Harbor survivors published by Turner in 1992.

The stories in this book are real, they are compelling, and they give a true picture of the December 7, 1941, attack on Oahu, Hawaii, by the Japanese Empire. I would like to thank Robin Greenlee, Kathy Young, and the men who were willing to share their experiences of the Day of Infamy.

Chapter 1

The Attack

EARLY MORNING, DECEMBER 7

At 3:42 A.M., the minesweeper *Condor* (AMC–14), on a sweeping station about a mile and a half from the entrance of Pearl Harbor, spotted an object off the port bow. The officer of the deck called the quartermaster and asked what he thought it was. The quartermaster studied the object through binoculars and agreed with the officer of the deck that it was a periscope. There were no submarines supposed to be in the area, so the Channel Entrance Patrol considered this a serious problem.

At 0357, the *Condor* sent a message by yardarm blinker to the destroyer USS *Ward* (DD–139) saying, "Sighted submarine on westerly course, speed 9 knots."

The USS *Ward* was cruising at 15 knots, patrolling a two-mile square just off the entrance to Pearl Harbor. The captain of the *Ward*, aware of the critical relationship between the United States and Japan, ordered general quarters and asked the *Condor* for the submarine's course and speed. The response was the last sighting, at 0350: the submarine was headed for the harbor entrance.

The *Ward* began a sonar search but did not make contact, and at 0435 secured general quarters.

The USS *Antares* (AKS–3), a stores and supply ship, with a lighter in tow, moved slowly toward Pearl Harbor. Her captain, Commander C.

Grannis, waited for a tug and a harbor pilot to bring *Antares* to her berth in Pearl Harbor.

At 0630, the captain spotted an object about 1,500 yards on the starboard side. The object did not resemble any submarine that he had ever seen, but its conning tower was above the surface indicating that it was a submarine of some kind. The submarine appeared to be having depth control problems.

The *Ward* was notified of the sighting and once again general quarters were sounded at 0640. The *Ward* set all engines full speed ahead and started toward the submarine. The *Ward* opened fire and missed with the first shot, but the second hit right at the waterline and the conning tower. The submarine quickly slowed and sank. The *Ward* passed over and dropped a depth charge set at 100 feet.

The captain of the *Ward* immediately contacted the 14th Naval District watch officer and made the following report. "We have dropped depth charges upon a submarine operating in the Defensive Sea Area." After thinking for a moment, he concluded that he should be more precise and sent a second message. "We have attacked, fired upon and dropped depth charges upon a submarine operating in the Defensive Sea Area." A Bishop Point radio station logged the message at 0653, one hour and two minutes before the Pearl Harbor attack.

The Coast Guard cutter *Tiger* (WSC–152), a sub chaser, was on station and patrolling an area between Barbers Point and Diamond Head in Mamalo Bay. Her assignment area was south of the *Ward*.

At 0400, the *Tiger*'s midwatch had just been relieved when the vessel received the news that the USS *Ward* had sunk a submarine in the harbor area.

As the *Tiger* reached the south shoreline, she picked up a contact on sonar and began tracking. The first assumption was that the contact was a whale, but this was disregarded when motor noises were picked up. It was definitely a submarine, and it was headed for the mouth of Pearl Harbor. The *Tiger* lost contact but continued to the open harbor. Just as she entered, the air attack by the Japanese began. The *Tiger* turned and headed full speed out of the harbor. Nonetheless, she was a target and took many strafings.

Army Radar

At 0530, Admiral Chuichi Nagumo of the Imperial Japanese Navy (IJN), First Fleet Commander, and his 33-ship strike force arrived at a point 200 miles north of the island of Oahu, Hawaii.

Admiral Nagumo made the maneuver signals, turned the ships into the wind, increased speed, and commenced to launch aircraft. These aircraft, the first attack planes, were launched at 0600.

The U.S. Army's five radar sites were at Opana, Kaawa, Kawailos, Koko Head, and the backup station at Fort Shafter. Opana radar was located near Kahuku Point on the northern tip of Oahu at 230 feet above sea level and was considered the best site.

At 0400, Privates Joseph L. Lockard and George E. Elliott were on duty at Opana. At 0700, Lockard began to shut the unit down because it was the end of their morning's scheduled work.

Suddenly the oscilloscope picked up an image that appeared at five degrees northeast of azimuth at 132 miles.

Elliott plotted the information and called it in to the Information Center at Fort Shafter, several miles east of Pearl Harbor and about 30 miles south of the Opana Station. Lieutenant Kermit Tyler recorded the information: he had temporarily been assigned as the controller of ordering aircraft for intercept.

Neither the permanent controller nor the aircraft identification officer was on hand. The lieutenant listened to Lockard's report that it was the biggest sighting he had ever seen.

The lieutenant remembered, listening to the radio at 0400, that a bomber pilot friend had told him that the radio station would stay on all night when B–17s came to Hawaii from the mainland, because it was a resource for navigation. The planes were coming in from the right direction, and for security reasons Tyler could not explain his belief about them being U.S. bombers to the Opana radar station, so he simply told Lockard and Elliott not to worry about it.

Opana's scope at 0720 showed the craft bearing three degrees and 74 miles away. Opana continued to observe until 0739 when the blips disappeared.

Not once had Lieutenant Tyler considered the blips to be enemy aircraft. In fact, they were the 183 planes of the first wave attack by the Japanese Empire.

JAPANESE BATTLE ORDER

Carrier Striking Task Force Operations Order No. 1
23 November 1941
To: Carrier Striking Force

1. The Carrier Striking Force will proceed to the Hawaiian Area with

utmost secrecy and, at the outbreak of war, will launch a resolute surprise attack on and deal a fatal blow to the enemy fleet in the Hawaiian Area. The initial air attack is scheduled at 0330 hours, X Day. Upon completion of the air attacks, the Task Force will immediately withdraw and return to Japan and, after taking on new supplies, take its position for Second Period Operations. In the event that, during this operation, an enemy fleet attempts to intercept our force or a powerful enemy force is encountered and there is a danger of attack, the Task Force will launch a counterattack.

2. The disposition of Force will be as shown on Chart 1.

3. The Operation of Each Force.

a. General

While exercising strict antiaircraft and antisubmarine measures and making every effort to conceal its position and movements, the entire force (except the Midway Bombardment Unit) in accordance with special orders will depart as a group from Hitokappu Bay at a speed of 12–14 knots. The force refueling en route when ever possible will arrive at the standby point (42 N, 165 W). In the event bad weather prevents refueling en route to the standby point, the screening unit will be ordered to return to the home base. Subsequent to the issuance of the order designating X Day (the day of the outbreak of hostilities), the force will proceed to the approaching point (32 N, 157 W).

Around 0700, X-1 Day the Task Force will turn southward at high speed (approximately 24 knots) from the vicinity of the approaching point. It will arrive at the take-off point (200 nautical miles north of the enemy fleet anchorage) at 0100 hours X-Day (0530 Honolulu time) and commit the entire air strength to attack the enemy fleet and important airfield on Oahu.

Upon completion of the air attacks, the Task Force will assemble the aircraft, skirt 800 nautical miles north of Midway, return about X+15 Day to the western part of the Inland Sea via the assembly point (30 N, 165 E) and prepare for Second Period Operations. In the event of a fuel shortage the Task Force will proceed to Truk via the assembly point.

The force may skirt Midway in the event that consideration of an enemy counterattack is unnecessary due to successful air attacks or if such action is necessitated by fuel shortage.

In this event, the fifth Carrier Division with the support of the Kirishima from the third Battleship Division will leave the Task Force on the night of X Day or the early morning of X+1 Day and carry out air attacks on Midway in the early morning of X+2 Day.

If a powerful enemy force intercepts our return route, the Task Force will break through the Hawaiian Islands area southward and proceed to the Marshall Islands.

b. Patrol unit

The patrol unit will accompany the main force. In the event the screening unit is returned to the home base, the patrol unit will screen the advance of the main force and the launching and the landing of aircraft. After the air attack, the patrol unit will station itself between the flank of the main force and the enemy. In the event of an enemy fleet sortie, the patrol unit will shadow the enemy and in a favorable situation attack him. The Midway Bombardment Unit will depart from Tokyo Bay around X–6 Day and, after refueling, secretly approach Midway. It will arrive on the night of X Day and shell the air base. The unit will then arrive and, after refueling, return to the western part of the Inland Sea. The oiler Shiriya will accompany the bombardment unit on this mission and will be responsible for the refueling operation.

d. Supply Force

The supply force will accompany the main force to the approaching point, carrying out refuelings, separate from the main force, skirt 800 nautical miles north of Midway, return to the assembly point by 0800 hours, X+6 Day, and stand by.

4. The Task Force may suspend operations en route to the Hawaiian area and return to Hitokappu, Hokkaido or Mutsu Bay, depending upon the situation.

Commander, Carrier Striking Task Force
Nagumo, Chuichi

Japanese First Wave Attack

At 0600 the Japanese launched the first wave of planes for the attack on Pearl Harbor. The first wave of 183 planes included 40 torpedo bombers, 49 level bombers, 51 dive bombers, and 43 fighters.

The Japanese, on the first wave, passed over Lahuku Point and paralleled the west shore where they divided into three groups at about Haleiwa Field. At a point somewhat off Lihilahi Point, as he swung around

The Naval Air Station at Pearl Harbor during the Japanese aerial attack. This is the explosion of the U.S.S. Arizona.

Barbers Point, Fushida gave a signal for the attack at 0753 when he sang out "*To! To! To!*" (Attack! Attack! Attack!). At 0755, Fushida sent another message, "*Tora! Tora! Tora!*" (Tiger! Tiger! Tiger!) to signify that complete surprise against the enemy had been achieved.

The level bombers and dive bombers along with the fighters attacked Wheeler Field, Kaneohe Naval Air Station, and Schofield Barracks, as well as the Naval Air Station at Ford Island and Hickam Field.

The torpedo bombers came straight into Pearl Harbor from a point near Haleiwa Field. When they were passing over the Marine Corps Air Station at Ewa Field, the planes split up into two groups of eight planes each and headed for the west side of Pearl Harbor. A second group of 24 torpedo planes flew south; ten swung north and northwestward in a large arc over Hickam Field and headed for Battleship Row.

The Second Wave

The second wave of 170 planes was launched at 0715. It comprised 54 level bombers, 80 dive bombers, and 36 fighters. The second wave came over Oahu at approximately 0845 from the north and divided into four groups, with the fighters going directly to Wheeler Field and the Naval Air Station at Kaneohe and then on to Pearl Harbor.

The dive bombers went directly to Pearl Harbor and Hickam Field. The horizontal bombers circled over Bellows Field and Koko Head to the southeast and in a long sweep to the northwest, crossed over Diamond Head, and turned north to Hickam Field.

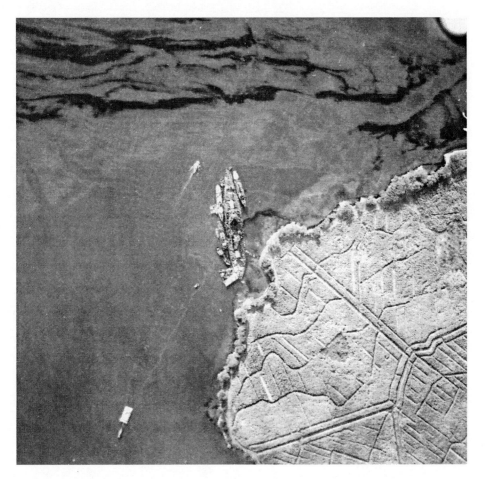

Ships at Pearl Harbor following the Japanese attack. Altitude 3,000'. USS Nevada *off Waipahu Point.*

*Ships at Pearl Harbor following the Japanese attack. Altitude 3,000'. Ships left to right:
USS Maryland; USS Oklahoma, capsized; USS Tennessee, inboard; USS West Virginia; and USS Arizona.*

At 9:45 A.M., the attack was over. In less than two hours the Japanese
had sunk or seriously damaged eight battleships, three light cruisers, three
destroyers, three small vessels, and 188 aircraft. Approximately 2,400 servicemen and 68 civilians were killed and another 1,178 wounded.

POINTS OF INTEREST

Interesting Facts

1. The Japanese attacked only the ships at Pearl Harbor Naval Base and airplanes at Hickam Airfield, leaving the surrounding areas such as repair facilities, the submarine base, and fuel oil storage areas unharmed.

2. The United States aircraft carriers, the primary target of the attack, were not at the base at the time. Because of this, the Japanese cancelled a planned second attack.

3. The United States declared war on Japan the next day, December 8, 1941, as FDR gave his famous "Day of Infamy" speech to Congress.

4. There is a conspiracy theory that FDR provoked the Japanese attack in order to sway American opinion and make it possible for the United States to enter the war.

Sneak Attack

The attack on Pearl Harbor was not intended to be a sneak attack by the Japanese. The last message sent to the Japanese embassy was to break off all diplomatic relations with the United States. The message was to be decoded and delivered to the White House at 1 P.M. on December 7. The Japanese then intended to attack Pearl Harbor. However, the Japanese clerk was a slow typist and simply did not have the message decoded and typed in time to get it to the White House. The attack began before the message arrived and was, for that reason, declared a sneak attack.

Myths of Pearl Harbor

Myths— The U.S. carriers were quickly moved from Pearl Harbor just before the attack to save them for the war that FDR already knew would be dominated by the flattop.

Fact— The two carriers operating out of Pearl were the *Enterprise* and the *Lexington*. Both were on missions to deliver additional fighters to Wake and Midway islands.

Myth— Pearl Harbor was not sent an urgent message on the morning of December 7 so the fleet would not be alerted. Variations include using commercial telegraph instead of military radio to transmit the message, in order to delay its arrival.

Fact— Atmospheric conditions prevented radio communications between Washington, D.C., and Pearl Harbor. That is the reason for the choice to use commercial telegraph.

Japanese Casualties

On December 7, 1941, the Japanese engaged in the attack with a force of 31 ships and 353 planes. They sustained 64 killed, 29 planes destroyed, five minisubmarines sunk, and 74 planes damaged. The number of wounded is unknown.

Chapter 2

USS *Maryland* (BB–46)

The USS *Maryland* was built at Newport News, Virginia, and commissioned in July 1921. A 32,600-ton Colorado class battleship, she participated in notable cruises to Rio de Janeiro in the summer of 1922 to participate in Brazil's Centennial Exposition, the U.S. Fleet's transpacific voyage in 1925, and President-elect Herbert Hoover's 1928 goodwill tour of Latin America.

Originally the *Maryland* was based at Long Beach, California, but she was transferred to Pearl Harbor, Hawaii, in 1940. She was moored at Battleship Row when the Japanese attacked on December 7, 1941, but unlike most of the other battleships, she received relatively minor damage. After she was repaired in 1942, the *Maryland* was sent later in the year to the South Pacific. She took part in the operations at the Gilbert and Marshall Islands in late 1943 and 1944, bombarding Tarawa and Kwajalein with her 16-inch guns.

In June 1944, she participated in the preinvasion against Saipan. During the battle she was torpedoed by a Japanese plane and had to return to Pearl Harbor for repairs. The *Maryland* returned to the South Pacific in September 1944, where she participated in the Palau operation. In October she participated in the Leyte invasion and not only bombarded enemy positions ashore, but engaged with Japanese warships at the Battle of Surigao Strait. In November she was once again damaged by a kamikaze or suicide plane.

Starboard broadside view of the USS Maryland.

The *Maryland* was repaired in time to participate in the Okinawa operation in March and April 1945, but was once again hit by enemy fire on April 7. She remained in action for another week and then went to the West Coast for overhaul. The overhaul was completed in August 1945, but by that time the war had ended. She spent several months transporting servicemen home from the mid–Pacific and was then sent to Bremerton, Washington, for deactivation. The USS *Maryland* was decommissioned in 1947 and remained in mothballs until July 1959, when she was sold for scrapping.

PFC OREN W. WRIGHT
U.S. Marine Corps, Seventh Division, USS Maryland

I enlisted in the U.S. Marine Corps in September 1940 in Ellensburg, Washington, and was sent to San Diego, California, for boot camp. I requested Sea School and after completion was transferred to Bremerton, Washington, aboard the carrier USS *Enterprise*. I went aboard the USS

Maryland December 6, 1940, then in dry dock.

The *Maryland* then sailed to Long Beach, California, for a training period, then to Pearl Harbor, Territory of Hawaii.

The *Maryland*, after some fleet exercises, sailed to Bremerton, Washington, where torpedo blasters were installed and new mess facilities were installed. We lost our family style dining, which was a major loss.

The Marines were in the 7th Division and were assigned four 5.51 inch broadside guns, port and starboard and some 20 mm. antiaircraft.

On December 7, 1941, I was on the Marine Corps Guard, standing by for colors. At 0755 we saw the first Japanese planes coming up. We were strafed by one of the first planes. He was so low he had to swing around the rear mast. The Marine bugler blew general quarters, after the officer of deck said to sound fire and rescue.

PFC Oren W. Wright, U.S. Marine Corps, Seventh Division, USS Maryland.

We Marines went to battle stations; mine was on the port side. I was on the phone asking for ammo. While doing that I saw the *Oklahoma* turn over. I then went to port 1.1 machine gun up by the Admiral's cabin. This weapon's main function was jamming; a gunner's mate lay under it to clear the jams, but finally gave up.

I don't remember all I did after that. I do remember being on the galley deck helping pass the 5.25 antiaircraft ammo. The chaplain was alongside with other personnel.

The *Tennessee* and *West Virginia* were aft of us and badly burning. I went to the end of the quarterdeck and helped a sailor keep the burning oil from the *Maryland*.

When the attack finally ended and for some time after that, I do not recall all that happened. Later we were on the 1.1 gun again for that night. Some Navy planes came down the channel and did not identify, so we opened up. A pilot said later, every inch of the sky had a bullet in it.

The *Maryland* was moved out of the box we were in and we were on the way to Bremerton, Washington, for repairs to the bomb damage on the bow.

We had just finished Christmas dinner when the storm hit. Our classmates' canvas cover over the guns blew off very quickly. All the classmates had about 2 feet of water and all hatches below the galley deck were sealed, so the Marines and sailors, to get warm, had to go to the vents around the stacks. I don't recall much of anything to eat for three days.

The waves were so big, when we were at the bottom of the swell, all we could see of the other battleship was the top of the mast. I generally was seasick in rough weather; this time I never felt anything except cold and wet.

At Bremerton we went under repair and remodel. Then to San Francisco for some time; we returned to Pearl Harbor for more exercises.

In November 1942, I went to the field hospital in Pearl Harbor for a knee operation and did not return to the ship.

I was transferred to Camp Elliott, California, then to North Carolina, then to Guada where the 6th Marine Division was formed and I was in Co F, 2nd Bn, 29th Marines. The 6th Division invaded Okinawa on April 1, 1945. I was in the second wave and we were point for the Division F Co. and 2nd Bn. On the Sugar Loaf Hill we were nearly wiped out. On June 19, 1945, I was hit by a grenade and shot through the head. I was later discharged in Bremerton, in November 1945. Since then I have been street and sewer superintendent and surveyor in Iran, Algeria, Saudi Arabia, South Vietnam, Zaire, and Bolivia.

Chapter 3

USS *Tennessee*

The fifth USS *Tennessee* was commissioned on June 3, 1920. The 31,190-ton vessel was sponsored by Miss Helen Roberts, the daughter of the governor of Tennessee. The new battleship was 624 feet long with a beam of 97 feet 3½ inches, was crewed by 1,401 men, and was armed with 12 14-inch guns, 14 five-inch guns, four three-inch guns, and two 21-inch guns.

The *Tennessee* and her sister ship *California* (BB–44) were the first American battleships built to a post–Jutland hull design. As a result, her underwater protection was much greater than the previous battleships'. Both her main and secondary batteries had fire-control systems. The *Tennessee*'s 14-inch guns could be elevated to 30 degrees, rather than the 15 degrees of earlier battleships, and her heavy guns could reach an additional 10,000 yards.

The *Tennessee* conducted trials in the Long Island Sound in October 1920, and during that time had a mishap when one of her generators blew up. The explosion destroyed the turbine end of the machine and injured two men. After the repairs she went on standard trials and then finally arrived at San Pedro, California, where she was assigned for the next 19 years.

Peacetime requires that battleships maintain a standard of readiness, and each year the *Tennessee* participated in maneuvers. In 1940, Fleet Problem XXI was conducted in Hawaiian waters during the spring. At the end of the exercises President Roosevelt assigned the *Tennessee* to Pearl

USS Tennessee *taken by the USS* Saratoga.

Harbor in hopes that the move might deter the Japanese from further expansion in the Far East.

On the morning of December 7, 1941, the *Tennessee* was moored starboard side to a pair of masonry mooring quays on Battleship Row, a row of deep water berths on the south side of Ford Island. The USS *Virginia* (BB–48) was berthed alongside to port. Just ahead of the *Tennessee* was the USS *Maryland* (BB–46) with USS *Oklahoma* (BB–37) outboard. The USS *Arizona* (BB–39), moored directly astern of the *Tennessee,* was undergoing a period of upkeep from the repair ship USS *Vestal* (Ar–) alongside her. The nests were spaced about 75 feet apart.

When the Japanese attacked, the first bombs fell on Ford Island. The *Tennessee* went to general quarters and closed her watertight doors. She began antiaircraft firing in a few minutes and started to steam up. That did no good, however, because the *Oklahoma* and *West Virginia* took immediate torpedo hits. The *Oklahoma* capsized and sank bottom-up. The *West Virginia* began to list heavily. She counter flooded and righted herself, but settled on the bottom. The *Tennessee,* still firing her guns, took hits and continued to fight back.

Japanese dive bombers were dropping battleship-caliber projectiles modified to serve as armor-piercing bombs. Several bombs struck the *Arizona* exploding magazines full of black powder. The fuel oil from the *Arizona* and *West Virginia* soon ignited and the *Tennessee* was surrounded by fire. The Japanese hit the *Tennessee* with some armor-piercing bombs doing extensive damage. One of the fragments killed the captain of the *West Virginia* who had just stepped out on the star wing of the ship's bridge.

By the evening of December 7, 1941, the worst was over. Oil was still blazing around the *Arizona* and *West Virginia* and continued to threaten the *Tennessee* for two more days while she was still trapped in her berth by surrounded sunken ships. Although her bridge and foremast had been damaged by bomb splinters, her machinery was in full commission and no serious damage had been done to ship or gunnery controls.

The *Tennessee* was finally moved out of the berth on December 16, 1941, and moored at Pearl Harbor Navy Yard. On December 20, 1941, along with the USS *Pennsylvania* and the USS *Maryland*, she departed for the United States. She arrived there on December 29, 1941.

The *Tennessee*, one of the old battleships, was unable to keep up with the carriers and was stationed in the United States until 1943. Although she was slow, she still had heavy turret guns and could still hit as hard as ever. In August 1943, she bombarded Kiska Island. The next morning, when U.S. troops landed, they found that the Japanese had already evacuated the island.

Soon after, the USS *Tennessee* returned to San Francisco.

SIGNALMAN 2C RICHARD E. BURGE
U.S. Navy, USS Tennessee

BEFORE THE WAR — 1940

In late 1940, Richard E. Burge and several of his classmates who were attending Dayton High School in Texas decided to join the Navy. Upon graduation, they made a trip to Houston, Texas, where the youngsters went through the enlistment process. After attending training at San Diego, California, Richard was assigned to the battleship BB–43, USS *Tennessee*.

Two weeks prior to the attack on Pearl Harbor, the USS *Tennessee* and other ships at Pearl had been at sea competing against each other in battle preparation. The *Tennessee* had had the record in gunnery, and had just won it again. It was rewarding for Richard and the crew because each member was awarded a $10.00 prize. This was a real bonus for Richard who

Richard E. Burge, Signalman 2C USS Ten-
nessee, witnessed the attack on Pearl Harbor
from the signal bridge of the USS Tennessee. He
witnessed the first two bombs of World War II.

was making only $56.00 a month. The bonus was great, but in just a few days the money would be forgotten and Richard's life would be changed forever. The Japanese were about to attack Pearl Harbor.

RICHARD'S STORY

A big part of the Navy was anchored at Pearl Harbor because it was the time of year of competition among the ships. Seven battleships were tied up in Battleship Row, and the rest of the harbor was filled with cruisers, destroyers, and all of the Navy's other ships. Each ship was in tiptop shape and full of fuel and ammunition awaiting a big Navy inspection.

One of my jobs was repairing rails and anything that required Turks heads, canvas, and varnish. The Admiral had a special chair on the navigation deck. It was made of pipe and finished with canvas covered rails and Turk heads. I worked late Saturday evening December 6th finishing the chair for inspection.

Late Saturday evening, three big aircraft carriers left the harbor loaded with Navy planes. No one knew where they were going, or at least no one would say. My job was on the signal bridge. My battle station was turret #2, with the gun crew. We had a 14 inch gun, and I was shuttle operator on the powder magazine door.

At nearby Kaneoke Naval Air Station seaplanes were stationed to patrol the Islands. On December 6th, I had made arrangements with one of the pilots to go on the 4 A.M. patrol. I failed to get my wake up call, therefore I was still around the next morning.

Richard Burge (right) and three other signalmen one week before the attack.

DECEMBER 7, 1941

I got up around 7 A.M. and ate chow—powdered eggs and beans. Strange as it may seem, I still like beans. I didn't have duty for the day, but went to the signal bridge to relieve someone for chow. I had just reached the bridge at 7:55 A.M. when the bugle sounded colors. Then I heard a plane in a hard dive. I looked up to see what was making all that noise during the changing of the colors. A plane came down out of the clouds and dropped something. I watched it fall on the Naval Air Station, blowing up the hangar and several planes. After that a second plane did the same thing. I didn't know whose planes they were or what was going on. At that moment, one of the planes came down alongside the battleships about 35 or 40 feet out, and started shooting and strafing the bulkhead all around me. The alarm to man your battle stations sounded and those famous words followed, "This is not a drill."

My battle station was the powder magazine for turret #2. I started for it, then all hell broke loose. Torpedoes and bombs were coming from every direction. I thought the end of the world had come. Just as I reached the powder magazine, a bomb hit turret #2, bursting the middle gun and putting the turret out of operation. The bomb shattered and killed the captain on the USS *West Virginia*, which was anchored alongside us. The explosion put the gun out of commission, so they sent us back to the top-side to help with fire fighting and rescuing the men who were thrown overboard from the ships that had sunk. I watched the fleet destroyed right before my eyes. The USS *Arizona* was anchored fifty feet to the stern of our ship. She took several bombs and torpedoes raised up and quickly sank to the bottom of the harbor. The USS *West Virginia* and the USS *Oklahoma* took several torpedoes. The *West Virginia* sank alongside us. The USS *Oklahoma* which was anchored forward of the *West Virginia* capsized completely. The USS *Maryland* anchored forward of us took a bomb and its bow sank.

I helped remove wounded and the dead from turret #2. I remember one sailor trying to talk. His flesh was falling off his face. The smoke from the burning oil fires created by the surrounding ships made it impossible to see, but it didn't stop the Japanese pilots. They came over and strafed us. I lay down on the deck and rolled back under the anchor chain for protection. The machine gun bullets were knocking sparks off the chain just inches from me. I thought my time had come.

Our ship was completely surrounded by burning oil. The officer of the day decided to fire up the engines and move up a little to get away from some of the oil. We were wedged in tight against the Quays and couldn't move. Our propellers sped up and pushed the oil and water away from us allowing us to get out of some of the fire.

The USS *Nevada* got underway and came around all the sunken ships. Then a second wave of Japanese planes came in and ganged up on her. The *Nevada* ran aground just ahead of us. Several other ships were sunk and then the attack was over.

For the rest of the day we rescued sailors from the oily water and picked up bodies and body parts.

That night I had midnight watch. One of the carriers was returning from Guam and sent two fighter planes ahead to return to the harbor. They were supposed to come straight down the harbor and land. The first plane did okay, but the second plane overshot his landing and tried to take off again. All the ships that had guns left opened fire on him. There wasn't enough left to identify.

December 8th

On December 8th, a crew came and pounded a hole in the bottom of the overturned USS *Oklahoma* and rescued 19 men, who had been trapped inside, the day before during the attack. A few days later they came back and pounded a hole close to the stern and rescued another sailor. He was still alive and very happy to be free again.

The USS *Arizona*'s superstructure was out of the water and the range finder that was off the forward mast was opened up and they took the body of a sailor out of it. That was the daily routine. Each morning we went out in liberty boats and picked up bodies and body parts.

One Jap plane was hit and exploded over Ford Island and the pilot landed just fifty feet from the USS *Tennessee*. We left his body in the water for three weeks before we picked it up.

Under Way

We were pinned in by the USS *Arizona* from the stern. The USS *West Virginia* was sunk beside me. The USS *Oklahoma* was capsized alongside the USS *Maryland* and was in front of our ship. We were pressed against the Quays and couldn't move. Ten days after the attack the USS *Maryland* was moved, ... and the Quays dynamited alongside our ship. We were able to move out.

We returned to San Francisco for repairs along with several other ships. Soon we formed a convoy.

The 1942 Battles

Over the next year Richard remained on the USS *Tennessee* which was involved in the Naval Battle of the Coral Sea, Midway, and the bombardment of several islands preparatory to the Marines going ashore. Then in the latter part of 1942, the USS *Tennessee* returned to Bremerton shipyard in Washington for repairs. While there Richard was transferred to the cruiser USS *Bush*.

Richard made several cruises with the USS *Bush* until he developed an infected heart and was hospitalized at Treasure Island. While he was there, the *Bush* went to sea, was attacked by three kamikaze Japanese planes, and was sunk off Okinawa. A few months later, Richard was discharged with permanent heart damage. Today he still remembers seeing the first two bombs that started World War II for the Americans.

Captain Charles Reardon leaving the USS Tennessee *after the Battle of Midway.*

POINTS OF INTEREST

USS West Virginia

The 33,590-ton Battleship USS *West Virginia* (BB–48) was berthed in F–6 on Battleship Row on the morning of December 7, 1941. She had 40 feet of water beneath her keel. The *West Virginia* was hit on her port side by five 18-inch aircraft torpedoes and two 15-inch armor-piercing bombs. The first bomb penetrated the superstructure deck, wrecking the port case mates and causing that deck to collapse to the level of the galley deck below. Four case mates caught fire and the ready service projectiles stowed in the case mates exploded.

The second hit further aft wrecking one Vought OS2U Kingfisher floatplane atop the high catapult on turret #3 and pitching the second one on her top on the main deck below. The projectile penetrated the four-inch turret roof, wrecking one gun turret.

The *West Virginia* was abandoned, settling to the harbor bottom on an even keel. The fires were extinguished by the following day.

The USS West Virginia *and the USS* Tennessee *after the Japanese attack on Pearl Harbor, December 7, 1941.*

During the battle, Captain Mervyn S. Bennion was awarded the Congressional Medal of Honor, and Mess Attendant Second Class Doris Miller was awarded the Navy Cross for his actions when he manned and operated a machine gun and directed fire at the Japanese despite the heavy strafing and bombing by the enemy.

The *West Virginia* rejoined the fleet in 1944.

USS Arizona

On the morning of December 7, 1941, the USS *Arizona*'s raid alarm went off about 0755, and the ship went to general quarters. Shortly after that, as well as can be determined, eight bombs hit the battleship. One hit the forecastle, glancing off the faceplate of turret #2 and penetrating the deck; it exploded in the black powder magazine, and this, in turn, set off other magazines. A cataclysmic explosion ripped through the forward part of the ship, touching off fierce fires that burned for two days.

The USS Arizona, *burning and damaged at Pearl Harbor, December 7, 1941.*

Three men were awarded the Medal of Honor: Commander Samuel G. Fuqua, the ship's damage control officer; posthumously, Rear Admiral Isaac Kidd, the first flag officer to be killed in the Pacific war; and Captain Van Valkenburgh, who reached the bridge and was attempting to counterattack when the fatal blast sank the ship and ended the lives of 1,103 of the 1,400 on board at the time.

The ship still remains at Pearl Harbor. A memorial built to it was dedicated on May 30, 1962. Approximately 1.5 million people visit the memorial each year.

Chapter 4

USS *Nevada* (BB–36)

The second USS *Nevada* (BB–36) was commissioned on March 11, 1916. The 27,500-ton ship was sponsored by Miss Elenor Anne Seibert, the niece of Governor Tasker L. Oddie of Nevada. The 583-foot vessel served on the Atlantic coast, and in August 1918 served with the British Grand Fleet in World War I. By December 1918 she had returned home.

The *Nevada* served with both the Atlantic and Pacific fleets in the period between the wars. In 1925 she participated in the goodwill cruise to Australia and New Zealand. Modernized at Norfolk Naval Shipyard between August 1927 and January 1930, she served in the Pacific Fleet for the next decade.

On December 7, 1941, the *Nevada* was moored singly off Ford Island and had the freedom of maneuver denied to the other eight battleships present during the attack. As her gunners opened fire and she got up steam, she was struck by one torpedo and two or three bombs, but was able to get underway. While attempting to leave harbor she was struck again. Fearing she might sink in the channel, blocking it, she was beached at Hospital Point. Fifty of her crewmen were killed in the attack and another 109 wounded.

In February 1942, the *Nevada* was repaired at Pearl Harbor and Puget Sound Navy Yard, then sailed for Alaska where she provided fire support for the capture of Attu on May 18, 1942. In June she sailed for modernization at Norfolk Navy Yard, and in April 1944 reached British waters to prepare for the Normandy Invasion. In June 1944, her guns pounded not only permanent

Port broadside view of the USS Nevada.

shore defenses on the Cherbourg Peninsula, but ranged as far as 17 miles inland, breaking up German concentrations and counterattacks.

Between August and September, she participated further in the invasion of France providing fire support. The *Nevada* returned to New York, had her guns relined, and sailed for the Pacific. She arrived off Iwo Jima on February 16, 1945, to give the Marines invading the island and fighting on its shores her massive gunfire support through March 7, 1945.

On March 24, 1945, the *Nevada* bombarded Japanese airfields, shore defences, supply dumps, and troop concentrations on Okinawa. She lost 11 men and had a main battery turret damaged when she was hit by a suicide plane on March 27. Another two men were lost from a fire from a shore battery on April 5, 1945.

Returning to Pearl Harbor after a brief occupation duty in Tokyo Bay, she was surveyed and assigned as a target ship for the Bikini atomic experiments. She survived the atom-bomb test in July 1946, returned to Pearl Harbor to be decommissioned on August 29, 1946, and was sunk by gunfire and aerial torpedoes off Hawaii on July 31, 1948.

The *Nevada* received seven battle stars during World War II.

SEAMAN SECOND CLASS CHARLES T. SEHE
U.S. Navy, USS Nevada

ENLISTMENT

Charles enlisted in the U.S. Navy in November 1940 in Geneva, Illinois, at the age of 17. After completing his recruit training at Great Lakes Naval Station in Illinois, he was sent to Bremerton, Washington, where he was assigned to the battleship, USS *Nevada*.

THE PEARL HARBOR ATTACK

At the time of the Japanese attack on Pearl Harbor, December 7, 1941, the USS *Nevada* was at the north end of Battleship Row moored to quay Fox 8 just astern of the battleship USS *Arizona*. Friday afternoon before that fateful Sunday, I went aboard the *Arizona* to visit Charles L. Thompson, a friend from St. Charles, a town near Geneva, Illinois. He requested a loan of one dollar for his liberty to Honolulu, and payment was promised Monday when we were to visit my ship. Tragically, Lee was among the 1,100 shipmates who perished in that fiery explosion aboard the *Arizona*. He even invited me to stay over on the *Arizona* Sunday but I declined because I was to have duty that Sunday on the *Nevada*. About 0730 December 7, 1941, I was eating breakfast with some of my division's shipmates, Bingham, Hubner, Stembrosky, Spear, Kirby, Fugate, and McGee. My division, the 5th, was assigned to the secondary gun battery 5"–51 used in gun casements [casemates]

Charles T. Sehe, USS Nevada *(BB–36), at Norfolk, Virginia, 1944, on his 21st birthday.*

against surface craft. At 0755 most of the *Nevada* crew had finished eating breakfast and the band members and Marine Color Guard were assembling on the main deck aft in preparation for raising the flag. I left the dining room to use the men's head. Moments later the concussions from the first bombs to hit the *Nevada* literally blew me and several other sailors from their seats. I was reading the Sunday comics from the *Honolulu Star Bulletin* at the time. As General Quarters sounded I ran forward to reach my battle station number #4 aft searchlight located high up on the main mast. Remembering the rule up starboard and forward and down [port and aft] was a must for everyone to remember to avoid confusion and delay. Already incoming planes were strafing the exposed deck areas with machine gun bullets and the color guard and band members were scattering for safety. Since the searchlights were not utilized during the daylight hours, all I could do was watch the terrible, alarming, and unbelievable nightmare unfold before my very eyes. Numerous torpedo wakes were already in the water streaking toward the double moored battleships. An aerial torpedo launched from one of the Japanese planes soon struck the *Nevada* on the port side near frame 40 causing the ship to lurch violently upward and shudder with a groaning sound. Our antiaircraft guns started firing.

The *Nevada* seemed to list slightly to the port and the *Nevada,* with some of its boilers already lit on standby, cast off her mooring lines and slowly got underway. Then many of us saw horizontal bombers approaching the row of eight battleships from the south. As the *Nevada* entered the channel, cheers came from the crews of the other ships encouraging us onward. Numerous misses by the bombers were evident by the high fountains of waterspouts appearing in the channel, but now that the Japanese concentrated on the *Nevada,* numerous bombs made their mark and several damaged the forecastle bridge and the boat deck area. As the *Nevada* passed the *Arizona,* one of those horizontal bombers hit their mark dead center because a fiery tremendous explosion ripped the *Arizona* apart, showering the open deck crews of the *Nevada* with hot searing metallic fragments, burning many of my shipmates to death.

As the now burning *Nevada* passed the *Arizona,* ahead lay the battleship *Oklahoma* on her side, capsized from the numerous torpedoes which slammed into her. My God, all along Battleship Row the ships were afire. The Wee Vee, *West Virginia,* outboard to the *Tennessee* had numerous explosions and fire aboard. As the *Nevada* passed by the dry dock, the destroyer *Shaw* moored nearby blew up by a direct hit, showering the *Nevada*'s open decks again with flaming metallic fragments. Our ship was now low in the water and was given orders to beach itself so as to avoid

The USS Nevada *after the Japanese attack on Pearl Harbor.*

blocking the channel to prevent other ships from entering or leaving. Assisted by two tugboats the *Nevada* finally came to a rest at Walpio Point. All of my ship's decks except for the watertight compartment below the second level were filled with floating debris in foul smelling water and mixed with sludge fuel oil.

There were still several fires throughout the open areas of the *Nevada* and, after the fires were put out, we turned our attention to removing the wounded and dead, who were transferred to motor launches which came alongside. My friend Roy Kirby was one of those badly burned from the explosions in the gun casements. I believe that the air attacks were over by 1030 or so and our casualties were 19 dead with over 100 wounded and 17 missing in action. Later I learned that 12 of those who died were from my division and six were at my breakfast table.

Some of us were given new, clean, shined, galvanized buckets to pick up the isolated, fragmented parts of fallen shipmates. In two of the 5th division 5"–51 gun casements were portions of the bulkheads which consisted of cyclone security linked fences. One noticed numerous body parts

USS Nevada *burning in Pearl Harbor, December 7, 1941. Courtesy of Chief Photography Mate H.S. Fawcett.*

which seemed to be strained through these partitions from the force of the explosions. I recall picking up several knee joints, shoulder pieces, and several torn and burned torsos that were unidentifiable because of their blackened and burned condition. The tremendous force of those explosions seemed to have literally strained the soft tissue through the chain-linked fencing, leaving the bony elements behind. I painfully realize now that some of those men listed as missing may well be some of those shipmates whom I spoke with at breakfast just a few moments before the Japanese attack.

Later, after all dead and wounded were accounted for, many of us took a survey of the extensive damage to our ship — forecastle, navigating and signal bridge destroyed.

All of us quickly realized that the *Nevada* gun compartment was inadequate against air attacks. At sea with another ship this would be acceptable but in an air war the *Nevada* was at a definite disadvantage. Our anti-aircraft guns were manually operated and the broadside 5"–51 casemate guns were completely ineffective against enemy aircraft.

THE AFTERMATH

I being a 2nd class seaman was among the 300 skeleton cleaning crew that remained aboard the *Nevada* whereas the other more experienced crew members were transferred to other ships for sea duty. From December thru February we labored during the daylight hours, removing floating debris and floating trash. By using gasoline powered pumps we soon drained the foul water and oil from the lower decks. The harbor water during the first weeks following the air attack was still laced with areas of heavy fuel oil floating on its surface. Following the initial attack that lasted two hours, many sailors suffered severe burns escaping from their ships, only to be covered with burning oil when they jumped into the water.

For three months following the attack many of us carried out debris in buckets, others using acetylene torches cut through damaged sections of the deck. In the evening we were transferred by launches to the mainland and were allowed hot soapy showers to remove the dirty grime and oil from our bodies. Hot meals awaited us at the mess halls and later we were berthed in the block area where sports events had been held earlier.

On February 12, 1942, the *Nevada* was raised and taken to dry dock in Pearl Harbor where temporary repairs were made. In May 1942, we went under our own power to Puget Sound Naval Yard, Bremerton, Washington. Here the *Nevada* underwent extensive repairs, remodeling and became fitted with the latest modern antiaircraft battery weaponry and radar detection apparatus.

I remained aboard the *Nevada* all this time and became a radar operator for one of the ten 5" twin gun mounts guided by the automatic control in our new directions, situated high above the main deck.

LATER ASSIGNMENTS

My later assignments for General Quarters station was as a 20mm gun captain at Utah Beach, Iwo Jima, and Okinawa. Hundreds of Kamikaze planes daily. I was slightly wounded at Okinawa.

A FINAL THOUGHT

The only thing worse than growing old is to be denied the privilege. Here today, I am a very grey-bearded grandfather at 77 years. My dear shipmate James Robert Bingham, Jr., is eternally lying in a grave at Punch Bowl cemetery in Honolulu along with many of the *Nevada* casualties. This once 18-year-old sailor still cannot erase those tragic events witnessed at Pearl Harbor, December 7, 1941, and the Kamikaze attacks on our ships at Iwo Jima and Okinawa. Perhaps in some cases, memories would be left better stowed away. For some veterans like the Marines and infantrymen taking those Pacific islands like Guadalcanal, Tarawa, Peleliu, Iwo, and Okinawa it could be very painful to relive the experiences. I returned to the United States on my birthday February 26, 1946, four years and two months after the Pearl Harbor attack. My best youth years lost.

SEAMAN C/1 WILLIAM ARTHUR RODDA
U.S. Navy, USS Nevada *BB–36*

I was on the USS *Nevada* on December 7, 1941. I was back on the fantail when the colors sounded. The band was playing the *National Anthem.* They did that every Sunday morning. I was saluting colors and started hearing explosions and machine gun fire behind me. I don't know if the guys in the band could see what was going on or not. When they finished, I turned around to see what was going on. A torpedo plane came down and dropped a torpedo. I asked the sailor standing beside me if that guy didn't drop a torpedo and he said it looked like it. We stood there and looked and the plane came over so low we could tell it was the Japs. About that time the torpedo hit. Everybody started running for their battle stations. I thought it hit the *Arizona* but some say a torpedo never hit the *Arizona* so it must have been the *West Virginia.* We went to our battle stations in # 4 turret. When we got inside we hollered down to some guys on the shell deck that the Japs were attacking us and of course they didn't believe us and hollered a few four letter words back. A few moments later the General Alarm sounded and the word came over the loud speaker that this was not a drill. After what I had seen, it was still hard to believe. I was a trainer in # 4 turret. We wanted to look through the sights to see what was going on but they made us get back. After a while we got underway and started out of the harbor. We didn't get very far. The Japs tried to sink us in the channel. The tugboats pushed us up in the shallow water next to the bank. It is now known as Nevada Point.

I don't know what time it was when Hodges, our 1st class boatswain mate, told me to go to the boat deck and fight fire. I went up to the starboard side. When I got to the top of the first ladder there was a Filipino sailor lying on his back. All his arms and legs were broken and bent the wrong way. I stepped over him and, at the top of the next ladder, there was a sailor on his back with a handful of guts sticking out through his t-shirt. After I stepped over him I looked around and there were dead sailors lying everywhere. I got a hose and started putting water on the fire. After a while the water stopped. The tugboat *Huge* was fighting the fire too.

After the Japs left we started carrying the dead back to the fantail. I was on the Quarter Deck when our Captain came aboard. He had an expression on his face you would not believe. This was after the attack was over.

I never knew any of the dead. I would see them every day because the shower was in the stern and they had to go through the 45th division quarters to get there.

Late that afternoon, I guess it was about dark, they took us over to the mess hall on the beach for supper. You could see the men on the bottom of the *Oklahoma* cutting through to get the trapped sailors out.

After we got back to the ship, I went to the shell deck in # 4 turret and lay down. After a while I heard a lot of gunfire. I went back up topside to see if the Japs had come back. It was our own planes from the USS *Enterprise*. They were shot down.

We lost 50 men on our ship. I was 20 and the average age was 19 on the *Nevada*.

What made this so bad is we went from peace to all of the death and destruction in about an hour. I think it took a few days before most of us could believe it really happened. I can write about this, but I still have trouble talking about it to another person. I still think about it every day. While it was going on I thought about what my family would think when they heard about it. They knew I was in the islands.

There were four of us from Sutter there that day. We all made it through the war and we are all good friends today. Sutter only has a population of about 300.

Chapter 5

USS *Oklahoma* (BB–37)

The USS *Oklahoma* was commissioned on May 2, 1916, in Philadelphia. The *Nevada* class 27,500-ton battleship was 583 feet long with a beam of 95 feet 3 inches, and it had a 20.5 knot speed. She was armed with 10 14-inch guns and 20 five-inch guns.

The *Oklahoma* joined the Atlantic Fleet with Norfolk as her homeport. She sailed many times to Europe and twice to South America. In 1921, she was involved in exercises with the Pacific Fleet. She joined the Pacific Fleet around that time and spent six years in it. She cruised with to Australia and New Zealand in 1925 as part of the Battle Fleet. The *Oklahoma* joined the Scout Fleet in early 1927. She continued extensive exercises during the summer's Midshipmen Cruise, voyaging to the East Coast to embark midshipmen, carrying them through the Panama Canal to San Francisco, and returning them by way of Cuba and Haiti.

The *Oklahoma* was modernized at Philadelphia between 1927 and 1929. She then rejoined the Scout Fleet in the Caribbean and returned to the West Coast in June 1930 for fleet operations which lasted through 1936. In July 1936, she sailed to Spain to rescue American citizens and other refugees from the Spanish civil war.

She was based at Pearl Harbor on December 6, 1940, for patrols and exercises. She was moored in Battleship Row when the Japanese attacked on December 7, 1941. Alongside the USS *Maryland*, the *Oklahoma* took

The USS Oklahoma

three torpedoes almost immediately after the attack began. As the ship began to capsize she was hit with two more torpedoes, and the crew was strafed as they abandoned ship. Within 20 minutes of the attack beginning, she had swung over until the mast touched bottom and stopped her; the starboard side was above water.

Many of the crew stayed in the fight after they climbed aboard the USS *Maryland* and returned fire against the Japanese with antiaircraft guns. Twenty officers and 395 enlisted men were killed or missing, 32 others were wounded, and many were trapped within the capsized hull.

In March 1943, the *Oklahoma* was salvaged and entered dry dock on December 28, the same year. She was decommissioned on September 1, 1944. Her guns and superstructure were stripped and sold. On May 17, 1947, she parted her towline and sank 549 miles out, bound for San Francisco from Pearl Harbor.

She received one battle star for her World War II service.

Ensign Adolph D. Mortensen
U.S. Navy, USS Oklahoma

My December 7th story really begins at midnight December 6, 1941, when I reported to the quarter deck at 2345 to relieve the watch. I had been assigned the midwatch as Junior Officer on Deck (JOD) and as was the custom we relieved 15 minutes before the watch was to start. I in turn could look forward to being relieved at 0345, December 7, 1941.

I found myself in the company of Lt. J.G. Bill Ingram then football coach at the Naval Academy, Annapolis. I always enjoyed Lt. Ingram's company. He seemed to me a very professional officer. He was fair, businesslike, and had a good sense of humor. I knew of no one who didn't look up to Bill Ingram. He had also been a football star as midshipman.

The watch was uneventful. A very few sailors had missed the last liberty boat and had straggled in by hitching a ride any way they could, logged in, condition noted, intoxicated, disheveled uniforms, black eyes, split lips, etc., and told to turn in — that they would be dealt with later. They lucked out — or did they?

The watch could be described as being very quiet — close to perfect. It was not cold — no clouds or wind — just clear black starry sky. There were only the noises of occasional small boats travelling the harbor. In the distance there were the anchor lights of ships and the lights of various areas of the base and the navy shipyard shone — so quiet and peaceful and yet to be disturbed so violently in just a few hours.

At 0345 December 7, 1941, I was relieved by Ens. Joe Spitler and handed the spyglass which was the symbol of the office for JODs. The symbol of authority for Officer of the Deck (ODs). was a .45 caliber pistol. Off I went to my room located on the second deck port side forward in junior officers' country. I undressed, put on my pajama bottoms and climbed into the top berth. My roommate Ens. Bill Morey, the junior aviator on board, was fast asleep in the lower bunk. Even in December in Pearl Harbor, being on a battleship is usually hot and although the porthole in the room is wide open, very little air circulated and I never wore more than PJ bottoms. In a moment I was fast asleep.

My intention for Sunday, December 7 was to sleep a little longer than usual since it was a free day for me. I planned to eat a leisurely breakfast in the JO mess which would be open till 9 a.m, then leave the ship and spend part of the day in town with my friend Ray Hefty, his wife Mabel, and their four year old daughter, Carolyn. The day would consist of church, lunch, and a swim at Waikiki. Usually Ray, Carolyn, a little neighbor friend, and I would swim. Mabel never went to the beach with us. After that it was dinner and back to the ship. But Sunday December 7 was to be different, the usual pattern completely broken.

"Air Raid! Air Raid! This is no drill — real bombs — no shit — get moving!" — followed by the raucous noises of the klaxon sounding "General Quarters!" Which meant "Battle Stations!" That was the announcement which startled me and brought me completely awake at 0750.

I recognized the voice of Ens. Herb Rommel and instantly knew without a question that this was for real and serious. The PA system was always manned either by a boatswain's mate or a quarter master — not an ensign. But this was December 7 not April 1 and Rommel was a person who didn't play jokes.

Ens. Morey had gotten a full night's sleep and was out of his bunk a few seconds before I was and took time to at least put on a pair of pants. He was going top side and aft to his plane. I was going below to the forward boiler control — my battle station. When my feet hit the deck I put on slippers and grabbed my hat. An officer wearing his hat was officially an officer — the hat being the symbol of authority — even if he wore nothing else. I felt rather foolish but had not much choice. Neither of us looked around the room or closed the open portholes. We stepped over the threshold and out the door at about the same time — no good-byes — no good luck. We didn't know what was happening. We did not see one another again for six months and then just for one fleeting second in Pago Pago Harbor, Samoa, when a Navy motor launch passed by the stern of the USS *Mackinac*, on which I was a passenger. Just as we were leaving the harbor, we saw each other. I called out "Morey" and he looked up at me and said, "I thought you were dead." We were rapidly picking up speed and soon were out of range of conversation. But back to December 7.

As I left the room, I hurriedly crossed from the port side to the starboard side over the ship's gleaming red linoleum deck that had been so highly polished on December 6th. The occasion for the polishing was a ship's inspection to be held on December 8th — an inspection that needless to say never took place. I passed by the starboard stateroom doors and into the JO mess. No one was in sight. Some breakfasts were partially eaten and some places were still set with dirty dishes on the white linen tablecloths. On my right side was the massively thick barbette of the # 1 turret in its very light pea green paint.

I was four or five feet into the JO mess when the first torpedo hit. It was an explosion that I will never forget. The noise was a very well muffled blast. You could tell it was deep in the bottom of the ship as the ship was lifted rapidly straight up a considerable distance. I don't think I would be far off in estimating it as 24 to 30 inches. My legs almost buckled and I reached out my arms to avoid being thrown to the deck. I did not fall, but caught myself and then knew for sure this was "no drill." The day of infamy had arrived.

The first torpedo explosion made a huge impression on me and was the only one that I distinctly remember. As I hurried aft, I passed the door of the JO galley, now empty, and through the doorway into the very clean warrant officers' country with its slightly darker shade of green, past the staterooms of the four commissioned warrant officers and past the four empty army style cots temporarily occupying passage space and used by four ensigns who recently reported aboard, then into B Division living space. The next eight or nine torpedoes that hit the ship came as a slow hitting swarm. I had lost count.

B Division living space, where breakfast had been completed was where for weeks chipping hammers had been working — hour after hour, day after day — chipping 28 coats of lead-based paint off the bulkheads and overhead down to the bare metal, where you could see a complete rivet head, not just a small bump where a rivet was supposed to be. This was all to reduce the fire hazard from the highly flammable and toxic paint. Only parts of the ship had gotten to the zinc chromate stage. Each division throughout the entire ship was eventually to do this. It was never completed. Even the beautiful red linoleum was to be stripped off. It never was.

Second deck, where the JO mess, warrant officers' country, and B Division lived was an armored deck. A plate of steel six inches thick covered those places; below that needed protection from bombs. The hatch through the second deck to the third deck and the fire rooms was located just inboard of B Division living spaces. I rigidly travelled between benches and tables, not yet put away after breakfast and down the ladder to the third deck and midship to the forward boiler control. Men assigned to the forward boiler control were already there and most of those assigned to the forward fireroom had already gone through the airlock and were down below. One more person who belonged below was a little late and as he opened the hatch and stepped into the airlock, I watched the spinner handle spin and lock the hatch. I wondered to myself — what is he going to find down there? What are the others doing down there? Can they possibly light off the burners and even if they could, what good would it do? How could this ship possibly get underway? The list was too great.

The ship had already picked up a considerable list. Some say it went to 45 degrees and hung there but that's not true since we were still able to stand and move on the deck and didn't need to seek the stability of the corner where the bulkhead meets the deck. We had a voice tube to the bridge but no one answered our calls. A "talker" manned the powered telephone but no one answered his rings. The ship's lights flickered off and on, but were mostly on. We didn't need to use the big dry cell lantern. The blower over our heads still functioned, drawing in cool air, but it was not fresh. It was laden with smoke — the white smelly smoke of exploded torpedoes. We quietly waited for more explosions. There were none.

Minutes passed with no communications, no words, no orders, no contact with the outside. We could here explosions, knew they were not hitting our ship and wondered. I must have looked an odd person, PJ bottoms and an officer's billed hat but no one laughed or said anything as I told the talker to ring the bridge again. We called through the voice tube and received no answer. I knew we could not do anyone any good in our location. There was nothing we could do but breathe foul air. The thought ran through my mind, can we abandon ship? Would it be legal for us to try? Or would we be in big trouble if we did try? We had never been trained in any drills for abandoning ship. It had never been mentioned in any instruction that I could recall. Fire drill, man overboard, yes, but not abandon ship. We just waited for more torpedoes to hit.

I noticed the dog handle to the passageway bulkhead hatch which led to the main boiler control turning and when the hatch opened all the way, out poured the five or six men from the main boiler control. They appeared to come through the hatch all at once, although that would have been impossible. For the first time that day I saw the division officer, Ens. Joe Hittorf and our Warrant Machinist, Bill Goggins. Joe looked at me and said, "Abandon ship." I felt some relief. Finally someone over me had said it.

The very heavy deck hatch just to the side of our heads, which had been dogged tightly from our side was soon released and flew open. It did not have to be pushed as was normally the case. Since the ship had a huge list to port and since the heavy hatch, even with springs and dampers and counters was hinged to the port, it flew open when the last dog was released. I hate to think what our problems would have been had the list been to the starboard.

It was difficult to climb the ladder to the second deck as it was now hanging almost vertical. But such a problem was very minor at the time. Eight or nine people from B Division had at least reached second deck. On reaching B Division quarters, I found an incredible mess. Tables and benches which were stored overhead when not in use had slid to the low side of the

The capsized USS Oklahoma *and the USS* Maryland *after the Japanese attack on Pearl Harbor.*

compartment and formed a big jumble. Berths attached to the bulkhead had come loose and were swinging on their chains making walking difficult. The remainder of breakfast food, coffee, pots, dirty dishes and food trays, platters of uneaten sliced baloney covered with the usual tomato sauce had spilled and made an incredible slippery mess through which we had to walk. I was still viewing the chaos and attempting to decide on the best course of action when Hittorf said, "Let's try to go back to Chief's quarters. They have 15 inch portholes back there." (The rest of the portholes to the ship were 12 inches.)

I thought that was a good idea because the three or four ports in B Division each had two or three men lined up to try to squeeze through. Each of these ports had a person half in and half out and I could see in one port a person on the outside pulling to help someone escape. He must have secured himself with some kind of line because the slope of the side was still greater than 45 degrees. If no one assisted in either pulling or pushing it would be very difficult to get your hips through such a port. There was no place to get a purchase to push with your feet.

As we started aft, I witnessed Chaplain Lt. J. G. Aloysius Schmitt pushing one person out. Two more were beside him. I understand he tried to squeeze through but was unable to fit so came back inside and spent the last few minutes of his life helping others escape. I don't think more than one more could have gotten out because shortly thereafter the ship rolled and he and the others were trapped in the rising waters. I doubt if that particular area had enough of a prism [*sic*] of air to sustain life for long. I could have very well been the last person to see the chaplain alive. He was awarded the Navy's highest honor for his heroism — the Navy Cross.

We went aft, Joe Hittorf, Bill Goggins, and I past the ladder which led to the first deck. The deck hatch was closed but it did have a round escape hatch in the center. The escape hatch was open and men were crowding and pushing their way up the ladder in an attempt to get to the main deck. It probably took 30 seconds per person to negotiate the tight squeeze. It was not meant to be a means of mass exodus. This was the only incident of panic I saw.

Five or six feet from the foot of the ladder and forward was one of our B Division sailors sitting in the corner where the bulkhead meets the deck. I can't remember his name but he was one of our water tenders— a good worker who usually came back from liberty with a split lip, bloody nose, black eye, or disheveled uniform with his friend from another division. They seemed to be inseparable. Here he was, sitting on the deck with his friend's head in his lap, his body stretched out on the deck. I couldn't see anything wrong but he seemed to be unconscious. When our eyes met, I said, "You better get out of here." He gave me an anguished look as he answered, "No. I'm not going to leave my friend. He's hurt." This scene and act of devotion made an indelible impression on me. What loyalty!

I turned my attention to making my way aft to Chief's quarters. Hittorf and Goggins were just ahead of me. We had gone 15 or 20 feet to a point just past the medical department and operating room located on the starboard side. I was even with a door that led to what the pharmacists refer to as the pharmacy. From this part of the ship it was possible to cross over to the port side and you could see two or three portholes just aft of the engineering office located on the port side. When I reached this point the ship began to roll over and as I looked, water flowed in along the deck and the deck began to disappear as the water rose and the deck descended.

Our ship was moored outboard of the USS *Maryland* and secured to her by the huge hawsers that battleships use for mooring. These had been doubled up sufficiently to hold the *Oklahoma* at least somewhat upright even with nine torpedoes in her hull. Not wanting to be trapped, the *Maryland* used axes to cut through these lines, allowing the *Oklahoma* to roll 152 degrees from vertical. There is no doubt in my mind that had we been given 15 or 20 minutes additional time, our crew could have abandoned ship in a more orderly manner and our casualties would have been far fewer than the 448 that we lost. Could the *Maryland* rightfully do what it felt it had to do? I believe the answer to be yes. Did it prove to be necessary? My answer is no!

The water was blue and clear and soon one open port reached the surface of the water on the outside of the ship. For a short time a small waterfall existed as water poured in. It did not take long for the porthole to descend into the water as the ship sank and slowly rolled. The water continued to rise inside and the ship continued to slowly roll. I soon found myself treading water and watching the ship as it rolled slowly above my head. I looked around quickly and could not see Hittorf or Goggins. I assume that in time I averted my eyes and watched the ship. They both slipped beneath the surface and drowned. I was told later that neither could swim.

As I treaded water, the ship continued to roll and I was carried into the pharmacy. As the door rolled over me, the glass-faced doors of the medicine cabinets on the bulkhead opened and I was showered with a deluge of medicine bottles both small and large. As I continued to tread water, I watched with anticipation. The starboard bulkhead rolled up, over, and down into the rising water. The deck broke the surface of the water and rolled over my head. I knew I was in an upside down ship. The deck was made of old-fashioned, small, white, hexagonal tiles just like my bathroom at home. As it rolled, it came to a slow stop at an angle over my head. The ship had rolled 28 degrees from being exactly upside down. The masts had buried themselves in the mud at the bottom of the harbor. I had also seen the one porthole in the compartment descend below the water line. But it was secured — how tightly I did know not know. The battle port was dogged shut, but I knew that if any of us were to escape it had to be through the porthole.

I put that out of my mind as the prism of air in which I found myself was growing smaller and smaller. As I watched the scupper area descending and the bulkhead and the deck areas getting smaller and smaller, I said to myself "I hope this space is airtight" as I knew that sooner or later the inside and outside pressure would equalize but we would have some time — how much I did not know. At the same time that the rolling and sinking were occurring, the light disappeared almost, but not quite, to zero.

As I looked around, I noticed that the others were with me. I had been the first to be carried into the compartment. I recognized WO John Austin, the ship's carpenter. He always carried a long five cell flashlight with him. He turned it on for a short time, then turned it off. There was a low blue glow of light coming in through the open door now underwater. Evidently there was enough light coming in from the portholes along the starboard side to allow some light to penetrate the interior of the ship. The whole port side had rolled into the mud and the starboard side was now outboard, but upside down and 28 degrees from being vertical. Consequently, light was entering the ship through the open ports and a little was entering our compartment. I recognized one other person — fireman Gayle Kelley from B Division, a tall very slender sailor. There were two others I did not know.

Finally we had a stabilized ship. The Japanese had done their job. Nine torpedo explosions, possibly ten, had indeed been effective. The water level rose inside but slowed and came to a stop with the prism of air approximately eight feet long — the triangle being approximately $2\frac{1}{2}$ x $3\frac{1}{2}$ x 4 feet. This was about 40 cubic feet of air for five people. I knew that we didn't have much time, although I knew that the cavity of air we had was compressed so there was something more than 40 cubic feet of air. I didn't know how much more.

I knew that if we were to get out it had to be quick. Our only hope was the porthole that I had watched descend below the surface. I located it with my foot — I'd lost my slippers treading water. I still had my PJ bottoms on and my hat. John Austin had his hat on and one sailor had his white hat on also. Kellogg and the other person did not.

I ducked my head under the surface and felt around for a dog wrench. None was there and I hoped the porthole was just hand dogged. I felt relief as I tried the dogs and they easily unscrewed. After the last dog was loosened, the battleport dropped with a muffled thud. Normally the battleport has to be held open, instead this was just the reverse of what is supposed to happen. Holding the glass open with my left hand and with my chin just clearing water level, I said, "Okay, who's first?" In one second the sailor with the white hat whom I did not know dove and swam past my knees, bumping me three or four times, he finally went through. I could tell he had a hard time but I said to myself, "If he can fit, I can too." At least he had made it outside. I then said, "Who's next?" Kellogg dove and had trouble getting through.

There were now three of us remaining and since I was holding the port and knowing John Austin weighed in excess of 200 lbs and was only 5'8" tall, I pointed to the third sailor. I didn't know him other than he was a lad from Guam, small in stature, a senior ward room steward. He was treading water with his feet only and praying. The palms of his hands were clasped together under his chin but his eyes were open. "You're next," I said but he replied, "No! No!" Obviously he was a swimmer. He was within reach of my right hand so I put my hand on his head and pushed it down to the vicinity of the port. He did not have a choice. I gave him none and through he went. I had to assume that the kid from Guam could swim.

It is difficult to judge the amount of time we had been in the compartment. There was still a glow of light and our eyes became accustomed to the dimness. It seems reasonable to assume that 10 or 15 minutes had passed from the time we found ourselves in the compartment until three people had escaped to the outside. The water level appeared to have stayed the same but the air seemed to be getting stale and it had an oppressive feeling.

Now there were two of us, myself at 144 lbs and John Austin, a man my height but rotund, weighing over 200 lbs. I was still holding the port open. It seemed I didn't want to let go, maybe it was the fear of not getting it opened again. At this point if John had weighed 144 pounds or even 160 pounds, it would have been his turn and I would have been alone. I would have given everything I had to get outside and I still believe I could have done so, but John must have known he had no chance. He did not say a word but moved over the few feet necessary and just reached down and held the port. I looked at his face but cannot describe the look of anguish it contained. It is a look that has never left me. And the fact that I had to leave him behind has always troubled me. John was awarded the Navy Cross.

I knew from the difficulty breathing thing that I had to get out. I took the deepest breath I possibly could but it felt as through my lungs were not filling so I dove and lined myself with the port going through first with my left arm outreached, then my head and left shoulder, then my right shoulder with not much problem until my hips reached the port. A push and some wiggles got them through. I was soon completely outside. I opened my eyes to see a golden brown glow above and I knew the surface was up there somewhere. It never occurred to me that the normal color should have been bluish. I had not anticipated oil on the surface or worse yet burning oil on the surface. I pushed off with my feet on the edge of the porthole and headed for the surface. It seemed like an eternity before I got there and actually had to swim to reach it. I had been to the bottom of pools that had been 10 or 12 feet deep but never had I experienced such great depth as this. The port must have been 18 or 20 feet from the surface.

But break through the surface I did and when I opened my eyes I could hardly believe what I saw. There were a few planes in the sky but very high. The sky was covered with the lingering bursts of AA fire and across the surface of the harbor were many small splashes—remnants of AA shells returning to earth and making small geysers wherever the shrapnel hit. Some were close, too close for comfort. Three or four inches of thick, smelly fuel oil covered the surface. The *West Virginia* at our stern was engulfed in flames. The harbor surface was ablaze 75 yards away.

The ship was a few feet away, since I had come straight up from the port. Since the ship was at an angle, I reached the surface perhaps eight feet from the side of the ship. I swam to a group of perhaps six or seven people hanging on the side. Everyone was covered with a very thick bunker oil. The only parts not black were eyes and teeth. I could not recognize anyone. One person spoke my name and when I looked very carefully, I could see Ens. McLellan. I looked to see if any of the other three who had been with me could be there but I couldn't identify them.

We were debating about what to do. We couldn't climb the side of the ship to the very bottom. It was too steep and we were slippery. Someone suggested we should go astern and swim to Ford Island, a long messy swim. I did not like that idea. A 40 foot navy motor launch was approaching but for some reason would not come all the way to the side of the ship but stood off 20 plus yards. I swam breaststroke carefully to the launch and was the first of the group to get there. The launch was manned by three Marines. Their uniforms were spotless. One Marine reached down as I extended my right arm as high as I could. Grabbing my filthy black oily arm, he tried to pull up but was unsuccessful. He did succeed in scraping off some of the oil. After doing this twice, my arm was scraped clean enough that he could hold on and I managed to get my right hand on the gunwale. That was all that was necessary and I pulled myself up and swung into the launch.

The launch was spotless so I thought I had better not sit down on their clean thwarts. I noticed for the first time that I was stark naked. I must have lost my PJ bottoms when my hips scraped the porthole. My hat must have been left in the dispensary. Three or four more were pulled into the launch but not all of the group by the ship attempted to swim out. I didn't believe the Marines particularly wanted to remain in such an exposed place very long and we soon took off for the Merry Point liberty landing. I was standing but after my feet went out from under me, I said to myself, "the hell with their clean boat" and sat down directly opposite a very clean Marine. We hadn't travelled more than 200 yards when the Marine across from me must not have liked what he saw. He didn't say a word, just stood up, took his pants off, then his skivvies, put his pants back on, and tossed me his skivvies.

In 10 or 15 minutes we were at the liberty landing and someone said to go to the receiving station and take a shower. I noticed for the first time a bleeding gash on the inside arch of my left foot. It was superficial and didn't hurt, but had a burning sensation as did my eyes which had a good quantity of oil affecting them.

The second deck of the receiving station had a large shower room with a quantity of showerheads protruding from the walls. Some people were already there. The floor was flooded with water and a thick black film of oil was over everything. It would have been much worse had there not been two five-gallon cans of kerosene just outside where I washed most of the goop off using rag waste before showering. But even with soap and water, it was days and showers later before I became acceptably clean.

After the shower we were directed to a pile of dungarees and shirts, no underwear, and a pile of shoes. None of these were new and I picked a pair of pants and a shirt that somewhat fit and a pair of shoes that didn't fit. No hat, no insignia, no socks. I went outside to see what was happening. I walked away from the water towards the main road and main gate. I no sooner had stepped clear of the building when a Zero, barely clearing the top of the main gate and the trees that bordered the main road, came zigging and zagging, strafing, his bullets hitting gate, pavement and cars on the road. I stepped back to the protection of a building in a hurry!

Shortly thereafter, I happened to run into Lt. Bill Ingram and Ens. Adam Demers. Bill said, "Let's go out to the ship." He was dressed in khakis and wearing two pearl-handled revolvers—one on each hip. We had stood the midwatch together just six hours before, so quiet and peaceful. At the liberty boat landing, Bill literally commandeered a 26' motor whaleboat. The coxswain in charge of the boat said no but we three boarded and off we went back to our upside down ship. This was the first opportunity to really get a good look at the destruction that had occurred. The second wave attack was just starting but no one seemed to be around the battleships. The Japanese had already devastated them and they knew it.

As we approached the upside down hull, I could identify Boatswain Bothne, Commander Kenworthy, the ship's executive officer, dressed in whites, Ensign Davenport also dressed in whites with a JO spyglass under his arm, a few yard workers, and a few *Oklahoma* sailors—perhaps 12 men total—standing on the bottom of the hull looking, pointing, conversing. Cdr. Kenworthy, Ens. Davenport, and some others had just walked around the ship as she rolled. They didn't even get their shoes wet. Ingram called to Cdr. Kenworthy and asked if he could help. The reply was, "No. Get out of here. The yard will take care of things." We motored back to Merry

Point liberty landing. I told Bill my foot was hurting and he said, "Go to the hospital and then report to the sub base." Everyone who could be found should report and check in with Lt. Cdr. Hobby.

I walked to the hospital located on Hospital Point. Some badly injured were already there. When the nurse saw me, she said, "We have to wash those eyes out!" After doing that and cleaning and dressing my foot, she advised me to stay off my feet for a while. I was dismissed and walked the long way back to the sub base.

It was easy enough to locate the *Oklahoma* group. I logged in by signing my name on a list. It was lunchtime and a large tray of sandwiches was brought in. This was the first time I had eaten since 1800 Saturday dinner aboard ship. Someone gave me a sheet of paper and a pencil and told me to write a statement of my experiences. I did, but to this day I don't know what I wrote.

In the early afternoon I walked to the sub base piers just to see what had happened. My ship, upside down, the *Arizona* with its two tripod masts tilted at crazy angles broken in two, smoke and fires. I had nothing, some dirty clothes, a pair of ill fitting shoes, and a turquoise ring on my finger. The stone had been smashed and the ring all bent out of shape. It was the only thing I had when I left the ship.

In my wandering about the sub base, I found a nickel coin lying on the ground. I tried to use it to call my friend Ray Hefty. I knew he could get a message to my wife. Unfortunately I dropped the coin in a phone that was out of order, but it gave me the idea to search slots for coins and I found a dime. I made sure I used a working phone and made a call.

It was very fortunate that I soon ran into Ens. Fred Brooks, a former classmate of mine who had a room at the sub base BOQ. Seeing I was not dressed properly, he gave me a pair of his khaki pants and shirt. I felt much better. Since his roommate was on a cruising sub, I slept in his bed Sunday night. At 2200 hours we thought there was another attack when planes from the *Enterprise* tried to land at Ford Island and every gun in the harbor opened up. We had parted the blackout curtains to be able to see the action. It didn't take long for "friendly fire" to shoot four planes out of the sky.

The rest of the night was relatively quiet. I tried to sleep.

Chapter 6

USS *California* (BB–44)

The USS *California* (BB-44) was the fifth ship to bear the name. The battleship was launched on November 20, 1919, by Mare Island Naval Shipyard and commissioned on August 10, 1921. She reported to the Pacific Fleet as flagship and served in that role from 1921 to 1941. She was active in, among other things, joint army-navy exercises, tactical and organizational development problems, and fleet concentrations for various purposes. During that time she won several awards for battle efficiency.

In 1940, the *California* was assigned to Pearl Harbor. On December 7, 1941, she was moored at the southernmost berth of Battleship Row and was with the other dreadnoughts of the battle force when the Japanese launched their aerial attack. At 0805, a bomb exploded below decks setting off an ammunition magazine and killing 50 men. A second bomb ruptured her bow plates. Despite valiant efforts to keep her afloat the in-rushing water could not be isolated and the *California* settled to the bottom with only her superstructure remaining above water. When the attack was over 98 crew men had been killed and another 61 wounded.

In March 1942, she was refloated and dry docked at Pearl Harbor for repairs. On June 7, she departed under her own power to the States for major reconstruction.

She departed Bremerton on January 31, 1944, for shakedown and sailed from San Francisco on May 5, 1944, for the invasion of the Marianas. She

Manning the rail on the USS California.

participated in the bombardment of Saipan in June and was hit by an enemy shore battery which killed one man and wounded nine. In July and August, she participated in the assaults on Guam and Titian. On August 24, 1944, she arrived at Espiritu Santo for repairs to her port bow, damaged in a collision with the USS *Tennessee.*

On September 17, 1944, she sailed to Manus for the preparation for the invasion of the Philippines. In October and November, she was involved in the destruction of the Japanese fleet in the Battle of Surigao Strait. On January 1, 1945, she sailed to the Philippines to provide artillery support from her powerful guns. She was hit by a kamikaze plane during the operations, and 44 of her crew were killed and 155 were wounded. She made temporary repairs and remained on station carrying out her duties. Finally she returned to Puget Sound Naval Yard for repairs, then again returned to action when she arrived at Okinawa in June 1945. In August she departed Okinawa to support the landing of the sixth Army occupation force at Wakanoura Wan, Honshu. She remained there until October

1945 when she returned to the U.S. She was placed in commission reserve on August 7, 1946, out of commission in reserve on February 14, 1947, and sold July 10, 1959. She was scrapped later that same year.

The USS *California* received seven battle stars for her World War II service. Today her ship's bell rests in a memorial in Capital Park in Sacramento, California.

JOHN H. MCGORAN
U.S. Navy, USS California

The morning of December 7, 1941, was typical of any Sunday morning aboard the battleship USS *California.* My billet for meals was the Marines' casemate #8 (an armored enclosure for a gun) located on the port side midship, just where the forecastle breaks and a ladder leads down to the quarter deck. Breakfast over, I took the dirty dishes to the scullery below. Lamentably, that's the way peace ended. Just then a sailor ran by crazily singing. "The Japs are coming — hurrah, hurrah!" I don't remember the alarm that sounded General Quarters. I only knew that suddenly I joined in a rush to battle stations.

When hurrying to our battle stations, to reach the decks below, we were trained to leap into the hatch instead of using its ladder (ladder is ship talk and most often refers to a steep iron stairway). Then, grab onto a bar attached to the overhead (ceiling) of the deck below and swing one's body into a run in the lower passageway. That's roughly the way I arrived at my battle station in the lower powder handling room where a first-class petty officer, named Allen, was in charge.

Allen was one of those old-time petty officers referred to as "the backbone of the fleet." Now, he was busily giving orders we couldn't carry out because no one had the keys to the powder magazines room.

Suddenly, a violent lurching shook us all, tossing us around like so many unmuscled puppets as the ship seemed to rise up a foot, then settle back. Allen grabbed at his ear phones. "We're hit," he cried. "A torpedo!"

"So what?" I thought foolishly. "Enjoy it!" The armor plating around the USS *California* was at least a foot thick.

My idiot elation was brief. A torpedo had hit us. Three in all hit below the armor plating and made huge holes. The fuel tank next to our port magazine ignited in flames and there we were, surrounded on three sides by powder-filled magazines.

Immediately orders came to check the temperature of the bulkhead separating the magazine from the fuel tank. We forced the lock on the

The USS California *after the Japanese attack.*

magazine off and inside saw that some of the cans containing the 14-inch powder bags had been broken open and that the aisle was strewn with ripped open bags of gunpowder.

Anxiously, I entered, walking carefully over the debris to feel the bulkhead. I returned and reported to Allen that the bulkhead was cool. Allen in turn passed the reassuring word over the mouthpiece of his headset to the bridge.

Whatever reply came back over the phones was reflected in the strain on Allen's face. He couldn't seem to comprehend, perhaps he didn't want to believe. He turned to us and almost in a whisper said, "The *Oklahoma*! It has capsized." Frighteningly, our ship was beginning to list dangerously.

We had no time to grasp fully this impossible situation, for a report next came over Allen's headset of a fire in the upper handling room. Our access to this space was a vertical ladder leading up the side of the column, which also contained the powder bag hoist, and which was centered, where we stood, in the lower handling room. The column was the pivot point for the entire gun turret complex above. The turret complex turned from port broadside to starboard broadside, in the direction desired to fire the guns.

I volunteered to carry a fire extinguisher up the ladder but found it difficult hauling that heavy container with one hand while climbing vertically, with the other. When I reached the upper handling room, I found no fire, nor any people. In fact, there was no reason to stay, but on the way back down this crazy thought struck me. "No one will believe all this when I tell them someday. And since I have no memory for dates, it will really sound silly." So I sat down and with my pocketknife, scratched on the back of my wristwatch: Pearl Harbor Dec. 7, 1941.

Back in the lower handling room the smell of danger was in the strafing air. The ship shifted heavily to port. The people in the engine room reported that they were working feverishly to correct it, and with a sense of relief we soon felt the ship begin to check the deadly roll and slowly inch back toward a safer situation.

But the danger was far from over, for Allen received a report that our antiaircraft ammunition supply line broke down from an explosion. The break was reported to be in "CL" compartment, my sleeping quarters, and when the call came, I said I'd go. Two others seamen also volunteered for the job.

As I was about to start, however, the lights in the handling room flickered and went out. For a few minutes we were in total darkness. Then red battle lamps came on, dimly, but giving enough light so I could make my way about.

Before leaving the handling room, I went over to shake hands with my friend Edwin "Ed" Halcrow. Although Halcrow and I had been together for six months and kidded each other a lot, when we shook hands, he started to cry. I didn't know what to do and in my embarrassment made it worse, saying, "If I don't see you again, Halcrow, be good." Halcrow burst out in tears afresh as I turned and quickly climbed a vertical ladder to a passageway above that led forward on the starboard side to "CL" compartment. We never saw each other again.

The passageway was narrow with several watertight bulkhead doors to open, pass through, and close behind us. A conveyor belt system ran along the inside of the passageway, so when ammunition arrived by elevator/hoist from the magazine below, into "CL" compartment, the men there would divide it and manually carry it to either of the two conveyors, port or starboard. From there it ran on the conveyors to other hoists which took the shells to the 5 inch guns on the boat deck.

Because of the dim lighting we made our way slowly and reached

"CL" compartment without trouble. But here a shock awaited us. As each of my companions looked into the "CL" compartment, he turned and backed off. Then came my turn and what I saw was pure horror, my first realization that the game was now for keeps. I saw bodies— many bodies— some of which I knew, just by their eyes, were lifeless. We stopped to reconnoiter.

While we stood at the door of "CL" compartment, my companion, a seaman named "Smitty," called to me. I turned to see him on the opposite side of the conveyor trying to help a shipmate whose back was against the bulkhead, but who was slowly slipping to the deck. His eyes were rolled back into his head. He looked like he was dying.

"This one is still alive," Smitty said calmly. Smitty was a small fellow but he managed to wrestle the wounded shipmate to me and I pulled his limp body over the conveyor into the passageway. If on December 6th anyone had asked me to help save the life of this offensive guy, I would have answered, "To hell with him." I had known this fellow since boot camp, and he was one of the most overbearing individuals I had ever met. But now, unconscious, he had no personality. His was a life to be saved.

To reach the first-aid station, Smitty and I backtracked aft on the starboard side. Now and then, we had to stop and lay him down, so we could rest. Catching our breaths, we moved on again. As we trudged along, we had to again open and close the watertight bulkhead doors while making our way back through the passageway to a ladder up, which was near the man-hole down to number three lower handling, from where we had started. The hatch cover at the top of the ladder was dogged down — another Navy term for closed and watertight. But, it was the nearest escape to the decks above. We undogged the hatch and pushed it open. Smitty took the injured man's legs and started up the ladder. I got him under the arms again and just as I'd taken a second or third step up the ladder an explosion again rocked the ship.

The blast of air compressed by the explosion thrust the three of us back down the ladder, landing us in a pile at the bottom. Picking myself up I found my right leg had a laceration. Blood was oozing from my shin. It stung. However, I soon dismissed it. There was too much to contend with at this time to be concerned about it. We knew we were in a life-threatening situation.

The explosion frightened us. We realized that we must make a decision. We immediately closed the hatch cover and debated what to do, which way to go.

Suddenly, a steam pipe nearby blew out. In a stunning moment of chaos that followed, I heard the cry, "Gas!" Unquestioningly, I held my breath until I could fit my gas mask to my face. The gas mask was very uncomfortable and it was difficult to cope with. Finally, I lifted it a bit to sniff the air to determine whether or not it smelled safe to breathe, it did. Then I looked up in alarm.

Incredibly, three Negro men we had thought dead, staggered toward us from the direction of that gruesome morgue, "CL" compartment, we had just left. Two of these men were helping a third one who kept repeating insanely, "Moses is dead. Moses is dead." [Moses Anderson Allen, STML.] Moses was a large man, an officers' mess attendant. He was liked by everyone on board, and the Negro crewmen looked up to him as a leader.

Smitty and I debated whether to try to escape by going back to "CL" compartment and try a ladder there or opening this hatch again and trying to escape here. Hesitatingly, we again tackled this ladder. We again opened the hatch cover and saw no evidence of damage from the explosion.

What actually happened was a bomb penetrated the decks above and exploded in front of the ship's store, several feet forward of the ladder. It killed "Boots," one of the masters-at-arms [ship's policeman]. It bent a heavy steel hatch, coming flush with the deck.

We picked up our injured shipmate and carried him up. This time, we were lucky and got him to the first aid station.

Some station! It was normally the crew's recreation room, but now a state of incredible confusion prevailed. We laid our shipmates on the deck. A chief petty officer, whom I recognized as one of the "black-gang" (engine room crew), asked if he was alive with great authority. "We think so," I said. "Then get him out of the way." (Later in the week, I learned that the fellow's back had been broken, but he would recover.) Then the chief went back to directing and sorting the living from the dead. As men brought in casualties, the chief would say, "Dead or alive?" If they're dead, take them into the other room and throw them on the dead pile." He repeatedly made rounds of the room inspecting bodies. "This man is dead — Get him out of here." Normally this cold, hard manner would have been resented. Now, I could only feel admiration for his efficiency.

As I stood, trying to comprehend all of this, someone handed me a bottle of root beer and a sandwich. Ordinarily I would have retched at the sight of so much blood, but I ate and drank, completely amazed at my appetite under such conditions and decided it was all incomprehensible. As I ate, one of the ship's seaplane pilots hurried into the room, presumably to pass right on through and on out an opposite door. Instead, he slipped on the bloody deck and fell across the wounded bodies. I watched, and feeling nothing, wondered: Does nature have the power to anesthetize? Or, am I in shock?

Then Father Maguire, Catholic chaplain for the fleet, strode through the doorway. In the past weeks, this priest had succeeded in getting permission for my brother's transfer from the USS *Detroit* CL–8, a light, four-stack cruiser, to the *California* so we could be together. Bob's transfer, Father Maguire had told me, was due to occur around the 14th of December.

Though dirty, and looking tired, Father Maguire walked with dignity. A gas mask that looked like a strangely shaped hat was propped on his hand. He passed on to someone to whom he could administer last rites.

While I was in the first aid station, word came to abandon ship. Whether or not this was an official order, I don't know. But instead, the chief petty officer in charge, and a warrant officer, named Applegate, formed a work party of ten men to search for antiaircraft ammunition, since ours could not be reached, due to a bomb explosion.

Our work party first went aft to the door which exited onto the starboard quarter deck. We were about to proceed across the quarter deck to board a motor launch when someone warned us that a wave of strafing Japanese planes was passing over. The planes came low, firing their machine guns. Between sorties, men from nearby battle stations raced out on the quarter deck and dragged to shelter those who had been struck by the machine gun fire. Then, as soon as we felt it was safe, we ran for the motor launch, which was waiting for us at the port quarter.

Normally, we used a ladder to step down to the boat, but now the ship was so low in the water, it seemed strange that we could jump from the quarter deck, right into the boat. Swiftly, we piled into the motor launch and headed in the direction of the battleship, USS *Maryland*.

The *Maryland* was next astern of the *California*, in Battleship Row, (the USS *Neosho* was moored at a fuel dock between the two battleships), and it was moored inboard of the *Oklahoma*, which earlier in the attack, after taking nine torpedoes, had rolled over. I'm sure the coxswain of our launch chose the *Maryland* because she seemed unscathed. Certainly, she must have the ammunition that we so desperately needed.

En route, we could see the strange angle at which the USS *Nevada* stood near the drydocks. She seemed to be out of the channel. Perhaps she had turned to avoid a bomb.

Our coxswain took our launch into the space between the capsized *Oklahoma* and the port side forecastle of the *Maryland*. Shouting up to sailors on the *Maryland*'s forecastle, we tried to convey to them that we needed ammunition, but we could rouse no support. Their problems were far greater to them than what we were shouting up to them about from our motor launch. Had we approached the officer's accommodation ladder at the *Maryland*'s starboard quarter deck, and spoken to an officer there, we might have been more successful.

Once it became clear that we could expect no help from the quarter, we gave up trying to board the *Maryland*. The coxswain maneuvered the motor launch from between the two battleships and motored around the whale shaped hull of the capsized *Oklahoma* and went to the USS *West Virginia*.

Carefully, the coxswain nudged the motor launch's bow against the *West Virginia*'s forecastle, just forward of # 1 turret. By keeping a little power on, he maintained the position without actually tying up to the battleship.

By the time, the *West Virginia* had sunk deep enough so that it was with little effort that Warrant Officer Applegate, and the five men he picked, could clamber aboard. I watched as they crossed the ship's forecastle, walking under the barrels of the 16-inch guns, and walk aft on the starboard side. We never saw them again.

Within minutes the forecastle shot up in smoke and flames. It may have been the bomb that hit the turret of the *Tennessee*. An officer in his white uniform appeared engulfed in the fire. Someone on board shouted, "Get out of there. The ship can blow up any minute."

The explosion frightened us terribly. The coxswain began backing the launch away from the burning battleship. Suddenly, I saw that the coxswain was not aware of the danger immediately behind our launch; we were backing straight for one of the large propellers of the capsized *Oklahoma* sticking high out of the water.

I yelled at the coxswain, "Reverse your engines." At the same time, two of us chambered to the tiller deck, and scrambled over the taffrail. With one hand grasping the taffrail, we reached with our legs spread eagle-like and with our feet shoved against the propeller. Unquestionably, our effort prevented the motor launch from being damaged; but we just did what the situation required.

The coxswain now had the launch underway forward. Then we saw a man struggling in the water near the midship's section of the *West Virginia*. A picture of this rescue was snapped probably by the USS *St. Louis* and it is part of the pictorial record of the Japanese attack.

"We're going in after him," he told us. Another sailor standing beside him objected. I too, murmured disapproval. I felt that since the *West Virginia* was expected to blow up as the *Arizona* did, it wasn't reasonable to risk the lives of the eight of us in our boat in an effort to save one.

Our coxswain was firm; he ordered both of us off the tiller deck. I said no more, and stayed right where I was. Actually, I was becoming so frightened I don't think I could have moved. The coxswain maneuvered in to pick the man up from the water, bringing us dangerously close to the perimeter of the burning oil that was closing in.

By now I was overwhelmed by all that was happening around us and for the life of me, I can't recall whether that man made it into the boat. We headed for 1010 dock at the Navy shipyard.

And there was, indeed, reason to feel overwhelmed. On every side were almost unbearable sights. Battleship Row was devastated. From the direction of the dry docks, an explosion shook the harbor. This was the destroyer *Shaw*. Just two weeks before, I had visited my brother's ship in that same dry dock.

As we headed for the center of the channel, we saw that the cruiser *St. Louis* was underway, switching from sternway to headway, after backing out from the Navy Yard, and intending to make a run for the open sea.

The *St. Louis* was gaining speed, but we were able to come alongside her starboard quarter where we tried to clamber aboard the gangway which was still hanging over the side. An officer on deck denied us permission to come aboard. Frustrated, we abandoned the attempt to board the *St. Louis* and headed for 1010 dock at the Naval Ship Yard, where everyone went their individual ways.

Points of Interest

USS Pennyslvania

On December 7, 1941, the USS *Pennsylvania* was sitting in dry dock at the Pearl Harbor Naval Ship Yard. When the attack started, the *Pennsylvania* was one of the first ships to open fire. Japanese planes tried to torpedo the caisson of the dry dock but never succeeded. If they had, the dry dock would have been flooded and caused severe damage to the ship. The Japanese were successful in dropping a medium bomb on casemate number nine and the entire crew of the 5"–51 were killed. Two destroyers in the dry dock, the *Cassin* and *Downes*, were severely damaged. A portion of a torpedo tube weighing about 1,000 pounds was blown onto the forecastle of the *Pennsylvania*. However, she received relatively little damage compared to the battleships on Battleship Row. She arrived in San Francisco on December 29, 1941, for repairs and by early 1942 was back in action.

SHIPFITTER 3/C HOWARD JUHL
U.S. Navy, USS California

DECEMBER 7, 1941

On December 7, 1941, we had just finished breakfast when we heard some sort of unusual noise going on outside. A kid from Louisiana came running in, General Quarters was ringing, and he said, "Them planes have little red spots on their wings." Looking at him, I knew he wasn't kidding and immediately realized this was the real thing. Shortly before, I had read how the Russian Japanese war started in 1904. The Japs had conducted a surprise attack under similar circumstances, on Port Arthur in Manchuria. Knowing it would take five minutes to secure the hatches, I couldn't resist running out 200 ft. along the passage just to have a last look. This was a complete reversal for anybody, both mentally and physically. The hundreds of hours of training at General Quarters in the sunny Hawaiian waters and elsewhere meant that you automatically went to your station, just like a robot.

It was interesting how I had to fight my own instincts to go outside and take a quick glance. It really only took 3 minutes and I did not see much for I allowed only brief seconds before I headed for by battle station. As the hatches were secured, there were a number who did not see another ray of sunshine.

My station was starboard, aft, below the armor plate on the third deck. Not too much smoke or bad air at first, because we were on the opposite side of the torpedo hits. I went forward to locate some oxygen for our reserve apparatus, and as I came up to the forward repair looker, I noticed a well-built gunner's mate coming through the hatch with a glassy look in his eyes. He fell at my feet completely out. I had suspected it could be carbon monoxide poisoning, but rumors were running rapid that it was poison gas. Things became chaotic and caused a lot of hysteria.

My job was to get full tanks. I went through the lot and all were empty, meanwhile trying not to breathe and watching myself for signs of passing out. I came back to the repair group and they were in the process of counter-flooding. The effect of the carbon monoxide was beginning to be evident, and I was told to get better air, so at 9:30 A.M. I was lying down on the deck in the wardroom when the bomb exploded in the area midship. There was a tremendous rumble of smoke and dust and I looked up and a sailor was standing in front of me with burns on his arms and legs. He begged me to do something for him. I was lucky to be where I was and I was very incapable of assisting anyone else at this moment. I began to pray that the attack would stop.

I found myself topside trying to close a hatch up forward, then realized the combined pressure of water made it impossible to close a normal cover. Later I began to develop a splitting headache and ended up near the side of the scuppers trying to vomit. I looked up and there was Captain Bunkley in his white and gold braided splendor. I thought, "What a Royal prick," as he had came aboard hours after the attack had started. He ordered some men to give me some help.

At about 10 A.M. I was out on the stern area when the oil caught fire from the *Arizona* and it seemed the entire surface was on fire. It appeared that the fire would engulf the whole ship and so the order was given to abandon ship. Standing where I was, I knew it was stupid to do what I did, but I jumped into the water with a one-half inch film of oil on top. There was a boat nearby picking up anyone they could.

Chapter 7

USS *Detroit* (CL–8)

The USS *Detroit* was on the northwest side of Ford Island in the first northern position; then came the USS *Raleigh*, the USS *Utah*, and the USS *Tangier*, an aircraft tender which was astern of the *Utah*. On the *Raleigh* Ensign Donald Korn was turning over the watch to Ensign William Game. The officer of the deck couldn't see much of what was happening at Ford Island, but he did have a good view of the valley up the center of Oahu and Pearl City. About 0755, he noticed some planes flying low from Pearl City and East Loch. The planes split up — two headed for the USS *Utah*, one for a battleship, and one for the USS *Raleigh* and the USS *Detroit*.

Ensign Korn called off the antiaircraft battery because he thought it was marine aircraft on maneuvers. Torpedoes were launched, two for the *Utah* and one for the *Raleigh*. The *Utah* was hit and began to list quickly. The crew begin to leap from her decks only to be strafed by Japanese planes.

The first torpedo against the *Raleigh* struck the cruiser at frame 58, flooding the forward engine room number one and two fire rooms. The launch that was alongside the gangway to take the church party ashore was destroyed. A seaman pulled the general alarm but it did not sound because of electrical problems.

A dive bomber hit the *Raleigh* with an armor-piercing shell that went through the ship and exploded in the mud beneath her. This bomb

The USS Detroit

creased the pom-pom gun tub and went through the support leg of a three-inch antiaircraft ammunition box. It barely missed an aviation gasoline tank.

At 0800, another torpedo was launched and passed between the *Raleigh* and the *Detroit*, burying itself harmlessly in the mud. *Raleigh*, at 0805, had listed hard to port and in spite of counterflooding continued to list dangerously fast. To alleviate the situation, the plane on deck went off on scouting missions; torpedoes, booms, ladders, boat skids, chests, stanchions, anchors, chains, rafts, boats, and anything nonessential was removed. Pumps were used against the flooding, but to no avail. The ship's bottom ultimately came to rest on the sand of the harbor. However, her antiaircraft guns were manned and defended to the end of the attack.

The USS *Detroit* and the USS *Tangier* were not appreciably damaged and were later able to get underway.

SEAMAN JACK J. LUSCHER
U.S. Navy, USS Detroit

PEARL HARBOR

Jack was born on August 29, 1921, at Mt. Olive, Illinois. He joined the navy on February 6, 1940, and was sent to Great Lakes, Illinois, for training. He then shipped to the USS *Detroit* which was docked at Pearl Harbor, Hawaii. Jack was aboard the ship on the morning of December 7, 1941.

THE PEARL HARBOR ATTACK

The attack started at 0755 on December 7, 1941. No warning was given but the authorities in Washington, D.C., knew more than they told us in Hawaii. It was strictly a political thing and there will be a day of reckoning. Too bad I won't be there.

We left the harbor about 1200 noon and started out of the channel. We had a report that a midget sub was in the canal and one of the destroyers was sent to blow the thing out of the water which they did.

We patrolled our area in the South Pacific until December 12 and then head back to Pearl for supplies and ammunition. That was a sorry fleet that left Pearl on the 7th. A small enemy force could have taken the islands without too much trouble. Think of all the ships and troops that were lost in the Pacific and if these were used on the 7th it would have been a different story in the way the war was fought in the Pacific.

On our arrival in Pearl the sight was sickening. Bodies floated in the water — fuel oil all over the surface. Ships sunk and no immediate plan to right them. Of course the *Arizona* was a complete loss. Ironically when the *Arizona* blew up we went under her smoke screen and out to sea. The scene was indescribable and we wondered in awe that we did not know the dignity of their birth but we did know the glory of their death.

POINTS OF INTEREST

USS Utah

One of the first vessels attacked by the Japanese was the USS *Utah*. Japanese pilots had been ordered to ignore the training ships because they were noncombat vessels and not worth attacking. However, eager pilots dropped two torpedoes on the *Utah* and nearby *Raleigh*. A torpedo hit the *Utah* on the port side at 8:01 A.M. as the colors were being raised. A short time later a second torpedo hit in the same area and the ship began to list. The crew was ordered on deck and to the starboard side for their protection from loose timber which had been stored onboard for practice bombing. Within five minutes, she listed to 40 degrees and orders were given to abandon ship. By 8:12 A.M. the ship had capsized.

Efforts were made in 1943 to salvage the *Utah*, but after many problems, these were given up.

The USS *Utah* is located on the west side of Ford Island about a mile from the USS *Arizona*. Six officers and 52 enlisted men are entombed in the ship.

Early in 1970, supporters from the state of Utah and shipmates from the USS *Utah* proposed a memorial to honor the dead. On May 27, 1972, Senator Moss from Utah dedicated the memorial. The monument is a 40- by 15-foot concrete platform connected to the northwest shore of Ford Island by a 70-foot walkway. A naval color guard raises the flag each morning in honor of the men entombed in the *Utah*. Although there are over a million people a year who visit the *Arizona*, few have visited the *Utah*.

FC/3C ARTHUR G. HERRIFORD
U.S. Navy, USS Detroit

THE PEARL ATTACK

I was in the "F" Division, which was comprised of people responsible for the operational readiness of all the offensive weapons systems within the ship. I was a Fire Control man Third Class and my battle station was operator of Main Battery Rangefinder No. 1.

I had just sat down to breakfast when a loud thump was heard and felt. Then, several seconds later another such occurrence. Someone made the remark that a boat coxswain would certainly get chewed out by the O.O.D. for bumping his boat against the ship.

However, a chief gunner's mate passing through the mess-deck happened to look out a porthole and exclaimed, "It's the Japs! This is the real thing."

Then, the General Alarm sounded, calling all hands to battle stations! I dropped a spoonful of cereal without taking a single bite of breakfast and dashed for my battle station. Proceeding up number one hatch on my way to "Range One," in the superstructure, I saw a sailor who had just missed being strafed. He was hugging the port leg of the tripod foremast seeking protection.

Range one was situated one deck level above the pilothouse. A thirty-six inch signal lamp mounted on a platform approximately eighteen inches above the deck had to be crossed in order to climb higher into the superstructure.

I was on the signal-lamp platform, when Vulmer Dates, who was squatted down behind the rangefinder, yelled at me, gun forward, and fired several rounds in the direction aft, the concussion popped covers off the ports on either side of the pathfinder housing. Dates, his index fingers in his ears, leaned against me. I asked him what the problem was. He didn't answer right off. Finally, removing them, he remarked, "That was the biggest damned torpedo I have ever seen!" Apparently, the Japanese torpedo plane was making its approach from the direction of Pearl City and was foiled in dropping its torpedo by the concentrated fire from our .50-caliber machine guns.

We were in the rangefinder just a few minutes when we decided to go outside and have a look around. The first things that we noticed were two grooves across the deck showing six or eight bright, shiny gouges surrounded with the dust of red-lead and grey deck paint. Here was evidence that when Dates yelled at me, "Duck!" he saved me from being strafed.

We observed the Japanese plane that crashed into the USS *Curtis*. It had been taken under fire by both the USS *Detroit* and USS *Raleigh*. We were looking directly at the USS *Arizona* when she exploded. At first, we thought it was a fuel tank over by the submarine base, but soon decided it was one of our battleships. There was a corona of a shockwave, but I don't recall hearing a loud report, just a slight rush of air a few seconds following the explosion. Range one was approximately 65 feet above the water line. Dates and I had a clear view of the entire harbor. We had nothing we could do except watch the destruction take place.

The uniform of the day was white shorts and t-shirt. Although we were in the tropics, I remember being extremely cold; actually, I was shivering, possibly augmented by fright. Had I been one iota more scared, I believe I would have dropped dead on the spot.

A torpedo missed the stern of the *Detroit* by about 10 feet and ran up on the beach at Ford Island, less than 200 feet from our ship. That happened during the first phase of the attack. The second phase consisted primarily of high level bombers. During one wave, two sticks of bombs narrowly missed the *Detroit*; when they exploded in the water, mud from the harbor bottom was splashed onto the *Detroit*'s weather deck. About 0945 the attacking planes withdrew.

We were very lucky. Although the *Detroit* was strafed from stem to stern, she only sustained superficial damage. On at least two occasions the Japanese missed the *Detroit* in their attempts with torpedo attacks. Furthermore, they missed us during their horizontal bombings.

At least four of the crew are known to have been wounded: Paul Lombardo by a machine gun's bullet, Walter Huff, radioman, by shrapnel, Lester A. Siva, by shrapnel and Bill Knotts was injured in an explosion that occurred aboard the USS *Nevada* as the USS *Detroit*'s motorboat was alongside that battleship dropping off some of her officers.

Over on Battleship Row, each time a torpedo struck one of the battleships, geysers of water would rise four or five times higher than their fighting tops, which were approximately 135 feet above the water line.

We watched as the Battleship *Nevada* got underway and steam by the carnage along Battleship Row and we watched as numerous Japanese planes swarmed upon her as she made her way toward Hospital Point. Due to the damage she suffered, she was intentionally run aground to prevent blocking the channel.

The destroyer USS *Shaw*, in the floating dry dock made a spectacular sight when her forward magazines exploded blowing off her entire bow. Fourth of July fireworks were never more spectacular. Two weeks before, our *Detroit* was in that dry dock for repairs.

By this time, Dates and I were in a state of shock. I requested permission to secure the rangefinder and go below to assist on the AA battery, the idea being that it would give us something to do. The request was denied. We were instructed to keep Range-One manned, as the ship was making ready to get underway. Normally, Range-One was manned during Special Sea Details in order to provide navigational ranges while entering or leaving port. Little did we know, then, that it would be almost 30 hours later before we would secure General Quarters.

During the early part of the attack, I remember looking down onto the starboard wing of the signal bridge and seeing Rear Admiral Milo F. Draemel, Commander Destroyers Battle Force (COMDESBATFOR) issuing orders to various staff officers for the orderly getting underway of destroyers under his command. Scared as I was, it was reassuring for me to note the calm demeanor of the Admiral and his staff, almost as if the attack was commonplace.

The *Detroit* got underway from the berth F–13 at 10:10 am, without benefit of tugs. Rather than circle Ford Island clockwise, as we usually did, Captain Wiltse turned the ship around in the channel, on the Pearl City side of the harbor. However, after completing the turnaround, the ship was ordered to return to berth F–13, where the ship tied up, this time, portside to the cays.

It was about this time that Dates and I first noticed that our sister ship, USS *Raleigh* moored next astern, had a heavy port list. Her crew was stripping ship. They had jettisoned her catapults and additional mooring lines were bound to the cays. The USS *Utah*, moored stern of the *Raleigh* had capsized.

Finally, the *Detroit* received orders to get underway and leave the harbor. As the ship passed by the *Raleigh*, her crew yelled over, "go get those yellow, sneaky sons of bitches." The Detroit steamed out the channel entrance at about 20 knots, a speed unheard of under normal circumstances, but now considered necessary to avoid torpedoes.

No sooner did the *Detroit* clear the channel entrance of Pearl Harbor than she received a flashing light signal from a destroyer that two torpedoes were heading toward the ship. Captain Wiltse took evasive action. Later, two end-of-run detonations were observed on the horizon. Rumors abounded. One of them, a possible enemy landing on the western beaches of Oahu, was investigated but found to be just that.

Admiral Draemel was made Commander Task Force One, which included the USS *Detroit*, a light cruiser, USS *St. Louis*, also a light cruiser, and several destroyers that escaped Pearl Harbor. His orders were to seek out and engage the enemy. The task force formed up and commenced a search for the attacking forces.

About midnight, I overheard Admiral Draemel remark, "Give them another 10 seconds to identify themselves. Then, if they don't, open fire." Almost immediately, I saw a blinker light sending a message to us. I detected a sigh of relief down there on the bridge.

Dates and I accidentally dozed off for a short time. That scared the hell out of me; I could just see us being shot for sleeping on watch. In the wee hours of the morning I really got a jolt. My CPO banged on the shield doors to wake us up. It seems that Forward Control couldn't raise us on the sound-powered battle telephone circuit. We had been at General Quarters for almost 16 hours without food or water. Everyone was so exhausted that they fell into catnaps. Somehow we got through the night. About midmorning, sandwiches and hot coffee were distributed. I remember taking a wonderful looking ham sandwich and a cup of hot coffee, but it was all I could do to force down a single bite. I gave most of it away.

On the afternoon of the 8th, Task Force One rendezvoused with the aircraft carrier USS *Enterprise*. Until Wednesday, 10 December, our combined force searched the quadrant South and West of the Hawaiian Island. In the afternoon of the 10th, the *Detroit* returned to Pearl Harbor to a sight that almost turned my stomach. Oil and debris of every description littered the harbor. Blackened ships with various degrees of list were resting on the harbor bottom or capsized. On Ford Island, damaged hangars and charred and wrecked aircraft, were a terrible sight to behold.

On the *Detroit*, all hands were ordered on a working party to offload all the target ammunition. It was replaced with service ammunition. The evening meal was served in two shifts so that the work at hand would continue without interruption.

For the next four years, the USS *Detroit* played her role in WWII. At first she served as commander of convoys plying the waters between San Francisco, and the Hawaiian and Samoan Islands. Then she spent two years patrolling the Bering Sea and retaking three Japanese held Aleutian Islands. She served several months during 1944 patrolling the West Coast of South America. In early 1945, she was assigned to the South Pacific Theater as flagship of Commander Service Squadron Six, consisting of some 200 supply ships assisting in the seizure of Japanese-held Iwo Jima, Okinawa, and the main islands of Japan.

The *Detroit* was honored with being the "Ship of Honor" at Japan's surrender which took place aboard the battleship USS *Missouri*, in Tokyo Bay, Japan, September 2, 1945.

Chapter 8

USS *Neosho*

The USS *Neosho* finished discharging fuel at Hickam Field the evening before the attack on Pearl Harbor. At midnight, the ship was moored at Berth F–4 at the Ford Island Navy Shipyard. She had delivered 500,000 gallons of aviation gasoline to the Tank Farm and had that much left in the tanks on board. On December 7, 1941, when the attack began the USS *Neosho* was in danger of being hit by Japanese torpedoes which, with the amount of gasoline fuel aboard, endangered the *Maryland*, *Tennessee*, and *West Virginia*.

The ship opened fire at the attacking planes at 0805. The captain, realizing the danger he placed the other ships in, began to prepare to get underway. By 0842, she was on course to berth M–3 at Merry's Point.

SEAMAN HARRY D. OGG
U.S. Navy, USS Neosho

I enlisted in the Navy in Corpus Christi, Texas on June 3, 1941. I took my training at San Diego Training Center. I was assigned to the USS *Neosho* A.O. 23 and went aboard the ship in Bremington, Washington. Our duty was to provide Pearl Harbor with fuel. The *Neosho* was a fleet tanker which operated between San Pedro and Hawaii.

USS Neosho *after preliminary conversion. Pictured from port broadside at the Navy Yard in Philadelphia, PA, two years before Pearl Harbor.*

We departed San Pedro on November 29, 1941. We arrived on December 6. We delivered fuel at Hickam Field that morning and later that evening we got underway to Ford Island to start pumping fuel ashore.

I myself was on duty that morning of December 7. My first duty was to assist my third class petty officer to make colors by raising the flag at 0800. We were standing by to do so when we were attacked by the Japs' dive bombers, torpedoes, low and high dive bombers, and zeros. They hit Battleship Row with a surprise attack. We were the first ship to get underway as we still had some 90 percent octane gas aboard. We went to Merry's Point fleet landing for liberty boats. We were the only oiler there at the time. The oiler *Ramapo* was there also but they did not participate in our first task force to engage the enemy.

Later we went to the Gilbert and Marshall Islands in search of the Japs, but we never were able to make contact with them. We fueled ships during the war including the *Lexington* and *Enterprise* and the rest of the task force.

I was sent back to the States to go to mine sweeping school in Yorktown, Virginia, and that is what I was doing until the end of the war. The USS *Neosho* was sunk at the Battle of Coral Sea. I lost a lot of my shipmates. I will never forget them.

Chapter 9

USS *Raleigh* (CL–7)

The USS *Raleigh* was in the position between the USS *Detroit* and the USS *Utah* on the northwest side of Ford Island. The events that then transpired were described previously at the beginning of Chapter 7.

SEAMAN 1/C GLENN R. NICHOLS
U.S. Navy, USS Raleigh

On Friday, December 5, 1941, the *Raleigh* returned to Pearl Harbor after antiaircraft gunnery practice and was scheduled to continue practice on Monday December 8. Permission was given to retain ammunition in ready boxes near the applicable gun rather than return the ammo to the appropriate storage.

My battle station was a pointer — turn hand wheels to point the gun vertically and fire the loaded gun when on target — on the 3 inch antiaircraft gun number 7 near the ship's stern. On December 7, 1941, at 0756 hours the ship was hit at frame 55½, port side by a Japanese Ariel torpedo. At the time of the hit I was on the 1 inch platform, the deck below the main deck, at frame 98. I travelled up three ladders and aft to frame 114 to number 7 three-inch gun. Gun 7, unlike six other 3 inch guns aboard, did not have an awning covering the gun-tub area, but only a few weather covers

74

Torpedoed and bombed, the 7,050-ton light cruiser USS Raleigh *is held afloat by a barge near her anchorage in Pearl Harbor. The capsized USS* Utah *is in the background. The* Raleigh *later rejoined the fleet.*

over critical parts of the gun, allowing quicker gun loading and firing. I was the third gun member of the crew and in seconds the gun was loaded and fired at Japanese planes.

During the attack our gun crew shot the tail off a Japanese plane as it crossed the ship's stern, the plane crashing into the water. Another of the ship's three-inch antiaircraft guns shot down another attacking plane that crashed into the USS *Curtis'* crane. Three other attackers received *Raleigh's* gunfire. At 0908 hours our gun was firing at attacking dive bombers. One of their 500-pound bombs struck our ammo ready box, penetrating the ship's hull before exploding.

Despite all the seekers of being first, the *Raleigh's* number 7 three inch gun crew can claim to be the first to shoot a 3-inch anti-aircraft at a Japanese attacker at Pearl Harbor. USS *Raleigh's* official deck log Sunday December 7, 1941, last sentence reads, "Went to general quarters and opened fire with A.A. battery." The honor of being first could be shared,

UNITED STATES SHIP _____ RALEIGH _____ Sunday _____ December 19_41_

ZONE DESCRIPTION ____ +10½ ____   REMARKS

0 to 4
Moored starboard side to Berth F-12 with 1 to 5 manila lines, in 6½ fathoms of water. Boiler #9 steaming for auxiliary purposes. Ships present: U.S. Pacific Fleet, less various detached units plus yard and district craft. S.O.P.A. COMBATFOR in U.S.S. CALIFORNIA. 0245 ARGEMENT, W., BM1c, returned from duty with the shore patrol in Honolulu, T.H. 0245 POOLE, T.S., WT2c, returned aboard having been A.O.L. since 0100 December 7, 1941, a period of 1 hour 45 minutes.

           J.M. WERTH, Ensign, U.S. Navy.

4 to 8
Moored as before. 0520 SMITH, W., Sea2c, was returned by shore patrol. Charge staggering. 0655 received for use in general mess from The Provision Co., Ltd., 500 pieces ice cream. Inspected as to quantity by D.L. KORN and as to quality by PETTY, W.E., PhM3c. 0735 U.S.S. HELM underway and stood out. 0745 sound of gunfire heard. 0755 Japanese torpedo plane attack on ships in Pearl Harbor. RALEIGH hit by torpedo at frame 58. Forward engine room and 1 and 2 fire rooms flooded. No personnel casualties. Went to general quarters and opened fire with A.A. battery.

           D.L. KORN, Ensign, U.S.N.R.

8 to 12
Engaged as before, firing on several planes to starboard pulling out of attacks on battleships or air station. Planes approached from general S.E. direction altitude 700 - 1000 feet. 0805 ship listed heavily to port. Commenced counter flodding in compartments A-107 and A-115. Compartment A-108 flooded due to leakage from A-107. List to port continued to increase. 0805 to 0820 following enemy planes taken under fire: plane No. 1 which had just completed attack on battleships or air station; general course N.W., altitude 1000 feet, bearing 200° true. Plane hit on bearing 220° true, caught fire, swerved sharply to left and crashed on after deck of U.S.S. CURTISS. Plane No. 2, astern, flying in general direction from air station to Pearl City, was hit by 3 inch shell and blown to pieces in air approximately over Buoy No. 5 at altitude of about 1200 feet. Plane No. 3 flew over bow of RALEIGH from direction of air station, was hit when about overhead and swerved in a westerly direction and crashed in direction of Pearl City. Plane No. 4, flying North over Ford Island altitude 1000 - 1500 feet was hit and crashed between BALTIMORE and DOBBIN off starboard bow. Plane No. 5, flying cross stern, was struck and had its tail blown off, swerved to the right and landed north of Peninsula Point. Plane No. 6 approached from over Ford Island dropped bomb which landed less than 100 yards to port. 0830 secured #9 boiler and cleared personnel from engineering spaces. 0900 relighted fires under #9 boiler. 0908 enemy bombing plane attack from direction of Ford Island dropped two bombs, one of which struck RALEIGH aft at frame 112, glanced off ready ammunition box, went through carpenter shop, oil tanks, pierced the hull on port quarter below the water line and detonated about 50 feet from ship. Second bomb landed less than 100 yards to port. Plane machine gunned ship. After compartments flooded. List increased. Hoisted out planes by hand and sent them to Ford Island with aviation detail. 0915 counter flooded compartments A-117, A-118 and A-119. 0920 plane dove on ship from northeast and dropped bomb at altitude of about 1000 feet. Bomb landed in water off starboard quarter between ship and beach - no damage. Secured #9 boiler and cleared personnel from engineering spaces. 0945 list 10° to port. Failed in attempt to relight fires under boiler #9 due to water in fuel oil. 1015 cleared personnel from engineering spaces. 1035 list 11° to port, mean draft 21 feet. Cruisers and destroyers commenced sortie. 1100 sent party to U.S.S. UTAH to cut out man trapped in hull. 1105 commenced jettisonning topside weights. Torpedoes beached at Ford Island. Torpedo tubes, catapults, cargo booms, boat skids, davits and stanchions put overboard by hand.

Approved:
R.B. SIMONS
Captain, U.S. Navy,
Commanding.

Examined:
D.F. MC LEAN
Lieut-Comdr.,
U.S.N., Navigator,

(Original (ribbon) copy of this page to be sent to Bureau of Nav...

Glenn Nichols was the Pointer on #7 3" AA Gun, by happenstance shot the tail off the # 5 plane and also Fired the gun while viewing through a crosshaired scope at the planes dropping the bombs.

ADDITIONAL SHEET

U.S.S. RALEIGH   Date December 7 19 41.

8 to 12(Cont'd)
Let go both anchors. Ran all available wires and manila to quays. Following ammunition expended during engagement: 3"/50 caliber - 266 rounds, .50 caliber - 9990 rounds, 1.1 - 3270 rounds. The following men were injured or wounded during the engagement: HOFFMAN, Joseph Daniel 256 06 32, O.R.M. F-4-D, U.S. Navy. Wound, lacerated, 2" right forehead (Falling object after torpedo explosion #2563 Key Letter "K". Disposition: Retained on board; PRIEST, Eugene O'Neal 316 60 17 Yeo.2c., U.S. Navy. Wound, Gunshot 2" right thigh. #2576, Key Letter "K" (Shrapnel). Disposition: Transferred to U.S. Naval Hospital, Pearl Harbor, T.H.; SMITH, Leonard Dale 342 35 83, Sea.2c. U.S. Navy. Contusion, left hip #2512 Key Letter "K" Cause: Explosion of bomb near motor launch in which he was passenger. Disposition: Retained on board; WILLIAMS, Charles Raymond 316 57 60, M.M.2c., U.S. Navy. Wound, Gunshot, 6" right deltoid (Shrapnel) #2576 Key Letter "K". Disposition: Transferred to U.S. Naval Hospital, Pearl Harbor, T.H.; WORKMAN, Carl (None) 265 94 76, G.M.2c, U.S. Navy. Wound, Gunshot, 1" left thigh (Shrapnel) #2576, Key Letter "K". Disposition: Transferred to U.S.S. SOLACE.

D.F. MC LEAN, Lieut-Comdr., U.S. Navy.

12 to 16
Moored as before. List 10° to port. Continuing to remove topside weights. Ship in very unstable condition. 1235 list 9° to port. 1300 commenced removing water from main deck at frame 88 with handy billys. 1325 SUNNADIN secured to port quarter with barge carrying four pontoons. Commenced running steel hawsers from pontoons under and around ship. 1338 list decreased 7° to port. 1400 successfully lighted fires under #11 boiler. 1405 commenced pumping out compartment A-115 with submersible pump. SUNNADIN took suction from compartment D-301. 1440 list commenced to decrease rapidly. 1455 ship rolled to starboard and steadied with 8° list. Secured #11 boiler. Cleared personnel from engineering spaces. 1500 relighted fires under #11 boiler. Commenced freeing after fire rooms and engine room of water. Took suction from compartment D-301 with two handy billys.

D.F. MC LEAN, Lieut-Comdr., U.S. Navy.

16 to 20
Moored as before. List 9° to starboard. 1700 AVOCET moored to port side forward and commenced furnishing power for radio transmitters and receivers.

D.F. MC LEAN, Lieut-Comdr., U.S. Navy.

20 to 24
Moored as before. 2105 five planes showing running lights crossed Ford Island in direction of battleships. Battleships opened fire followed by other ships and shore batteries. One plane crashed in flames at Pearl City. Expended 80 rounds 1.1 , 3 rounds 3"/50 caliber, 1200 rounds .50 caliber. 2130 list 7° to starboard.

D.F. MC LEAN, Lieut-Comdr., U.S. Navy.

Approved: R.B. SIMONS
Captain, U.S. Navy,
Commanding.

Examined: D.F. MC LEAN
Lieut-Comdr.,
U. S. N., Navigator.

This photograph was taken from Ford Island (inside Pearl Harbor) and shows the starboard side of the USS Raleigh CL-7 after being hit by a Japanese aerial torpedo on the port side at frame 55½ (a front edge of #2 stack) at 7:56 a.m. At 0908, a 500-lb bomb penetrated the ship at frame 112 and she was machine-gun strafed a number of times by Japanese aircraft. The following is in reference to numbers shown above: 1. Gathering of crew members for their body weight masses. 2. Main deck where ariplane catapult was mounted, jettisoned overboard. 3. Captain's gig — was loaned with his gear. 4. Dual 3" .50 caliber AA gun tub. 5. Port holes of the first platform (deck). 6. Location of the officers' gangway, jettisoned overboard. 7. Canvas awning from the top of the two gun tubs that was cut from outboard side at the attack, covering the guns and delaying their firing.

if all the other vessels at Pearl Harbor, having 3 inch .50 caliber anti-aircraft guns, had deck logs for December 7 which read the same as the *Raleigh*'s. Due to water in fuel tanks, the ship lost all power and, the two aircraft aboard were boom lowered by hand, all other activity to jettison topside involved pushing overboard by hand.

During the initial firing of our guns, numbers of officers and chiefs became ammo handlers until the enlisted crew could takeover. After torpedo explosion causing much flooding below decks crew and officers not manning critical areas were lined up in mass from stem to stern on the mandioc. This human mass moved by shouting from the bridge, "All Hands to Port," then "All Hands to Starboard," heaving most of the heavy items over the side and to the bottom of the harbor. The tug USS *Sannadin* AT–28 came alongside and its divers had wrapped cables around the ship and the adjacent barge.

Raleigh crew members being near the stern of the ship and less than 100 feet from the bow of the USS *Utah*, witnessed deaths of USS *Utah* sailors trying to abandon their ship, which had taken three torpedoes. Our rescue crew cut a bottom section of the ship to allow a *Utah* sailor to escape. To this day there are still 58 sailors aboard the *Utah*, whose bodies were never recovered.

Chapter 10

USS *Trever* (DD–339)

The USS *Trever* DD–339 was originally built as DD–16 at Mare Island Navy Yard and commissioned in 1922. This 1,190-ton, 314' 4"–long ship had a speed of 35 knots. She was built with four 4" .50 caliber guns, one 3" .23 caliber anti-aircraft gun and twelve 21" triple torpedo tubes. In 1940, the vessel was converted to a Fast Mine Sweeper DMS–16 USS *Trever* (ex-DD–339). The *Trever* was docked at Pearl Harbor on the morning of December 7, 1941, when the Japanese attacked.

NORMAN ROBARR
U.S. Navy, USS Trever *DD–339*

I enlisted in the U.S. Navy September 17, 1940 at Lockport, New York and shortly thereafter received boot camp training with company 34 at the Naval training station in Newport Rhode Island.

It was late November that year when I arrived at Pearl Harbor, Hawaii and I was assigned to my first ship the destroyer USS *Trever* DD 339. The Trever was a four pipe flush decker commissioned in 1922. Her main armament consisted of four 4 inch single purpose guns that could fire at surface targets only. For air attack defense she mounted four .50 caliber water cooled machine guns and for anti submarine work, she carried under water sound gear and depth charges.

A port bow view of the USS Trever, *six months after Pearl Harbor.*

A few months before the attack of December 7 the *Trever* was converted to a high speed destroyer mine sweeper and became DMZ 16. The USS *Trever* was in Pearl Harbor the weekend of the Japanese attack. Moored to buoys in West Loch facing Pearl City landing, she was outboard port side ship in a nest of four destroyer mine sweeps.

Four ships were tied together side by side with one ship keeping boilers lighted to supply steam and electricity to the others. *Trever*'s boilers were shut down and secured and it took hours to start up the boilers once they were shut down. Our customary procedure was to light off the night before the day we went to sea.

On Saturday, December 6, 1941, we stood a Captain's inspection and that Saturday morning found our crew like many others, lined up in neat rows wearing our cleanest white uniforms—hats squared, shoes shined, and looking spit and polished.

The Captain inspected the ship, checked out all quarters and gear and then left ship to spend the weekend ashore. The Captain was soon followed by most of our other officers and Sunday morning when the bombs began to fall, our senior officer was our engineering officer Lt. Shay.

It wasn't long after the officers left when the enlisted men begin to pack it up for the weekend. These are the guys who know how to fire a gun, light a boiler, steer a ship, and in no time they were gone for the weekend. Before they left they put most of the gear away, greased guns down, and secured them for next week's inspection.

That Saturday night I was excited. I was writing letters home to my girlfriend, my parents, and my friends. I was telling them the good news that we had gotten word that the *Trever* was going back to the States for R and R and East Coasters would get leave preferences. Wow! I was going home!

Sunday morning December 7 1941, four ships the USS *Trever*, USS *Wasmuth*, USS *Perry*, and USS *Zane,* were tied together in a nest moored to buoys off Pearl City landing. Breakfast is over and it is about a quarter to eight. Someone sticks his head over the hatch to forward crews' quarters and hollers, "Bum boats alongside."

A bum boat is a civilian launch that sells things to ships moored in the harbor. I go up topside for the Sunday morning newspaper. I brought a copy, took it down to crew's quarters, sorted out the junk, and got into the important stuff.

I was reading the funnies when the general quarters began to ring. "Sunday morning! What kind of a drill are they pulling on us now?" I thought. I left the paper behind and started up the ladder for topside. On the next deck up, a sleepy looking Lt. Shay opened his cabin door, stuck his head out and says, "Sailor, what's going on?"

I answered, "I don't know sir," and continued to the main deck.

Topside with several more "What's going ons?" with no one knowing, I decided to do a bit of looking around and then, looking between the well decks of the ships on our starboard side, I saw what I thought was the reason for the general alarms ringing—fire! Fire over at Ford Island Naval Air Station. There were flames and clouds of black smoke coming from the hangars near the seaplanes' ramps. So that's it! Away fire and rescue party, now I know what to do. I immediately proceed to my assigned station, a huge and heavy chest of tools kept right there in the well deck. The chest is so heavy it takes two men to carry it, but no one is coming to help. What is going on?

I ran forward, but on the forecastle I still can't see because I'm under those pretty white awnings that cover all our decks. I looked forward up to the front point on the ship where the Union Jack is located. It was lying on the deck. "This can't be," I thought.

I look over at the big ships moored over by Ford Island. One prep at the yardarm and we execute colors when the senior ship present in the harbor brings that flag down. I stand there at the bow holding that Union Jack wondering why Ford Island is burning and where is the messenger of the watch who's supposed to be here with this flag.

I didn't have to wait long. Airplanes flew in on the port bow very low. They were not familiar — shiny metal, red trim, and round red emblems. I've never seen airplanes like these before but I have seen red triangles on some Dutch PBY seaplanes that came to Pearl Harbor a while back. I wonder if these planes are Dutch.

They're crossing our bow real low; then it happened. I saw torpedoes fall. My God! They're aiming them at the battleship *Utah*. Then a thought came to me. Torpedoes dive deep before they establish running depth and I know there is a reef in front of those torpedoes because we ran a motor whale boat aground there one night cutting channel markers coming back to our ship.

As I watched a huge column of water rose high in the air as those torpedoes hit the *Utah*. A fifty-foot launch alongside her instantly disappeared and it didn't take more than a minute till the *Utah* was bottomside up.

I quickly secured the Union Jack and ran aft to the fair weather under the bridge. I heard pretty music coming from the radio shack. It was tuned to KGMB Honolulu. By the time more of the crew was topside everybody was running around all excited, nobody knowing what to do. I didn't go to my battle station. The four-inch gun on the forecastle would not elevate to shoot in the air and, under the white awning, it wouldn't have done much good anyway. "Machine guns," I thought. That's where it's at — machine guns! Heck, we have four of them, two on the gallery deck house and two on the after deck house. Does anyone know where they keep the ammunition?"

It didn't take long before someone got down in the forward magazine and found out where it was kept and a few minutes later we began hauling these funny-looking wooden boxes up on deck.

It said .50 caliber ammunition on each box, but what do we do with it? We opened some boxes, found tin boxes inside, opened them and discovered loose rounds inside the tin boxes. The ammo had to be put in belts and placed in drums before it could be used. We didn't have a gunner's mate or the clips we needed to belt with.

I heard a horrible boom from aft and I felt the ship lurch forward and suddenly I found myself sprawled on the deck at least ten feet from where I had been working. They said later that the bomb was so close it sunk the buoy we were moored to aft. Later the afterdeck force slipped the wire cable to get us underway. They couldn't unshackle us from a sunken buoy. The other whaleboat tied under our screw guards was swamped and left behind when we put to sea.

Back on the well deck with the ammunition, I now hear a voice on the radio shouting "Air Raid — Pearl Harbor!" We've hauled up more .50 caliber ammunition, found some clips, and the gadget used to join rounds and clips together. Trouble is that the process is slow. We picked up the loose clips from under the guns as rounds were fired.

I grabbed a strip and ran with it up to the galley deckhouse. There Jimmy Riggs was on the port side gun. He knows how to fire the thing. He lifts the cover and loads, pulls the trigger and bang! One round and it quits. Do it again and one round. We look inside and see if we can figure this one out. What the heck is this? Grease! Heavy black grease inside the gun. It is full of it. We take it apart. We don't know a thing about it. We've never seen one of these guns fire. Oh, how I wish I could talk to the person who put all the grease in the gun. It may be ready for next Saturday's inspection, but it ain't going to fire right now.

I learned an awful lot about .50 caliber machine guns in the next few minutes when we pulled the thing apart and cleaned it. We put some light oil on the moving parts, loaded the strip of ammunition, and found that the gun did fire.

Next we discovered that all .50 caliber ammo is not the same. It came in boxes of armor pierce, common ball and tracer. All we knew was that we couldn't see where them shots were going. We put some tracer rounds in to give direction when we fired.

Wow! A plane just blew into small pieces right in front of us and a bit to starboard. He wasn't too high and he was coming our way, but we weren't shooting at him. Sheets of burning gas were falling. The right wing breaks off. Parts are fluttering — junk and gas. It hit on the beach right at the water's edge astern of us.

The barrels of the guns are smoking because they are so hot. We need water for them. I look way up in the sky. A plane with four engines and a narrow slip of wing is coming over. It isn't ours. We are firing from all guns now at the Jap planes flying low over our bow. Then I look up and a P–40 is in a dogfight with a Jap Zero. They go behind a line of trees and an explosion is followed by a yellow flash. Up comes the P–40.

Here comes another Jap plane, low crossing our bow from starboard. He's flying slow. He looks okay, no smoke or fire, no parts missing that I can see. He keeps getting lower as we begin firing at him. I am holding a strip of ammunition. The tracers are hitting the plane and bouncing off.

He's getting lower and lower. I can't see bullets hitting him. He was just off the water then suddenly hit the water and quickly sank.

Our ship's officers had come aboard. We are going to sea. The Japs are gone. As we finally pull out, I looked at the harbor. Ford Island is burning. The ships alongside the island are on fire. It is nothing but a big mess of burning ships and black smoke. The *Utah* is sunk. I wonder what Battleship Row looks like. Can't see it, there is so much smoke.

We were finally at sea. There were a few other ships out there. I'm on gun four, but there are no Japs. We were out for a short time and a PT boat approached and asked us to return to the harbor. They were afraid there were mines.

When we returned, the channel was full of junk. We come in closer. I can see Battleship Row now. I have forgotten about the mines. It is unbelievable. All the ships are sunk or upside down. There are no mines and we went back to sea.

That night I was on watch. Suddenly the harbor lit up with tracers and firing everywhere. We learned the next morning that planes from our carriers were coming in. Our men opened up on them and shot all of them down. They thought we were being attacked again.

One night about a week before the attack I was aboard the battleship *Arizona* watching the ship's movie. She was moored at 10–10 dock in the Navyyard. It was our custom to go around the yard asking what the ship's movie was for that night. Then finding one we wanted to see we'd ask permission to come aboard.

I'd like to quietly go aboard *Arizona* again. And there be alone with my own thoughts. Then I'd like to take a small boat and visit a couple of anchorage areas. Then I'd like to get on the plane and leave — never looking back.

A CHRISTMAS REMEMBERED

Christmas— to me it's a time for memories and a time of awe and wonder of God's gift to us and to His world.

I'm a grandfather now, and today it's a time for the little ones, the excitement of Santa Claus, the presents, things to be stored for future memories.

But somehow the memories that seem to me like yesterday — so real, so vivid, that every act, every word, will be with me forever — are of a time when there was no peace on earth, when brotherhood had a different understanding — World War II.

December 25, 1941. I'll never forget it. That was the Christmas that wasn't — it didn't go away or anything like that — it just didn't happen.

Our destroyer, the USS *Trever,* had been at sea in the area around Hawaii since the air raid on Pearl Harbor December 7th. Time had lost all meaning with watch following watch and day following day. We had survived the attack with minor damage, none of our crew was injured, the ship was strafed and one bomb had hit so close astern that it capsized our motor whale boat and sank the bouy we were moored to. Somehow we had managed to shoot down a Japanese plane with our .50 caliber machine guns. Then in the days at sea following the attack, we'd had three torpedos fired at us (all missing). We had attacked and probably sunk an enemy submarine and had the sad experience of picking up survivors from a torpedoed cargo ship.

Then the order was received to proceed to "Pearl," tie up at the submarine docks, fuel, provision, spend the night in port and return to sea in the morning. We were standing full condition watches then, even in port. One third of the ship's company was on watch.

I will always remember that night — a midnight watch on a gun crew. It was quiet and it was good to be safe in port. One of the fellows was writing a letter home when he asked a question only a serviceman can understand. "What's the date?" after a brief discussion (and some finger counting) someone said, "Why it's December 26th." There was a long pause before someone quietly said, "Then yesterday was Christmas."

But things do change, and time does move on. I remember Christmas 1945 and the ships party we had at the former Japanese Navy enlisted men's club in Yokosuka, Japan — lots of beer, fun, laughter and good food. It was great. We'd won the war and survived. It was good to be alive, to be young, to be making plans for the future.

We had a grand time that night. I remember the Japanese entertainer who, with his young lady assistant, put on a comic skit using gestures and whistling. We spoke a different language, but we understood and we all laughed.

Then I thought of people who had little to celebrate that Christmas— the Japanese. I thought of the plight of homeless people living in rubble — of the pitiful sight of innocent little children living in a culvert —cold, hungry.

Then an idea occurred to me — we're going to spread a little of this cheer around! I had no trouble recruiting a couple of helpers— and then we did it — we stole a United States Navy turkey. I mean we stole the whole thing — a huge juicy, still hot from the oven, roasted bird, roasting pan and all.

Now — have you ever thought of running with a thing like that? Well, run I did (and successfully). I managed to slip unnoticed past the Marines guarding the base and into the darkened streets outside. As I left the area I became aware of the freezing rain that was falling, and that I'd forgotten my coat.

I called to several Japanese I met and I still wonder what they thought, but one thing sure — they weren't going to stop! Finally I saw a young fellow like me. I called and he stopped, somewhat apprehensively, but he did stop.

It took some doing to make him understand that I wanted to give him the huge, juicy, still hot, roasted turkey, I just happened to have with me.

I don't believe he knew a word of English, but he learned one that night. Offering him the turkey I said "Christmas" and we each repeated it several times before the look of bewilderment began to leave his face. Then with the beginning of a smile turning into a broad grin he said, "Christmas" and bowing politely took his turkey (pan and all) and quickly disappeared into the darkness.

— Norman Robarr

0755–7–12–41

The Bosun's call Has long Been Still
A call That Piped To War
By the Mark Five In A Shimmering Deep
Its sounds Heard No More

Prep's Ready At The Yard Arm
Jack And Ensign Halyards Bent
When From Above The Fury Came
And Mornings Calm Was Rent
Confusion Came With Terror
New Orders Of The Day
Load, Fire, Prepare For Sea
We're Getting Underway
Deck Crew Slip The Hawsers
Let Go The Buoy Wire
Oh God! Ford Island and Berths
The Ships, The Smoke, The Fire
Sinking, Burning, Or Turned Hulls
Decks Awash, Oh Edge The Beam
Friends we Knew As Shipmates
Gone To Fiddler's Green
For Sights And Sounds And Memories
Of That December Day
We've Set The Watch, The Duty's Ours
They Shall Not Pass Away

— Norman Robarr

Chapter 11

USS *Boggs* (AG–19) (EX DD–136, DMS–3, AG–103)

The destroyer USS *Boggs* was first commissioned on September 23, 1918. She saw little service before she was decommissioned in May 1922. After being decommissioned for nearly ten years, the *Boggs* underwent extensive overhaul in preparation for conversion to a radio-controlled high-speed destroyer target unit.

She was then commissioned on December 19, 1931, as the AG–19. The ship visited many ports including Cuba, Haiti, Norfolk, and New York, to name a few. In 1939, she was used as a high-speed mobile target unit and then in 1940 reported to Pearl Harbor. There she was first used as a high-speed target towing vessel. As DMS–3 she was converted to a minesweeping vessel. She was then assigned to Mine Squadron Two as flagship of Commander Mine Division Six.

On December 7, 1941, the USS *Boggs* was at sea when the Japanese attacked, but quickly returned to Pearl Harbor and conducted minesweeping operations.

Throughout the war the *Boggs* operated in the Pearl area making a few cargo trips to Palmura Island in operations with Task Group 44.1.

When those operations were over in 1943, she returned to Pearl Harbor with Task Group 66.7.

In 1945, she was sent to the Marshall Islands and then to Toyko, Japan, where she was part of the Japanese occupation forces.

After a 27-year career she was decommissioned and sold in November 1946.

SEAMAN JAMES D. SYLVESTER
U.S. Navy, USS Boggs

At the time of the attack on Pearl Harbor we were out to sea off of Oahu. We got the message that the Japanese had attacked. We went to General Quarters immediately, anticipating a possible attack if the Japanese spotted us. We headed back to Pearl Harbor and by the time we got there the attack was over.

It was a shocking sight. Just unbelievable. It looked like every ship in the harbor had either sunk, was sinking, or was on fire. As we past the *Oklahoma* I was looking at the hull of the ship. I glanced over at one of the other crew members. Neither of us said a word, but both of us silently with our eyes said, "This can't be possible." Much of the water was in flames from the burning oil. Sailors were running in all directions helping the wounded, trying to put out fires, watching for

James D. Sylvester pictured on December 7, 1991— 50 years after Pearl Harbor.

the Japanese, or in some cases just running in a shocked and confused state. The airfield at Ford Island was in flames. The water was full of debris— mattresses, parts of ships, uniforms, other clothes, bodies. There were still boats picking up men from the harbor both dead and alive.

We rapidly began mine sweep operations in the harbor. By dark we had finished with the harbor being clear of any mines. We headed back to sea. None of us said much to each other. The looks of shock and disbelief were enough. It was conveyed as we looked at each other. I tried to sleep that night, but all I could see was the sight of Pearl Harbor on fire.

POINTS OF INTEREST

USS Helm (DD–338)

On the morning of December 7, 1941, the destroyer USS *Helm* was the only ship underway in all of Pearl Harbor and she was in the main channel about to turn into the West Loch when the attack began. Planes

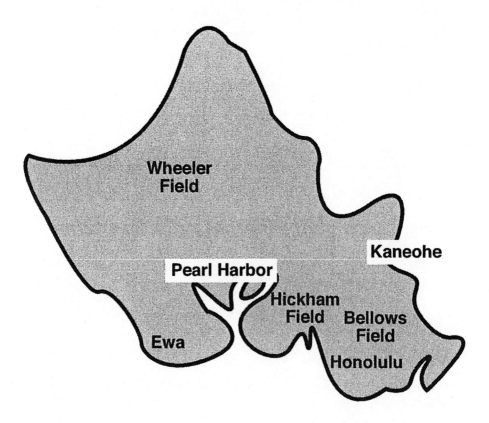

The submarine base at Pearl Harbor.

passed the ship at about 100 yards and casually waved as they passed over. A short time later, when the explosions began, the *Helm* turned around quickly and headed for the channel and open sea.

USS Vestal *(AR–49)*

The USS *Vestal* was moored with the USS *Arizona* for repairs. When the attack started, the *Vestal* sounded the alarm. At 0805, she opened fire on the Japanese. One bomb hit her at frame 110 portside, and a second hit her at frame 44 starboard.

The bomb that hit forward went through four decks and exploded in the general storeroom. The bomb that hit the afterpart of the ship went through the carpenter's shop and on down through a double deck. Both started fires in the magazine areas.

In bitter irony, the fires that destroyed the USS *Arizona* saved the *Vestal*. The concussion from the fatal explosion on the former put out the conflagration on the latter.

About 100 men were thrown overboard from the *Vestal*, among them her captain.

Chapter 12

Submarine Base

SEAMAN BM 2/C M.C. ESCARENO
*U.S. Navy, Captain's Driver for Commanding
Officer of the Submarine Base*

On December 7, 1941, I was a BM 2/c attached to the U.S. submarine base, Pearl Harbor. I was the captain's driver for Capt. Daubin, commanding officer of the submarine base and also the commander of submarine squadron 4. I had just had chow and was walking across the submarine barracks and I looked towards the bay. It was approximately 7:55 A.M. and I saw two torpedo planes flying very low at the end of the submarine piers. I noticed the black planes with the red meatballs on the wing. Thereafter, they hit the battleships which were moored at Ford Island. I ran up to the third floor of the barracks which overlooks Kahua Island and Ford Island. It was a mess. The *Oklahoma* was hit and turned over upside down. The *West Virginia* was torpedoed pretty bad and the *Arizona* at the same time. I ran down and got into the, captain's car and drove out the sub base gate to Malacalors to the officers' housing. Soon as I drove up, Capt. Daubin came running out and asked me what was going on. I told him what I had seen. As we started to leave, Adm. Kimmel ran up to the car and asked Capt. Daubin if he could hitch a ride. The captain said yes. I got out of the car and opened the door for the admiral and he asked what was going on. Capt. Daubin told them that the Japanese were attacking. I drove to the sub base gate and told the Marine, "U.S. Fleet." As I stared around the sub base baseball field, a Jap Zero came down and tried to strafe the car. I drove off the road onto the baseball field and the planes missed us. I went around BOQ and to the Administration Building which was the headquarters for the U.S. Fleet. Captain Daubin asked the admiral if he would like to go up the escape training tank and see what was happening. They both went up the elevator which was approximately 150 feet high. In about 15 minutes they came down. The admiral looked at me and said, "Thanks for the ride." He was white in the face and very worried. They went up to fleet headquarters. My job was to wait for the captain.

TMC DEWITT BARHAM
U.S. Navy, Submarine Base

I enlisted in the Navy on June 8, 1940, at New Orleans, Louisiana. I was sent to San Diego, California, for twelve weeks of recruit training in October of 1940 and then transferred to the USS *Holland* AS–3 at San Diego. We sailed for the Hawaiian Islands in November 1940. In 1941 I was transferred to the MK–14 torpedo shop at the submarine base located in Pearl Harbor.

On December 7, 1941, I had the duty and was standing the 0400–0800 watch at signal tower located above Adm. Kimmel's headquarters. We received a few communications from ships moored and tied up in the harbor.

At 0735 I was relieved on watch and went to O.O.D.'s office located at submarine base barracks where we had to be relieved by the oncoming watch. While in formation waiting for the raising of the U.S. flag I heard this constant roar of airplanes from the north. Looking back over my shoulder I observed approximately nine aircraft in V formation headed toward Pearl Harbor.

Myself and one other sailor were told by the officer on the deck that we were at attention and were to remain that way. When one sailor told the officer that the planes didn't look like our own, the officer on deck informed us that they were our planes. They were just camouflaged and were on maneuver. By this time several men were watching the lanes. As they peeled off formation we saw their mob bay doors open and bombs coming down. Then explosions hit at Battleship Row and in the general area of Pearl Harbor Navyyard. Without being told anything, the men broke formation and headed for the armory underneath Adm. Kimmel's

The submarine base at Pearl Harbor.

headquarters. While en route to the armory a Jap torpedo plane flying about fifty feet off the water passed to the front of me and another sailor. The rear gunner put his hand to his nose and gave us a go to hell salute and then opened fire at us. The bullets went between us. We ran for the armory and a Jap plane crashed directly in front of us.

When we arrived at the armory it was locked and no one had a key. We broke the lock and the only gun I could find was a .30 caliber Springfield rifle. I filled my pockets with ammo, grabbed the gun, and headed for pier 2 and started shooting at torpedo planes flying down the channel at Merry's Point to launch torpedoes at battleships tied up at Ford Island.

Then the horizon bombers started coming over at a height of approximately six or seven thousand feet, dropping their bombs on Pearl Harbor shipyard.

I left the pier and climbed up on a roof of a building where Adm. Kimmel's headquarters were. There were three other sailors on the roof firing at the planes with a Thompson machine gun, a BAR, and a Lewis machine gun.

At approximately 8:30 A.M. Adm. Kimmel and his aide, a lieutenant, came up to the area where we were at and, speaking to no one in particular, said, "What in the hell is going on?" His aide looked around and said, "Admiral, I think we better go below." They hurried from the scene.

At this time I went down to the pier. A barge came in with a badly burned sailor. I directed them to the submarine dispensary. Then a few minutes later I met three sailors off one of the battleships. Two of the sailors were blind and the third was trying to get them to a doctor. I took them to the dispensary and returned to the entrance to the submarine base. There a sailor and Marine had about twenty Japanese civilians lined up. I stayed there for a short time until more Marines arrived. Then a boat came up carrying dead bodies of men who had been floating in the harbor.

As night approached we stayed in the torpedo shop with no lights. We did not do any work until the next night as we had to black out all buildings. It was Monday night before we got any food or any sleep.

Chapter 13

Camp Malakole

SERGEANT KENNETH K. LITTLE
U.S. Army

DECEMBER 7, 1941

I had a decision to make, a tough decision, as I snuggled under two army blankets on this cool Sunday morning, December 7, 1941. I was in my quarters in a barracks at Camp Malakole, Oahu, Territory of Hawaii. The decision: should I remain here half-awake or should I get up and go to the mess hall for breakfast.

I had been relieved from duty as regional sergeant of the guard for 24 hours ending Saturday at 4:00 P.M. Recently promoted to sergeant, I was new at this. Certainly, I wanted to do well. Not much sleep during that time.

On the other hand, Sunday was a good day for breakfast in the mess hall. No rush. No uniform. Plenty of time to talk over an extra cup of coffee or two. What a dilemma, but if I was going to eat, I needed to make up my mind promptly as it was getting close to 8:00 A.M., closing time for the mess hall.

But something unpleasant was beginning to invade my state. Faint at first, it was becoming louder. Now more distinct, I identified the noise as

Members of the 867th AAA A.W. battalion with 40mm gun at the Camp Malakole firing range.

gunfire. Why would the Navy be holding gunnery exercises so close to shore, especially on Sunday?

I was jarred back to reality by the unmistakable sound of machine gun fire coming from nearby. Then a scream of surprise and pain from the other end of my barracks— it was my best friend. I could only think that one of the guards had fired one of the machine guns mounted on a truck for local security. For a brief moment, I selfishly thought how glad this error didn't happen during my recent tour of duty.

The roar of a low-flying aircraft and another burst of machine gun fire and I realized this was no accident. I jumped out of bed, into some clothes and shoes, and out the door. Another aircraft was approaching from the south, but not an immediate threat to me at my position. As it roared over, I saw the rising sun of Japan painted on the underside of the wing. Time to get moving!

Never had I dressed so fast! Within minutes I dressed in the field uniform, including gas mask and rifle. Next, I had to gather my gun crew, get our gun, and drive to our prepared firing position, some five miles away at the Naval Ammunition Facility at West Loch, Pearl Harbor.

When promoted to sergeant, just a couple of weeks before, I was placed in command of a three-inch antiaircraft gun crew. I had inherited a good crew. Some of us had been together since our National Guard days back in San Diego. They were ready. Some went to the gun park to ready the gun for towing, others to the motor pool to get our 5-ton truck which towed the gun, others to get the chest containing additional necessary equipment.

The gun had to be hooked to the truck and readied for travel. The entire crew was exposed to the shuffling aircraft, giving Camp Malakole a few parting shots as they returned to their awaiting carriers to the north. But by now, we had a small supply of small arms ammunition, so we could deliver a weak, but nevertheless satisfying fire at these intruders. I was directing the final preparation for travel and watching for enemy aircraft. Seeing one, I would give warning, and the crew could duck behind the gun, and using their rifles fire at the enemy. The bulk of the gun gave adequate protection even though the air was filled with the sound of ricocheting bullets. As the plane passed over, we had a field of fire free from return fire that is except for once when the aircraft was occupied by a rear gunner. We hugged the gun in a hurry!

Later, we learned that small arms fire such as this from the regiment had resulted in the downing of two Japanese planes. This was welcome news. By the time any of the batteries were able to fire effectively with their main weapons, the enemy was well on their way back to Japan, toasting their unbelievable success with saki. This was indeed a sad day for an unprepared United States. Once we were ready to roll, the gun was towed to our normal "alert" position — a spot on the road near the camp. Normally, all towed weapons would line up in their prescribed position on this road awaiting orders to move out.

Nothing so far that day had been done in an orderly manner, and I decided that we wouldn't win any battles by waiting for the order to move out. We pulled out of Camp Malakole alone, a five-ton truck, with 13 people aboard, towing an, as yet, useless, 3-inch antiaircraft gun, en route to our awaiting, prepared firing position.

So far, we had suffered no casualties. We hoped to keep it that way. The canvas cover for the back of the truck where the crew rode was rolled back to give us aerial observation. Two crew members were posted as air guards, both with rifles ready, one looking forward, the other to the rear, to give warning of any air threats. In that event, the truck was to be driven to the side of the road and personnel dispersed. A low flying aircraft surprised us by firing directly over the truck. The white star on the underside of the wing was a welcome sight indeed.

The distance from Camp Malakole to our defense position was but a few miles over a paved, but narrow road. It was located on the Navy's West Loch Ammunition Depot, West Loch being an arm of Pearl Harbor. Nearby was the barracks of a Marine Detachment which provided ground security for this facility. There didn't appear to be any damage to the area.

The gun was placed and ready to fire in record time, but we had no ammunition. I reported that we were ready, the first of the four guns in the battery. Our reward was that we were instructed to bring the ammunition to the battery.

A short trip by truck to the igloo where our ammunition was stored followed. It was spooky going into this underground structure, covered by a thick layer of dirt, filled with high explosives. In addition to our ammunition, there were several Navy torpedoes stacked like shelves on the walls. They seemed to be suspended rather than attached and were moving about quite a bit as the building jumped about from several nearby explosions. Our small rounds of ammunition packed in cardboard containers which were in turn packed in heavy wooden boxes didn't seem to be much of a threat. But torpedoes!

This of all places is where I started smoking! I asked a crewmember for a cigarette. He pointed to one of the many, NO SMOKING signs around, but I just shook my head and gave him the "gimme" sign. He lit one and passed it to me. Soon, all smokers were puffing away as they handled the AA ammunition.

In spite of this flagrant violation of common sense, not to mention regulations, we returned to the battery and distributed the ammunition to the waiting crews. Now, we were ready to fire. But at what?

All of a sudden there was nothing to do. We were emplaced, had our ammunition, and were ready to fire at any target. There were none. To the south of us was a huge column of black smoke. Undoubtedly, the Japanese, in order to temporarily cripple the U.S. fleet had bombed several huge fuel tanks in that area. One of the crew members wanted to climb a tall water tank that served the Marine facility and perhaps get an idea of how much damage had been done to Pearl Harbor.

He climbed the tank and after a short while returned to the ground. He was visibly shaken when he returned to the gun. Pearl Harbor was a mess, he said. Not burning oil tanks, which were not damaged, but burning ships. This was a sobering revelation. I reported this to the battery commander. It was the first indication we had of just how serious the situation was.

In the battery command post (CP), there was a Zenith portable AM radio. It could get both of Honolulu's radio stations. I know, because I bought one just like it at post exchange. It could get a third station, I learned — the Army Antiaircraft Intelligence Service (AAAIS). This was our official source of military information — broadcast in the clear and over a readily available AM frequency.

Suddenly, it came to life. Perhaps they finally got set up, too. Had the situation not been so serious? We didn't know, but then the official intelligence reports began coming in. Reports were hysterical, in delivery and in fact. We were being overrun by Japanese forces arriving by ships, landing craft, parachute, aircraft, and gliders. For the rest of the day and most of the night we were searching for the enemy that had long gone.

Tension was relieved to some extent in the afternoon, which left me with a red face, but with a welcome pat on the back a few days later. In addition to my primary duty as gun commander, I was also the battery gas non-com. Two days of chemical warfare schooling, and I knew all there was to know about the subject. I caught the unmistakable odor of a chemical agent. I sounded the alarm. The rush for gas masks was on. The gas mask was the most maligned piece of equipment the soldier carried. It was in a canvas pouch, about a foot square, and perhaps three inches in depth. It was carried over the right shoulder to the left hip. It was cumbersome and according to most, just another unnecessary thing to carry around. It was often misplaced, and although forbidden, it did have a value as a depository for the soldier's toilet articles. With a gas alarm goes the immediate proper placing over the face followed by testing for proper seal. A number couldn't remember where they had left their masks and sought direction as to how to save themselves.

Well, military gas is always heavier than air, so I sent these unfortunates up the nearby water tower. That should keep them above the concentrated material. Once I had everything under control, I started to analyze the situation and it kept coming back to me, "Where was this stuff coming from?"

About that time, I heard a strange sounding truck starting up near the Marine mess hall. Pulling out of that area was a civilian truck with an open body and overloaded with garbage. Meekly, I gave the "all clear" and motioned for the unmasked soldiers to come down from the tower.

I could just see my new sergeant stripes being discarded in a convenient G.I. trash can although it was a good drill. I could see much improvement in the way many of the troops kept track of their masks. A few days later the C.O. came to me smiled, winked, and said it was a good timely drill.

We went out on a goose chase and, when we returned, we had a group of sailors. Their clothes were filthy, they were dirty and hungry. They told us that they were aboard the USS *Oklahoma*. The ship had sunk with only the keel exposed and a lot of men were trapped in the ship below.

We helped them the best we could and then assigned them to our gun crews. I got a chief petty officer who was three ranks above me, but I wasn't about to turn my gun crew over to him. Instead, I assigned him as a gun pointer. He had to match the gun's data indicator with that sent electronically from range section. When he moved the indicator, the gun moved to point at the predicted position of the target. A few turns and he had it down pat.

I've known a few chiefs, both personally at home, and while in the service. One thing to me that stands out about them is the chief's hat. No matter how dirty, sweaty or involved in a project, the chief would not be caught without his hat. It might be a little messed up, but never as dirty as the rest of his uniform should that be his situation. And so it was with our chief — no steel helmet.

Now dark, we were standing around the gun pointers keeping the gun where the range section indicated. Then, AAAIS reported, "Unidentified aircraft approaching Pearl Harbor!" We assumed our position on the gun. The gun moved following the directions transmitted by our range section. Suddenly, the sky over Pearl Harbor lit up. Tracers from every direction climbing into the sky. For a moment it was eerily silent. Then the noise reached us. Gunfire of many calibers. No longer eerie, it was just deafening.

One chief had been hoping for the return of the Japanese since coming to the gun. "I want to get even," was his battle cry. Now he saw his chance. Although the gun moved, we didn't get the order to fire, and to his disgust, I told him we wouldn't fire until given the order. Later, we were told that the "unidentified aircraft," were U.S. naval aircraft from the carriers which fortunately were out to sea at the time of the attack. The army did not fire one antiaircraft round that night.

Not long after that incident, we went out to suppress another false landing. When we returned our guests were gone. No AA fire from us, but a lot of sugar cane fell to our deadly small arms fire.

All battery personnel were back at the firing position when our unreliable intelligence network informed anyone tuned in to their channel that Japanese landing craft were coming up West Loch. My gun was sited nearest this body of water, so I was given the task of thwarting this attack — 13 of us. The rest of the battery would remain in reserve so they could move to any part of our position where reinforcements were needed.

We formed a defensive line between our gun and the beach on West Loch. We had the battery's two .30 cal. AA defense machine guns with us, one on each end of our meager force. Each of us carried our .30 cal M 1903 Springfield rifles with a five-round capacity. We were going to repulse an enemy amphibious attack so armed. It was dark. Quiet. Very nervous as we waited. Still quiet, until ... noise. It grew louder coming from Pearl Harbor into the West Loch. No doubt about it, it was a boat. AAAIS had finally got one right and here it was right in our backyard.

One boat was all that could be heard. Perhaps this was a reconnaissance party for the main attack. Now we could see the outline of the craft, a little darker than the darkness that surrounded it. Now a light showing. The boat would pass parallel to our line, perhaps 20 yards away. Even with our puny firepower, the occupants didn't have a chance once we opened fire. Now the boat was directly opposite our line. When it reached the center of the line I should have given the command to fire, but for some reason I hesitated. There was something familiar about the silhouette. By now, the boat had passed the center of our line, moving further up West Loch. A couple of the guys were whispering at me to give the command to open fire. My orders were to sink any boat coming up the Loch. It had to be done. We had to fire on it. I think I got as far as taking a breath preparatory to giving the command, when from the boat came a yell, "Ahoy there!" It was apparently a couple of U.S. sailors on a detail to pick up ammunition at the nearby depot. They were in a familiar Navy whaleboat. A collective sigh of relief went through the group. Had we opened fire it would have been a tragedy that would have been perhaps unnoticed in the overwhelming tragedy that was Pearl Harbor, but most real to us on that firing line. Intelligence had failed us again.

Things began to come together by Monday morning. We still had the patrols. They were just precautionary as we didn't get any more reports of enemy activity. Probably had a few reports of unidentified aircraft that kept us on our guns for long periods of time. Nothing to fire at though.

Tuesday, December 9, I joined the noon chow line, mess gear in hand. Now that the gear was filled with the meal, all jumbled together in typical field mess manner, I carried my dinner to a secluded shady spot and sat down. Gingerly, I took a small bite. Another. Then I really dove in. I was tasting the first food since Saturday night December 6.

Chapter 14

Hickam Field

In 1934, the Army Air Corps saw a need for another airfield in Hawaii. A 2,200-acre field adjacent to Pearl Harbor became the location of the new base. The airfield was dedicated in 1935 and named in honor of Lt. Col. Horace Meek Hickam, a distinguished aviation pioneer who was killed in an aircraft at Fort Crockett in Galveston, Texas.

Twelve men and four planes moved to the base while it was still under construction, on September 1, 1937. Hickam Field was then completed on September 15, 1938. It was the only airfield large enough to accommodate the B–17 bomber. Planes of various kinds were brought to the airfield until 1941, for defense measures in the Pacific. By December 1941, the base consisted of 754 officers and 6,706 enlisted men; 233 aircraft were assigned at Hickam and the Corps' two other primary bases on Hawass— Wheeler and Bellows.

During the Pearl Harbor attack, Hickam suffered extensive property damage, aircraft losses, and personal casualties totalling 189 killed and 303 wounded. It was important during the attack for the Japanese to destroy the planes so that they could not attack their task force.

Hickam served as the hub of the Pacific aerial network not only in World War II, but Korea and Vietnam as well. Its services included supporting transient aircraft, ferrying troops and supplies, and evacuating the wounded.

In 1957, Headquarters Far East Air Force completed its move from Japan to Hawaii and was redesignated the Pacific Air Force. The 15th Air Base Wing, host unit at Hickam AFB, supported the *Apollo* astronauts in the 1960s and 1970s; the return of prisoners of war from Vietnam during Operation Homecoming in 1973; the movement of 94,000 orphan refugees from Southeast Asia Operation Babylift/New Life in 1975; and NASA's space shuttle flights during the 1980s and 1990s.

In 1985, Hickam AFB was designated a National Historic Landmark in recognition of it being one of the most significant resources associated with World War II. The base was awarded a bronze plaque.

MASTER SERGEANT JOHN H. KOENIG
U.S. Army Air Forces, 17th Airbase Group HQ and HQ Squadron, Hickam Field

---

I graduated from high school in 1939. Then, the first big decision of my life — Cornell University or the service.

My father served in the famous infantry unit, the Rainbow Division, in World War I. After the Armistice, he was assigned to the U.S. Army of Occupation in Germany because of his fluency in German. Due to under-standing the language, he would listen to Hitler's speeches during his beginning conquest on our Phillips battery-powered radio. As a result, it was his opinion that the U.S. would be involved in World War II. There-fore, he suggested that I volunteer enlistment in the armed forces. Serv-ing in the bloodiest battles of WWI, he did not want me to be called and possibly serve with little training, as was his case.

I enlisted in the U.S. Army Air Corps in the summer of 1939. While waiting to be called, I returned to school for a thirteenth year, which some schools were beginning to offer for volunteers in situations similar to mine. I soon learned the meaning of the service hackneyed phrase, "hurry up and wait," for it was not until July 6, 1940, that I was sworn in to defend our country.

Having volunteered, I was given the choice of permanent assignment. I gather the assumption was that I would choose Hawaii over Ohio and Panama. Coming out of the Depression era with little money to travel, I decided not to go too far from home on my first venture, so I chose Ohio first, then Panama, and finally Hawaii. The response was, "Sorry, Ohio and Panama are full. You are assigned to Hawaii." By way of Syracuse, New Rochelle, Brooklyn, Panama and Angel Island in the San Francisco Bay, I arrived in Honolulu on September 19, 1940.

Basic training at Hickam Field was held on the aircraft parking ramp while still in our woolens. The shortage of khaki uniforms was indicative of a number of situations in the peacetime military at that time. Supplies and equipment were frequently in short supply, particularly in those areas where there was some movement toward preparedness.

As a result of basic training in woollens, a number of servicemen, including myself, developed a severe heat rash in the armpits and crotch. I was in a spread position on my bunk for nearly two weeks, frequently applying calamine lotion that was supplied for relief.

After graduation from aircraft mechanics school, it was "wait" to be assigned to an aircraft crew. No new planes were scheduled for arrival on the island, so obviously no additional aircraft crews would be needed for some time. This meant back to general peacetime details to appear busy. After such innocuous jobs as being on all fours, shoulder to shoulder and crawling on our hands and knees picking up cigarette butts on the parade field, I decided there had to be another school I could attend. An auto mechanics school was scheduled, but I had to be assigned to the 481st Aircraft Ordnance to attend, so I transferred.

Shortly after my transfer, troops were beginning to arrive more frequently on the island fortress of Oahu. Some B–18 bombers, flying whales, were being shipped to Gen. MacArthur in the Philippines for his first line defense. Japanese ambassadors Adm. Normura and Saburo Kurusu stopped on their way to Washington for conferences with Secretary of State Cordell Hull. They were given the "red carpet" treatment accorded all dignitaries. The military was put on twenty-four hour alert for two weeks prior to the surprise attack on December 7, 1941. The 481st Ordnance belted ammunition on twelve-hour shifts during that time. Friday before the Sunday attack, the two-week twenty-four hour alert was called off at 4:00 P.M. All but essential personnel were granted off base pass requests. Thirty-nine hours and fifty-five minutes later, the United States was humiliated beyond belief. The billion-dollar fortress on the island of Oahu, the strongest fortification in the world, was in near shambles. No U.S. military installation had suffered such mass destruction since the founding of the country in 1776.

Unfortunately, due to the pictures, press releases and the name Pearl Harbor, present-day accounts of the Day of Infamy would lead one to believe that the Pacific Fleet in Pearl Harbor was the only installation that suffered major destruction. When remembering December 7th, the public conception is reinforced by the usual one picture, the explosion of the battleship *Arizona*. Where the heartfelt sympathy goes to the 1,000 plus sailors entombed in the *Arizona*, the mass destruction of other installations, equipment and evidence of unpreparedness should also be remembered in addition to military and political situations that attributed to the entombed servicemen in their eternal grave.

All aircraft hangars, including the two huge repair depots on Hickam Field were completely destroyed or severely damaged. The huge barracks, "The White Majesty," was bombed and strafed. The post exchange and chapel were completely destroyed including smaller buildings, trucks and other equipment. Wheeler Field, the pursuit base, sustained similar damage to aircraft hangars, buildings and equipment. The smaller airfields, Kanehoe Bay Naval Air Station and Bellows Field were also hit. In all, 188 planes were destroyed and 159 damaged. Aside from the airfields, Schofield Barracks, the home of ... [the infantry] was hit. There were some 40 explosions in the city of Honolulu and an estimated $500,000 worth of damage.

Where there are questionable military and political decisions prior to the surprise attack, the following are most frequently raised:

1. What rationale prompted the two-week twenty-four hour alert prior to December 7?

2. With the awareness that negotiations were definitely not proceeding well in Washington between Ambassador's Admiral Nomura and Kutusu and Secretary of State Cordell Hull, why was the twenty-four hour alert called off at such a critical time?

3. Britain and the U.S. had deciphered the Japanese military code. Why were Adm. Kimmel and Gen. Short of the Hawaiian Command not privy to the deciphered information in Washington, particularly the tenor of the negotiations between Japan and the U.S. prior to December 7?

4. Gen. George Marshal, chief of staff and others were suspicious that the 14-part message from the Japanese government resulting from meetings with Cordell Hull contained a "time bomb." Being concerned that the scrambler on his telephone may be tapped, Gen. Marshall notified the Hawaiian, Panama, and Philippine commands via Western Union, without priority. The message reached Gen. Short via a messenger on a bicycle as the December 7 attack was ending. How can one not question the lack of urgency and low priority of such critical timely information when the tension between the two countries was such that the potential of a "time bomb" somewhere in the Pacific was a fearful possibility?

As a result of my transfer to the 481st Aircraft Ordnance, I had to move from the huge three-story White Majesty across the parade ground to a new two-story wooden barracks. I was still assigned to eat in the mess hall of the White Majesty.

Sunday, December 7, I was third from the door when it was closed five minutes early. On the way back to the barracks, I decided to stop at the post exchange for something to eat, but discovered I had forgotten my billfold, something I had never done before. After picking up my billfold and heading for church, a buddy still in bed, asked me to wait for him. While waiting, we heard the sound of aircraft. Since the base was virtually shut down due to the number of personnel on a weekend pass, the question was, "Where did they come from?" I stepped out of the second floor screen window onto the roof shielding the rain from the windows below and watched the planes approach from the direction of Honolulu. When overhead, we knew they were Japanese due to the red circles under the wings. As they flew overhead, we rushed to the opposite side

John Koering (left) 481st Aircraft Ordnance motor pool.

of the barracks and saw the first torpedoes drop in Pearl Harbor. Our bewilderment as to what was happening soon ended in a mad rush down the stairs and out the door when bullets came whizzing through the wooden barracks. After dropping their bombs and torpedoes in Pearl Harbor, pilots strafed adjacent Hickam Field. Since there was virtually no opposition gunfire, pilots were flying so low we could see the smiles on their faces.

Due to the surprise attack, mass confusion and no officers to direct action, I asked Carl Weissman to join me on a terrifying ride in an ordnance truck to the ammunition bunkers where we picked up a trailer load of six 300-pound bombs. After leaving the bunkers and nearing the then Rogers Airport, we encountered aircraft strafing from some of the last planes of the first raid. Construction crews were expanding the section of Rogers Airport adjacent to the Hickam Field runways. For whatever reason, a Caterpillar tractor was not clearing from the area for the weekend, so Carl and I left the trailer load of bombs and rushed for cover behind the tractor, switching to the opposite side when seen by another pilot.

When the skies appeared to be clearing of enemy aircraft, Carl and I continued on with our load of bombs to the Pearl Harbor entrance of the runways. As we wove through the aircraft looking for a flight crew and bombers that were not damaged or with flat tires, the only two officers we saw on the entire flight line suggested that we get off the runways because it was suicide to be there, especially with a load of bombs. Nevertheless we continued down the line of aircraft surveying the damage. When reaching the end, we saw a crew standing by a B–25. Some several weeks before the attack, I noticed two B–25s and two B–26s parked at the very end of the parking ramp. We informed the captain of the condition of the planes we had just surveyed, and that we were looking for a crew and undamaged plane to load. He asked if we had ammunition for the plane's wing guns because he was hesitant to fly without some protection. We did not have any belted ammunition. After some thought, he did grant permission to load the plane. The effort was an experience because the bomb bay mechanism to load the bombs did not work. Being from the farm and in weight training at the time, Carl and the crew were able to lift the bomb high enough so I could place it on my shoulder and raise the bomb to the shackles on the bomb bay rack. With limited space to work, we were exhausted when the fourth one was locked in place. After the aircraft was loaded, the four-member crew took off. Some twenty minutes later the crew returned. One was bleeding slightly. They departed the plane without saying a word and left in a command car that was waiting for them.

Herein lies another questionable situation, plus an unsolved "mystery."

Several weeks after the attack, there was a notice on the bulletin board for reports of heroic action during the raids. Carl and I related our story to an officer assigned to record such action. He did not appear to be interested in hearing our story, nor did he record our names and company. We made a second attempt to report our heroic action and that of the B–25 crew. The noncom in the office took our names, company and purpose for the meeting with the officers. We were never contacted. By then the base was a beehive of activity, so the effort was not pursued further at that time.

We know now that the B-25 crew did not see the enemy aircraft carriers or support ships. We do not know if the crew dropped the bombs in the ocean before returning because they were very silent when departing the plane, almost as though contacted and instructed not to comment because the crew was talkative when loading the aircraft with bombs.

It is very disturbing that historical records will apparently forever indicate that the enemy was so successful in damaging all aircraft bombers at Hickam Field that not one plane was capable of take-off during the raids. I finally contacted my congressman, the Honorable Sherwood Boehlert who forwarded my letter to Patricia M. Fornes, Lt. Col. USAF, Congressional Inquiry Division, Office of Legislative Liaison. She sent the letter the usual route, to the Air Force Historical Research Agency at Maxwell Air Force Base. It was then sent to Leatrice R. Arakaki, Historian, 15th Air Force at Hickam Field where the obvious response was no record.

John Koering after the attack. He was detached from Hickam Field to a wooded area. Here he is digging a trench in the coral for an outdoor latrine.

In an effort to apparently question my several attempts to correct the records, I was sent a transcript of an oral report taken from Maj. Gen. Brooke E. Allen during December 1965. (Oral History #566)

From the transcript: Question — Could you, Major General Allen describe for us your attempt to strike back against the Japanese? The General's response, "I wanted to save at least one of the three B-17s I had in my squadron. In the hustle and bustle to start the engines, I flooded them. I abandoned the idea of trying to take off since I had to take off across the coral, not on the runway. My comment, the General could not take off because of the damaged B–17s that had arrived from the States during the raids. He further states that when he did take off, the plane was loaded with bombs. Where Carl Weissman and I were searching for a crew and undamaged bomber during the raids, we were on the runway at my decision, not that of an officer because none were present. Since it was suicide to be towing a load of bombs during raids, to my knowledge, no bombs were delivered until after the raids. Furthermore, the general could not have taken off until the runway was cleared of damaged aircraft. It was possible for the smaller B–25 to take off.

Unfortunately, the questions asked and the general's answers did not specify time. A specific time would have at least corrected the present inaccurate assumption for the historical files that the general was airborne in a B–17 during the raids.

The heroic experience of Carl Weissman and I and that of the B–25 crew are obviously not in the historical records because of the "disinterest," for whatever reason, in not hearing and recording our story. Setting these facts aside, the Seventh Air Force and Congressional Investigation Records indicating all planes at Hickam Field before, during and after the attack, also, does not mention the B–25s and B–26s. The Congressional Report does include a B–24A, not assigned to Hickam Field, that arrived on December 6th for repairs.

There is some speculation that the planes may have been headed to China to reinforce Gen. Chennault's Flying Tigers. Wherever their destination, the "mystery" remains and the following questions are unanswered:

1. Where did these four bombers come from?
2. What was their destination?
3. Why were these planes not recorded in the records at Hickam Field and especially in the Congressional Investigation records of all planes at Hickam Field during and after the attack?
4. Why was there no interest in recording the heroic action of Carl Weissman and I, that of the B–25 crew and the fact that the B–25 was the only bomber airborne during the raids?
5. Would recording the B–25 story reveal the "mystery" of the presence and destination of the four bombers?

For anyone to assume the Day of Infamy was all over in a day, perish the thought. Rumors abounded. The Panama Canal was bombed. The West

Coast was shelled. The Japanese were landing and joined by the 150,000 Honolulu residents of Japanese descent. The confusion, stress and immediate transition from a peacetime military operation to a forced wartime situation after the shock of the surprise attack and having to start from piles of rubble can only be comprehended by those who were there. Communications were slow, compared to today, in debunking rumors, contacting detached units and co-ordinating the hurried transition to a wartime mode. Should one forget, 1941 was still the era of the radio, propeller-driven aircraft and travel to the Orient via flying boats, the Yankee Clipper and China Clipper.

Precautionary measures were extreme, but necessary due to the unknown whereabouts of the enemy and weakness of the fortress. The island was completely blacked out. Speaking only of Hickam Field, critical units were dispersed into wooded areas off the base. All were on twenty-four hour alert which meant, when one did sleep, it was in full uniform. When finally permitted to remove my shoes, what was left of my socks stuck to my feet. I still carry the remnants of foot fungus as a reminder.

A prepared meal was not even expected after the attack because the mess hall was bombed and completely out of commission. Our unit survived for a week on broken candy bars and crackers scavenged from the bombed post exchange.

Several weeks after the attack, when operations were getting somewhat back to normal and supplies were being rushed in, I transferred back to 17th Air Base Group. My assignments were aircraft mechanic, crew chief, and flight engineer on B–18s, B–17s, and B–24s.

The rush to train flight crews for reinforcements in the Pacific was conducted at night so the numerous spies on the island would have a difficult time recording activities. Due to the shortage of navigation instructors, new navigation graduates were not always accurate in their calculations without some instruction in live situations. Thank the Lord for experienced pilots or the island would have been missed on occasions when returning from missions. The error could have resulted in the loss of fuel and obviously, the crew and plane.

No radio contact flight aircraft to the airfield was permitted during flight or when returning from a mission. A handheld flasher was used to signal "friendly aircraft." There was always the fear of being blown out of the sky, especially when the flasher did not work. Trigger happy anti-aircraft gunners were ready for action since they "missed out" during the surprise attack.

Night flight training crews faced other perilous possibilities after the attack due to the uncertainty of the whereabouts of the enemy, particularly submarines. Should any plane have gone down during its mission, it was "hello" briny deep. Radio contact, signals, and flares were not permitted.

Due to increase in air activity and again, shortage of trained troops and shortage of supplies, parachutes were to be routinely checked, nor was there always a sufficient number on board the aircraft. Since the chances of being rescued were nil, crew members were not too concerned whether or not they had a parachute. Conditions were understood and accepted. Loyalty to country and giving of one's life for revenge and victory over the enemy was the unequivocal mission.

The four years of war that followed the mass destruction on the island Fortress that brought the U.S. into World War II and successive wars were all "hell," as is any war regardless of size and length. But the men and women on December 7, 1941, the Day of Infamy, did not have a fighting chance. It is also suspected that they were the victims resulting from Hitler's victories in Europe and the relentless destruction of air raids on England. As a result, England needed more than lend-lease support. But, President Roosevelt campaigned on neutrality in his re-election to the office. There-fore, if the needed expeditionary forces were to aid England, there had to be some serious provocation against the United States. Did military and political decisions surrounding December 7 lead to and result in the suc-cess of such provocation?

Looking back at the death possibilities within just a few hours of my nearly five and a half years of service, I have to believe in "angels."

I was moved from the White Majesty to the wooden barracks when transferred to the 481st Ordnance. The wing that I moved from suffered the greatest number of casualties from the enemy.

I was third from the mess hall door when it was closed five minutes early. There were a number of casualties from the bombs that came through the roof.

The post exchange that I stopped at for a bite to eat and had to leave because I did not have my billfold was flattened by a direct bomb hit. I never went anywhere without my billfold.

The chapel that I would have been in had a buddy not said, "wait," was a wooden barracks.

All construction equipment used to enlarge Rogers Airport was always removed at the end of the day. For whatever reason, the Caterpillar trac-tor that was left over the weekend saved the life of Carl and myself when strafed by enemy fire.

Thank the Lord for making the pilot so intent on strafing us that he did not hit the trailer load of bombs. Had that happened, I definitely would not be submitting my story.

The rush to train flight crews for reinforcements in the Pacific was on a "wing and a prayer" immediately following the attack. Shortage of some supplies, shortage of trained personnel, forbidden use of the radio and flares, complete blackout of the island, and night training missions were all accepted due to the strong revenge to defeat the enemy.

POINT OF INTEREST

Marine Air Station at EWA

The Marine Corps Air Station at Ewa is located southeast of Pearl Harbor. Twenty-one Japanese fighters attacked the base. As was the case with all the military installations on Hawaii that day, the element of surprise took its toll: approximately 49 aircraft were lost in the attack.

SERGEANT GEORGE G. SAWYERS
U.S. Army Air Forces, Hickam Field

On the morning of December 7, 1941, I started to the mess hall. Sunday breakfast was served at 8 A.M. We had just returned from Bellows Field after field exercises. The rumor was we were to go to Clark Field in the Philippines. I heard a group of planes. Thought it was the Navy having exercises. Suddenly, I heard explosions. We ran outside and saw the planes with the rising sun on them. We knew it was the real thing.

We had no place to hide. There were no bunkers or foxholes. The ships in the harbor were smoking or on fire. Planes on the ground, hangars, barracks were all being hit with planes carrying torpedoes, .30 and .50 caliber machine guns.

Sgt. George G. Sawyers, U.S. Army Air Force.

One of my buddies and I worked our way to a supply room and got some World War I rifles and a machine gun. He set up the machine gun and started firing. A short time later he was hit by machine gun fire and killed. I tried to stay out of sight of a group of planes that were strafing the barracks and airfield. A group of unarmed B–17s flew in from the States on their way to the Philippines and were all shot down or destroyed on the airfield.

It was a beautiful day and during the second wave attack I could see highflying planes open their bomb bay doors. Their targets were oil depots, large buildings, or ships that were still afloat. They flew over Pearl Harbor, Hickam, and Ford Island dropping their bombs. I got under a wooden building, but was uncomfortable there. I got up and ran across the grounds. Shortly after, a bomb hit the building and leveled it.

After the attack was over there were bodies everywhere. Everyone needed a medic. I helped anyone I could for the remainder of the day. There were 483 killed at Hickam Field. I don't know how many wounded. That night several planes from the carriers came in to land. We opened up on them and shot down at least four. It was a day I thought would never end.

PVT. EARL M. SCHAEFFER, JR.
U.S. Army Air Forces, 72nd Bomb Squad, 5th Bomb Group, Hickam Field

Prior to December 7, 1941, we, meaning Hickam Field personnel, had been on an alert which consisted of putting on the war paint, so to say. The planes were armed with machine guns, loaded with bombs and disbursed throughout the field. We had even been out on maneuvers somewhere on Oahu, when a certain Japanese statesman was on his way to Washington and was supposed to stop over at Hawaii. We took off the war paint, put the bombs and guns away and lined up the bombers inspection-style out on the flight line.

During the first week in December 1941, I had received word that my Dad wasn't expected to live and I was given an emergency furlough. I was to leave on December 8th by surface vessel.

On the evening of December 6, a buddy of mine was scheduled for switchboard duty from midnight to 0800. This switchboard had been set up in the communications shack at the time we went on alert and was still in operation at this time. This friend had a heavy date in Honolulu and was looking for someone to pull his shift. I agreed to do this for $2.00 which was accepted.

So my December 7, 1941, started real early on that day. Since it was late Saturday night and early Sunday morning there wasn't two much going on and I don't recall one phone call coming in on the switchboard. I slept most of the watch, which was okay to do, and went to early chow, and came back to finish my eight-hour shift. Must have been about 0730 when I turned on the radio and was listening to the Lutheran Hour coming from one of the Honolulu Stations. I also had a book on aerial navigating that I was reading as I was planning on Aviation Cadets in the near future. My plans were to be a fighter pilot. About 0800 I heard explosions and aircraft, not too loud as I was in the communications shack which was between two hangars, numbers 3 and 5. The noise became louder and when things started shaking and rattling and parts of the ceiling started coming down, I ran out in

Earl M. Schaeffer, in the summer of 1942.

the hangar, over to the end where the large doors were, to see what was the matter. Well, I saw many fires, aircraft burning, buildings afire, and much smoke coming from the Pearl Harbor area. It was too much! I just couldn't comprehend what was going on. I didn't have to wait long to learn the awful truth. Three aircraft came flying very low across the field firing their wing guns at our B–18s, B–17s and other planes. As they passed by, I saw the big red balls on the sides of their aircraft! The awful truth came home with a jolt and nausea in my gut. I knew from the aircraft identification classes we had that I was looking at three Japanese Zero fighter planes. I was completely disoriented and frustrated. Jap planes here! Where did they come from? What were they doing there shooting up the airfield?

At this time I was all alone in this big hangar. It must have been the beginning of the attack. I went back to the switchboard. I didn't know where else to go or what to do. Back at the communications shack, at the telephone switchboard I waited for something to happen. No one called in on the phone and I couldn't raise any answers on outgoing calls, so I just stayed at the post and waited. The radio program went off the air. I heard no information from it at all. Some time later, I don't recall, people started showing up at the hangar. This was Sunday morning and Sunday morning was sleep-in time. Other personnel were out on weekend passes and there just wasn't too much activity on an army base on Sunday morning. Eventually personnel did show up along with some leadership. The armament shack was broken open and weapons handed out. I was given a 12 ga. Winchester riot shotgun and told to get out there on the ramp and shoot at "those bastards." Before I could shoot at anything I was grabbed by someone in charge and told to help get what aircraft that wasn't burning disbursed. Our bombers were all lined up side-by-side in rows of 4 or 5, so the strafers could make a run on all 4 or 5 in one pass. I ended up helping move our B–17, which was the older type without tail guns. I think it was called a B–17–C. PFC Eddie Robbins was with me and we were told to get the .50 caliber machine guns set up in the side blisters of the 17. This was fine except I had never seen a .50 caliber before and what they dumped off the armament truck weren't even completely assembled. While trying to accomplish this assignment we were plagued with Zero strafing attacks. On several passes they made, I jumped out of the 17 and lay prone beside one of the 17's wheels. The good Lord or Lady Luck was with me that morning as Robbins and I both came through unscathed. Others on either side of us didn't fare so well, some being killed and others wounded.

There was a lull in the attack. I don't remember the time and then there was another warning and this time it was a high level bombing run. We could see the planes way up there. We watched the bombs drop and fall down and run across Hickam Field. Several hit our beautiful barracks, starting fires in several wings. There was a hit on the mess hall killing many airmen. All this time we could see Pearl Harbor catching "Hail Columbia." We saw many terrible explosions and it looked like the whole harbor was burning. It seemed the Japs were now ignoring Hickam and concentrating on Pearl.

Pearl was fighting back. We could see the antiaircraft shells bursting, but the accuracy wasn't too good. We also had men with machine guns up on the roof of our hangar. I might mention that nowhere on Hickam that I knew of was there any kind of protection from the air raids, such as strafing and bombs, no shelters or slit trenches.

Up to this time we had never left the flight line and were now told to go to the barracks and get our steel helmets and gas masks. The fact that I did not have my gas mask probably terrified me more than any other thing as we had plenty of gas drills and the possibility of a gas attack was driven home on more than one occasion. Robbins and I went back to the barracks to pick up our equipment at this time. We were dumbfounded and awed at all the destruction. Everywhere there was wreckage and fires. The barracks roof was burning and eventually I believe the whole roof burned off, or most of it did. This was a very large barracks for this time in history, made of mostly steel and concrete except for the roof. We lived on the second floor (there were three) of one of the wings that went out from the large mess hall in the center. Two bombs had come through the roof and third floor and exploded on our second floor. There wasn't anything left on the floor except twisted bunks and wall-lockers. Everything else was gone —consumed, obliterated. There was no steel helmet or gas mask. I did find a Planters peanut can with 17 pennies in it, all blackened by the fire. All our personal possessions were gone —clothing, personal items, my stamp collection that I had been collecting since I was 11 years old, my photo albums with the photos I had taken during the last year and a half, my record collection and radio/phonograph and other things too numerous to mention. We went back to the flight line and somewhere we were issued steel helmets and gas masks.

Now it is the afternoon of the 7th. We were told that there were three B–18s flyable and we would take off and find the Jap fleet (nobody knew where it was). I was picked to be the turret gunner on one of the planes. I believe Eddy Robbins was the radio operator and I'm pretty sure Lt. Rice was the pilot. I cannot recall the others. I do not recall the number of the B–18 I flew in. We took off about 1400 hours and I believe we went northwest. Not sure of this, rumors were that the Jap fleet was northwest of Oahu and others had the fleet southeast. We three B–18s each went out in different directions. Now I must tell you something about the B–18. Built by Douglas, a two-engine, slow, not very attractive creation protected by one each .30 cal. machine gun in the nose turret on front of the vertical stabilizer and in the belly. Not too much firepower considering what we might run into. Here I was, a 19-year-old kid from a farm in Berke County, Pa., all trussed up in a very heavy, large flying suit, stuffed into the rear turret. I was scared. I tried to remember all the things we were taught in gunnery classes like short burst, lead properly, etc.

When we took off we flew over Pearl, not directly, but close enough to see all the unbelievable ruin and destruction. It appeared that everything in the harbor was blown up, burning or destroyed. I had the feeling that the U.S. had had it. My stomach was full of butterflies. I had plenty

Ford Island, Pearl Harbor, August 1944, from an altitude of 10,000 feet.

of time to think. I didn't even know the Japs were mad at us. I thought of my slim chances of coming out of this flight alive should we run into some Jap fighters. Hell! They'd blow us right out of the sky in these very vulnerable B–18s. I thought about my dad, near death back in Pennsylvania. I'll probably not get to go on my emergency furlough now (I didn't) with all these happenings. We flew for 7½ hours and didn't see anything but a few whales which at first we thought were Jap subs, but closer examination disproved that belief.

It was dark when we returned to Hickam. There was total blackout down there on Hickam and Pearl. When Lt. Rice tried to land they wouldn't turn on the landing lights. We flew around in a holding circle and pretty soon people started shooting at us. I could see the tracers flying about us. They finally turned on what I remember was a large search light down the runway and we landed. I was very relieved.

I cannot remember eating anything since breakfast. I'm sure I did but can't remember. I recall that there were stacks of soda pop in the hangar and we were told not to drink any water but just soda pop. The rumor was that the Japs had poisoned the water system. There were other rumors, too. Jap paratroopers had landed in the sugar-cane fields, on the east side of Oahu was one. There were others which all turned out to be untrue, just rumors.

That night we stayed out under the wing of our B–18. Around midnight the air raid alarm sounded. We heard planes coming in and of course everybody assumed the Japs were back. The whole sky lit up with tracers and everybody with a weapon was firing at the noises in the sky. This was unfortunate as they, the planes making the noise, were ours. I believe they were Navy planes that had taken off from a carrier arriving from the States. The remainder of the night was quiet.

Chapter 15

Ford Island

RADIOMAN THIRD CLASS A.J. HOPKINS
U.S. Navy

THE DAYS BEFORE PEARL HARBOR

As an amateur radio operator I was in the Navy Communications Reserve and volunteered for active duty late in 1940. Eventually I joined a squadron (VP 24) of PBY (Catalina) airplanes at North Island Naval Air Station in San Diego as a Radioman, 3rd Class (RM3C). Those PBY's were long range patrol planes, designed especially to provide surveillance far at sea and to prevent surprise attacks. They were flying boats; they had no landing gear. We took off and landed on the water. Usually a crew of men would fit wheels (called side mounts) to the hull and a tail wheel and a tractor would pull the airplane out of the water. In forward areas the planes would be moored by buoys when not flying.

The squadron went to Pearl Harbor in October of 1941 and we had barely settled in our new hangar by December. It is sad to say that we were poorly trained and armed for the task assigned. That, coupled with wilful neglect from Washington made us, and the rest of the fleet, a "sitting duck" for the Japanese.

December 7, 1941

At Pearl Harbor, most of the Naval air activity was based on Ford Island which is located right in the middle of Pearl Harbor. Our hangar was on the seaplane ramp near the water and at the edge of Luke Field which was used for land based and carrier planes. Alongside the hangar there was an open ditch of varying depth recently dug for installing a new sewer or water line. This was a godsend since it provided the only shelter available from shrapnel and strafing planes. Our barracks were about two blocks away and parallel to Battleship Row. This was the line of battleships moored in a line; some were two abreast along Ford Island.

I was rudely awakened around 0800 that morning by the sound of roaring motors and explosions. I dashed to the lanai (screened porch) in time to see a Japanese plane drop a torpedo and pull up over the barracks. The torpedoes hit the battleship *California*, which was only a few hundred yards from the barracks. After that, all was confusion, everyone trying to get to their battle stations, if they had one. Mine was with a plane crew and at the hangar. I got there as quickly as I could through the smoke, with bits of shrapnel and bullets whizzing around.

There was little to do at the hangar since we were only a six-plane squadron and four of them were already flying somewhere on a communications drill or something similar. At any rate they were a long way from where the action was. Probably a good thing since we flew unarmed most of the time. They were diverted to a search sector but unfortunately, or perhaps fortunately, in the wrong direction.

Our ramp was covered with burning airplanes, ships were burning and exploding. A small submarine was attacked and sunk in the channel. The air was filled with dive bombers, fighters and torpedo planes, all Japanese. One crashed Kamikaze style into the sea plane tender, USS *Curtiss*, moored just across the field. The *Arizona* exploded with a terrible roar, as well as a destroyer in dry dock at the Navy yard. The water was covered with burning oil. One battleship, heavily damaged and on fire, got underway and came down the channel, guns firing. She had to be beached to prevent sinking and blocking the channel.

All in all a terrible day and no way to fight back. There were no antiaircraft guns on Ford Island and very few on the ships. In those days the question of what airplanes could do to ships was still undecided and antiaircraft defenses were minimal at best. Anyway, the Japanese decided not to launch a third attack so the one sided fight was over ... before we could use our defenses— fortunately we did not have to use them.

Some order was coming out of chaos by the next morning and for our part we flew many, many long search and patrol missions, taking off before daylight and returning after dark. Of course we never saw anything but at least we were alert and there was very little chance of anything like that attack happening again. In fact the attempted attack on Midway Island a few months later showed what could happen if they tried. I and several thousand others did little heroic that day, but we survived and were available and, when given the tools and leadership, we got the job done.

AVIATION METALSMITH 2ND CLASS ADOLPH KUHN
U.S. Navy

IN THE MIDDLE OF IT

I was born on a La Crosse, Kansas, wheat farm on September 5, 1921, ninth child of Lorenz and Karie Kuhn's. I enlisted in the U.S. Navy for a six-year hitch on May 26, 1940 at the age of 18. I breezed through my physical exam with flying colors, up to the point where my height was concerned. That Navy recruiting doctor scratched his head several times, as he studied his manual. I was becoming uneasy and feared I'd wind up back on the farm again, milking cows and slopping hogs.

He pointed out to me that the maximum height limit for that time in our history was six foot four and a half inches and I was a quarter of an inch over. He mulled it over for a while and then said, "Congratulations, you just made it." He leaned over and whispered in my ear, "You are the tallest man in the Navy." I thanked him and was on my way to boot camp at Great Lakes, Illinois, where yet more physical conditions awaited me.

The largest Navy shoes they carried in stock were size twelve, and I wore thirteens. Imagine going through three months of hectic training with undersize footware. I had the closest cropped toenails on the base, and yet had to draw my toes back while drilling and marching. Those ninety days seemed to drag along under those conditions. Off to Pensacola, Florida, for sixteen weeks of Aviation Metalsmith School, of living and breathing aircraft, day and night.

On January 20, 1941, aboard the Navy cruiser, U.S.S. *Boise*, I sailed for Pearl Harbor checking in to Ford Island Air Station on January 27, ten months prior to the Rising Sun's sneak attack.

Our island of Oahu in Hawaii was heavily laden with aircraft from all branches of the military service throughout. Airplanes were in my blood, day and night, riveting, repairing, patching, welding manifolds and hand facing tail hooks, etc. We supplied aircraft parts for Kaneohe Naval Base as well. Carriers in the Pacific would bring damaged aircraft to our A&R shop for complete renovation. Our test pilots had the most dangerous tasks of all. Phase after phase was thoroughly checked and rechecked for a one-hundred [percent] safety record. Too often the pilot and crew died in explosions which resulted in sea and land crashes. Every engineer on our base scratched his head, trying to determine the culprit of the explosions. After many funeral services, one aircraft mechanic discovered that vibration causes copper tubing to crystallize to the point of rupture, spilling high octane fuel on the hot engines. This matter was immediately corrected by replacing all copper fuel lines with annealed aluminum tubing.

We had a concrete sea plane launching ramp that extended far out into the Pearl Harbor channel for takeoffs. I was fascinated by this ramp and wondered where it ended. I found out the hard way on December 7, 1941. My second cousin, Andy Herrman of Liebenthal, Kansas, was employed as a civilian blacksmith in our shipyard across the Pearl Harbor channel from the Ford Island base. His crude Kansas forgings were a far cry from our Navy's close tolerances.

On the night of December 6, 1941, I arranged with Andy to spend the night at his wooden cantonment barracks in the sugarcane fields outside Pearl Harbor's main gate. I told Andy I would be in rather late, as I had planned to attend a dance at the National Guard Armory in Honolulu and Sunday morning Andy and I were to attend a Catholic mass at a Honolulu church, but Japan's plans drastically altered our schedule. At the dance, I bumped into an old buddy, Kellogg, from our boot camp days in 1940.

We had a pleasant visit as we danced the night away. He and his new bride were staying at a Honolulu hotel.

The clock was ticking away towards a major onslaught which would change our lifestyles forever. I asked Kellogg which ship he was assigned to, and when he said the USS *Oklahoma*, I immediately knew where she was docked in Battleship Row at Pearl, and that I would come aboard Sunday morning some time to visit him. Neither of us expected the Winds of War were about to blow in our faces. When I arrived at Andy's place, he and his associates were feeling no pain. A wild poker game was in full swing, with the booze bottles and smelly ashtrays all over the makeshift wooden table. Andy knew that I was not a drinker nor a smoker. We talked for a while before hitting the sack to be ready for our church service.

As I mentioned earlier, aircraft was my game and the sounds of planes was so instilled in me that I was almost unaware of their presence. We finally dozed off and in the wee hours of Sunday morning, December 7, 1941, we were just a hop-skip-and-jump away from all hell breaking loose. Andy and I both woke up at the same time as bullets came through the roof of the barracks. My first impression was the nearby Hickam Field Army base with very careless pilots on early morning maneuvers.

Andy and I sat up as he said, "Adolph, I wonder what it would be like to be in real war." The poker players had assumed their game, clad in their skivvies, when bullets hit their score pad on the table. They rushed outdoors with clenched fists, cussing our military pilots. I said to Andy, something is wrong and we canceled our church services and I was anxious to get to my base as soon as I could. Two sailors in a Model A Ford with a rumble seat in the rear saw me in uniform waiting at the bus stop. They pulled up and stopped, "Get in Mac. We are at war!" I was in shock as most were for the rest of the day. I was hanging on to my hat as that little Ford made tracks speeding toward Pearl. Huge explosions with billowing smoke and flames reaching high into our tropical sky was grim evidence of what was occurring. The sailors in the front seat spotted the red meatballs painted on the planes which we identified as the Japanese Rising Sun insignia. At about this time, our Secretary of State, Cordell Hull in his Washington, D.C., office, was shouting out pissants and scum at the two Japanese envoys who were trying to negotiate peace plans for both of our countries. We reached the main gate and the Marine on duty hastily flagged us through. The driver pulled over into parking lot and stopped. He said this is as far as we go, as we have to get to our ships in the Pearl Harbor channel. I thanked them both and started running across the officers' golf course trying to make way to our foot landing. A Nippon pilot spotted my white uniform on the plush green grass and started strafing bullets— the soft sod was flying up in all directions around me. I ducked behind a palm tree and waited for a clear signal from the plane's noise. At this point, I noticed a larger piece of shrapnel landing next to me and my curiosity was to examine it in more detail I picked up this hot rusty casting. I immediately dropped it. It had burnt skin from my fingers. My Guardian Angel was nearby, knowing I didn't miss Sunday morning Mass on purpose. I spotted a soldier and a Marine in uniform also running from one palm tree to the next, dodging stray bullets and flak as well. That poor soldier unfortunately was slain before our eyes, but the Marine and I kept pushing on. I kept thinking about Kellogg and my visit to his ship, the *Oklahoma*. Andy's face kept appearing before me as I wondered if he was safe.

As I reached the boat landing, all the dock and pilings were engulfed in flames from the spilled oil from our naval vessels. I looked across this carnage and devastation to my base on Ford Island and wondered how I would manage to get there. By this time, every other serviceman in the same dilemma, had gathered around this massive conflagration in the Harbor with 96 U.S. naval vessels packed in like sardines, and tremendous explosions from various vessels. We watched in awe with our mouths agape as sailors and Marines were flung over the rails into an inferno of flames and burning oil on the water.

We spotted tiny wooden craft out in the channel with a lone and highly confused civilian fisherman aboard. We yelled and flagged him down amid all the noise. He turned and came toward us, but had to stop a considerable distance from us, due to the burning boat landing. We immediately waded out into the oily water and all eleven of us scrambled to climb aboard, almost sinking this tiny vessel. We were so tightly packed, shoulder to shoulder, our feet and legs interlocked and practically sitting on each other's laps.

The pilot slowly revved up his small out-board engine and headed towards Ford Island, my base. Very little conversation was exchanged, as we could see the terror in each other's faces.

The cruiser, U.S. *Shaw* was docked near our overloaded fishing boat, when out of the blue, a Rising Sun Raider spotted us bobbing below. We watched his aerial bullets hit the foamy sea, rapidly coming towards us. The only protection we had to this point, was our bare hands over our heads, as the bullets hit our craft and were flying in all directions. Sea water was coming up through the floor boards.

We all checked each other for wounds, and lo and behold, that Guardian Angel I mentioned must have been right among us, as not one man onboard suffered as much as a scratch. We stared at each other and wished good luck. Over the side we went. Every man for himself, so to speak at this point. Shortly following the boat attack, I never saw any of the other elevens again. This tall lanky Kansas farm boy was frantically dog paddling toward my base, amid dismembered sailors and Marines floating in oil burning sea. I savagely groped onto various shipboard debris that littered the channel. The most vivid recording in my memory bank of that ordeal was the hundreds of white sailors' hats floating on the salty brine, with their black stencilled names in full view. Torpedoes passed me, heading for Battleship Row, and I witnessed the thunderous eruptions and heard the screeching sound of large steel plates ripping apart, spilling more supplies and humans into the Pearl Harbor channel. There were pots, pans, mattresses, galley supplies, wooden engine crates, canned goods, etc., which I clung to to keep afloat. My Guardian Angel was determined to see me safely through this massive onslaught, for which I am still grateful to this very day.

The battleship USS *Nevada*, the only ship of its class, managed to get underway and sail toward the harbor entrance, as I dog paddled nearby. She was listing and burning but her skipper deliberately beached her, to avoid blockage of the entryway.

The bombing of the fleet and my base and hangars continued relentlessly as I was trying to locate that seaplane launching ramp I mentioned earlier and wondered how far it extended into the channel. Well today I found out first hand. I had my bearings set and worked my way toward it. Three times I went under to see if I could spot it, but to no avail. I knew I was in the right place, so I tried again the fourth time in this helter-skelter sea, when my right toe on my undersized Navy regulation shoe, hit a solid and slimy algae-covered mass.

I stood erect for the first time since our small craft sank, and still no trace of the rest of the guys from that boat. The oily water was between my chin and lower lip at this time, as I again paused for a thank you prayer to my angel. Now for the first time I had a brief spell to check myself over, hair matted in oil, my uniform, far from fit for a captain's inspection. My undersized shoes had one big advantage this day. They clung to my feet despite the gooshy mess they were in. I had difficulty trying to inch my way up this slippery concrete ramp. My oily leather shoe soles didn't help matters much, as the bombing and shellings continued to rain down in a catastrophic barrage.

I finally managed to reach the shallow end where I could crawl on all fours, onto my Ford Island base. I paused and gave thanks again to my Guardian Angel. Now with both feet flat on the runway, I thought the worst was behind me.

I stared at those airplanes I worked on last Friday with mouth agape as flames spewed from the cockpits, and they were bullet riddled. An unknown photographer snapped my picture, which is now property of the archives of Hawaii. Years later, my oldest grandson, Dean Kuhn, spotted my photo in the *National Geographic* magazine, December issue 1991, marking the 50th anniversary of that Infamy Day which is indelibly etched in my memory. If our magazine collectors read this story, you'll find this twenty-year-old, six-foot-five lanky sailor in his oil-soaked uniform. Everyone asked me who the crouched sailor is by my side. I haven't the foggiest, as too much slaughter and carnage was everywhere. The USS *Shaw* I referred to earlier exploded at the same time as this, sending huge hunks of hot bulkhead steel past my head as I dropped to my knees on the tarmac. That hunk of shrapnel sliced through quarter-inch thick steel plate on our hangar doors as easy as slicing a newspaper with a butcher knife. Again my angel was on duty.

All the while this devastation is going on, a large portion of Japan's fleet is anchored off Oahu with more than 350 Kamikaze and Zero planes fueled up and eager for more flight. They had their radios tuned to our Hawaiian music station in Honolulu.

To add insult to injury, most of the low flying Nippon pilots grinned at the Americans as they made eye contact while strafing us below. Many of my buddies couldn't understand why I dogpaddled instead of swimming. My answer was that I was raised in Kansas and there was too little water to practice in. Too often someone would ask why I joined the Navy to begin with. My very valid answer was, so I can wear clothing no one else wore before. My hand-me-down clothing from my older brothers was now past history.

Shortly following the *Shaw* explosion, I crawled on my knees to a small steel door in one of our hangars, and ran inside and slid under a very heavy welding table, flat on my belly. I recounted all the events thus far for the day, especially wondering about my best pal Allen Hoffman, who was our electro-plotter in our shop of assembly and repair. It took a while before we made contact, both being thankful we made it this far. The hangar was totally dark and quiet. All electrical power was out of whack. I heard a loud crashing sound as a Japanese bomb tore through the steel roof tearing out Ginger supports and bracing. To myself I whispered, "no, not again." The bomb landed between ten to fifteen feet from my face, as it stuck to the concrete hangar deck at its angle of travel. It wavered and spewed an obnoxious stench when a sailor from the storeroom on the far end of the building shouted out, "Let's get the hell out of here before she blows!" It was a chemical bomb and several sailors on a disposal mission later suffered severe burns and open sores that resembled leprosy. Some perished.

I immediately slid backwards and darted out another door, only to find more of our planes and fuel storage tanks in a raging blaze. The majority of our ammo was under lock and key since Friday night for a long lazy laidback weekend. Some sailors busted the padlock to our ammo locker, and a young Navy ensign, gung-ho on regulations, wanted all the serial numbers on the rifles recorded before passing them out. A very impatient gob, at the end of a long waiting line, took matters into his own hands. He ran to the front, grabbed the ensign by the shoulder and moved him out of the way as he yelled, "Sir! Don't you know there is a war going on?" This sailor was an instant hero as he tossed guns and ammo to the crowd.

As a Kansas farm boy, I had nine years of tractor driving under my belt, and seeing all those burning planes next to out hangars, I yelled for a sailor to find a cable sling in one of the storerooms which he did. I mounted one of the little Minneapolis Moline orange colored tractors and backed up to a burning plane while they fastened the sling. I sped down along the lonely runway towards the Navy junkyard, better known as the Bone Yard. I glanced back and saw the tires on fire, and .30 caliber ammo belts erupting in the cockpits, sending bullets and shell casings in all directions, including my tractor fenders.

As I was about to abandon this lethal package of dynamite I was towing, a Japanese pilot swooped down low in front of me where I could see his bomb bay doors open. He released a huge bomb heading straight for my tractor. I said to myself, "Adolph, this is it for sure." With foot on my brake and hands on top of my head like I did in the little crowded boat earlier, I prayed again. After all I had missed Mass this morning. I saw the bomb enter the concrete runway, ripping out huge chunks of cement laced in reinforcing steel, which landed on nearby roof tops and equipment, while smaller pieces hit my tractor and bounced off, some hitting my arm and shoulder. Again I thanked my Guardian Angel. I stared at the deep crater in front of me. Just as I made the U-turn and headed back to my base, a tremendous explosion blew my burning plane to smithereens. I thought to myself, "Driving tractors in Kansas was never like this."

I sped to the first available hangar, abandoned the tractor, and ran to the entrance to pause and collect my thoughts. A young ensign appeared with a megaphone clutched in both hands, blaring out, "Now hear this, we need volunteers on a rescue mission aboard many of our badly damaged ships in the harbor." Some were the very vessels I saw exploding earlier and leaping out of the water like harpooned whales. Now I'm being slated for another perilous mission.

The USS *Arizona* was the nearest to my barracks, so I decided to make my way aboard this flaming and gallant lady of the seven seas. All walkways, railings, gangplanks, etc., were in a twisted and charred state which made it difficult to climb aboard, especially with all the hot steel I had to cling to.

Lying on her port side, smoke, flames, and hot steel caused my shoe soles to begin to smoke. I worked my way around all the twisted steel looking for survivors. At one point, a badly barbecued sailor next to a gun turret, both eyes charred shut, slowly extended his right hand in my direction, and muttered a few distorted words. I grabbed his hand and realized the hell and agony he suffered. He then slumped over into our Lord's care along with many others on that day of infamy. The minor explosions aboard this 1916 battlewagon made me cringe at every unusual noise, and I had an eerie feeling, learning that beneath my smoking shoes, lay eleven hundred and two including the Becker brothers who graduated from my La Crosse, Kansas, high school a year or so ahead of me. A third brother escaped the ordeal by being on a weekend liberty in Honolulu. Another story aboard the *Arizona* is the fact that all her band members competed the night before with other bands from various ships in port at a place called Bloch area, named after a naval admiral. The *Arizona* band members came in second place and all won the honors of "sleeping in" on Sunday morning, December 7, 1941.

God rest all those souls who have been sleeping in for almost 58 years. Elvis Presley, years ago held one of his concerts at Bloch Arena and all the proceeds were donated to the erection of the Arizona Memorial, which is visited by millions around the globe. To make matters even more eerie, one of their final tunes they played that night was "I Don't Want to Set the World on Fire," but forces from the empire of Japan, certainly set all these young heroes worlds on fire.

Seeing that I was no longer of any help aboard this crippled ship, I turned around and, before my eyes, I spotted a badly charred U.S. quarter on the deck. It was still very hot as I picked it up and plopped it into the pocket of my oil-stained Navy jumper, which left a burnt ring.

I wondered which seaman aboard lost this coin among all the chaos and panic. Fifty years later at one of our Pearl Harbor survivors' meetings, an ex-sailor named Clare Hetrick, who was a crewmember of the *Arizona* at the time of the bombing etc., spoke up and said, "Adolph, that's my quarter. I remember dropping it as I hurriedly abandoned ship that Sunday morning." He went on to say, he clearly recalls the markings of "In God We Trust."

Well, that quarter, almost 58 years later, is still in Adolph's good care, but to pacify Mr. Hetrick, I have paid him a penny interest per year for the past 57 years, and he doesn't hesitate to let me now the interest is due every December seventh.

The USS *Utah*, also a rusty relic from the sneak attack with fifty some seaman entombed aboard, has far fewer visitors than the *Arizona*. Lord, lay a gentle hand on the souls of those 2,400 plus Americans who had their dreams and goals snuffed out like a flickering candle in a Kansas windstorm.

As I made my way off this doomed ship, thousands of leaflets dropped out of the smoke-filled Hawaiian sky, as I set foot again on Ford Island. I gathered a handful of these messages from Hirohito's and Tojo's boys which read, "You damned, go to the devil" and "Wake Up Blind Fools Listen to the Voice of Doom."

I later mailed them to my mother for safekeeping along with many other artifacts, including the December 7, 1941, newspapers from Honolulu's two major presses, the *Honolulu Star Bulletin* and the *Honolulu Advertiser*. Some of my nosy nieces managed to find their way into my mother's attic and raided my large wooden footlocker. By the time I arrived back home in 1944 for a well-earned leave, my relics of past history were past history.

Scuttlebutt ran rampant on that December day at Pearl. Many U.S. servicemen were in agreement that our President Roosevelt and British Prime Minister Churchill were in on the Oahu onslaught. Fifteen minutes of pre-warning to the thousands of us guys could have drastically altered our history. I haven't seen any evidence over the past five plus decades to substantiate the Roosevelt-Churchill story. I am however well pleased with the recent decision to have Kimmel and Short exonerated as the two so-called scapegoats of the Pearl Harbor disaster. The humiliation their families suffered is despicable.

With wads of leaflets in hand, I made my way to my barracks which also was totally blacked out, and sailors had orders to break all the huge glass window panes on all the Ford Island buildings. If you ever wanted to see approved vandalism at its height, this was it. Those guys had a ball, smashing the panes with steel pipes and hammers, etc., and gloating over the results as the ground was littered with lethal shards, which otherwise might have played havoc during the raid.

I grabbed on to the handrails in total darkness making my way up these flights of stairs to my locker, when someone on a megaphone blared out, "Open your lockers and pass out blankets, sheets, clothing, etc. for all the misfortunate seaman fished from the channel. Many only have on skivvies."

They told us to keep track and the Navy would resupply us with new ones later, which they did. It was common to see a seaman second class wearing a coat belonging to a lieutenant, anything to accommodate their plight. Someone heard me talking by my locker, as I tossed that charred U.S. quarter from the *Arizona* in. He shouted out, "Is that you Adolph?" I yelled back, "Who wants to know?" "Kellogg," he shouted. With the aid of my flashlight I made my way down to the end of the dark building and, sitting on one of the empty beds, was Kellogg bleeding profusely from both shoulders and hips, after being squeezed through a small port hole on the sunken USS *Oklahoma*, the ship I was supposed to visit today. I said to my friend, at least I am visiting you today, but under entirely different circumstances.

He showed me his four wounds, scraped to the bone from that undersized port. I was amazed at his composure and jovial attitude, despite his horrible and painful wounds. He said he was very thankful to be there but spoke of some very gruesome events of his shipmates who perished. The skinny ones like himself were forced through the ports by a very portly CPO who said, "No need for all of us to have to die." Kellogg said that the Navy chief poked them through like sausages, knowing full well he would be among the four hundred plus entombed below. We chatted a while longer as some medics were treating his wounds. We discussed our fun at the dance we attended a few hours ago, and our boot camp days at Great Lakes, Illinois.

He asked me if I ever found shoes big enough to fit my feet. I showed him my oil-stained ones and we both chuckled. We wished each other good luck as I parted for my next mission. Little did I know we were never to meet again.

I scooted down below and into our mess hall and couldn't believe my eyes. All tables were jammed together in long rows, end to end and packed like sardines with the wounded, dying, and dead sailors and Marines. Most had been pulled from the channel I had been dogpaddling earlier. Makeshift stretchers and wheelbarrows were used to haul these badly wounded Gobs and Gyrenes. All services in the mess hall were in disarray. No flushing toilets, drinking water, electricity, etc. Some undamaged coffee urns still had lukewarm brew, for all the Navy lovers. One sailor filled about a half a cup and showed it to me, saying, "This is like Clorox. If I spill some on the cement deck, it will bleach it."

Looking outdoors from the mess hall to the channel, and seeing the carnage of our fleet from another angle, was enough to jar every ounce of sanity from within me.

The Nippon bombs and torpedoes certainly did a state of the art devastation on our Navy and all the poor souls whose dismembered bodies floated in the tons of debris.

The huge incinerator smokestack in the shipyard had two huge gaping holes blasted in the brick structure by one of our sixteen-inch guns from Battleship Row, which was trained on a low flying Zero or Kamikaze pilot. I have often wondered where that giant projectile wound up at. Looking at our lifeless fleet, I said to myself, "Thank God none of our aircraft carriers were in harm's way."

Earlier from my third deck barracks, I saw the upturned USS *Utah*, which occupied the berth of one of our carriers. Japan immediately gloated when the *Utah* was sunk, thinking they had put one of our carriers out of service. From that same window, I saw an enemy plane crash on our seaplane tender, the USS *Curtiss*, setting numerous fires and devastation. Fifty years later I met two survivors, Fernandez and Pitts, who were aboard at the time.

Those Rising Sun raiders had us all well mapped out. At a glance they could identify all our ship classifications, plus our harbor depths. Special wooden fins were attached to some of their torpedoes to keep them from sinking into the mud before they had a chance to level off when dropped.

More scuttlebutt circulated through Ford Island base, about the Japs coming back that night in barges to finish the remainder of us off.

I heard someone shout, "We need volunteers to fill sandbags and place them around our intricate machinery to keep it safe from shelling and flying flak." As a farm boy, I was well acquainted with heavy bags of sand mortar, etc., as we hurriedly filled gunny sacks of dry sand. Some of the weaker sailors had quite a struggle to bug them and asked for help. Demita from Arkansas placed one sack on each shoulder and ran to the drop-off site. Some used wheelbarrows to haul theirs. The Navy chief in charge of our sandbagging detail couldn't believe his eyes as he watched Demita in action.

The following morning he called Demita into our small office. Demita was nervously standing at attention, as Chief Grant asked point blank where he was yesterday when he was needed for this detail. Demita blurted out, "Sir! I was here!" The chief said, "Would you mind going to the sand pile and bring one filled sack to the office?" Grant and I watched from the window as Demita struggled to raise it to his knees. He then drug it all the way into the office with both hands. Grant said to him, "Didn't I see you yesterday with one bag on each shoulder and running?" Demita's face turned snow white as he fainted before us. Severe shock can sometimes muster up additional strength within during terrifying situations. Shortly following the sandbag detail, I ran across my best Navy pal, Allen Hoffman. He had his share of horrifying experiences with all the fires, etc.

Our base fire chief, also tall and lanky, crammed into a small vehicle with knees almost to his chest, when a large hunk of steel blown from one of the ships in the harbor plowed through the driver's door and out the passenger side. It ripped out the brake and shift levers as it passed under the chief's legs. Had he been a shorter guy, he would have had both legs amputated. As the old saying goes, a miss is as good as a mile.

We filled large cans of swimming pool water and hauled them all over Ford Island to quench the thirsty and smoke-filled throats. This water lasted for three days before some of our pumps became active again. We were very short on automotive equipment due to the destruction by fires. Along the road leading from Pearl to Honolulu in a dusty field were hundreds of brand new jeeps, trucks, cars, tanks, etc. Not one piece of this equipment ever turned a wheel in all the months I served at Pearl. I doubt if an act of Congress could have released some of that gear we so desperately needed on that Infamy day.

What must those two servicemen on the hill have thought when they were told to ignore their radar blips. A flight of B–17s were due from the States but gave different readings than the Kamikaze and Zeroes did. I detect a trace of coverup here.

The night of December the seventh was cold and a drizzling rain was falling, to make matters even worse. Elza Gerald Archibald, a Montana sailor, and I were selected for a very frightening task. Seventy-seven of our base aircraft were still out on their wee morning hour flights on Oahu Island. It was up to Archie and I to run all over the island, warning our trigger-happy sailors to hold their fire and let our planes land. They were running low on fuel and couldn't communicate due to power failure throughout. What must have gone on in the minds of those pilots when they saw only fires all over Ford Island, totally oblivious to our day of hell.

Archie and I could certainly feel those cold steel bayonets pressed to our chests as we blurted out, "Don't fire. Let our aircraft through."

To make matters worse, our landing field was completely cluttered with machinery, trucks, jeeps, road graders, tar pots, wheelbarrows, etc., to keep the enemy from landing, but our sentries couldn't tell one plane from another as some of our pilots died at Pearl Harbor from American bullets. It was a gruesome sight the next morning seeing our pilots bullet-riddled in their cockpits, shot by our servicemen. Under a blanket in our shop that night, Archie, with the aid of his cigarette lighter, jotted down in our shop logbook, "What a surprising way to return our scrap iron."

One sailor caught a piece from an old cast iron cook stove like Mom used in his shoulder blade, and another sailor caught a piece from tin snips in his upper arm. These are just a few cases: glass, nails, fence post staples, razor blades, ground up cast iron, and Australian beer bottle caps. I can recall only one such bomb hitting my Ford Island base.

One bomb dropped into the sun portion of our base dispensary causing extended damage to the building as well as the hospital equipment. Later on, a bronze plaque was placed on the new tile deck in the exact spot and at the angle of penetration. My buddy Hoffman and I visited that site regularly in the month ahead. One of my metalsmith pals, Sharrett, was on sentry duty that night on top of a large flat roof building when the moon and his shadow played peek-a-boo on the stone stack. Sharrett opened fire and brick and mortar was flying everywhere. It took many months for him to live this one down from his buddies. He was known on the base as the guy who "shoots at his own shadow."

One dedicated Marine sentry was discouraged later in the day still standing his post, awaiting his relief who joined St. Peter earlier. An ensign found a replacement for him and thanked him for his dedication to rules and regulations.

It was common in the aviation field to swap flights with other qualified personnel. One case in point, this terrified sailor was physically sick to the point of vomiting because he had flight duty on December 7 night. He asked a buddy to swap dates with him and his pal accepted. The flight crew was way overdue for their return and we learned that their planes went down into the Pacific Ocean. That poor sailor had a guilt-ridden streak throughout. He was immediately hospitalized and I never did learn what his outcome was.

After Archibald and I completed our frightful duty with those trigger-happy guys with bayonets, my pal Hoffman and I carried one of the bloodstained mattresses from our mess hall to our A&R shop for the night. We decided our barracks were less safe than the steel building. We found one of our large welding tables with the most floor clearing to accommodate the mattress and ourselves. It was now past midnight and we just couldn't ignore those rumors of a nighttime invasion by the Japanese. We huddled close together and whispered to each other. The rain on the tin roof and the creaking of the metal sounded to us like someone was already up there. We were convinced that our time had finally come this night. We talked about death and our families back in the States, not realizing at this point that over 2,400 Americans already lay dead throughout our area. As the night wore on, dozens of tiny bright lights appeared on the far wall in front of us. I said to Hoff, "They're already here in the building. "We lay absolutely still as our eyeballs stared, the closer they seemed to appear. At this point we were both praying for our lives. The steel roof continued to screech and bring on additional terror. Neither of us had a wink of sleep at this point, nor did we have a club, hammer or baseball bat to defend ourselves if we needed to.

Without an ounce of warning, my mind was totally clear of what those staring eyes were. I yelled out, "Hoff" as I slid out from under this massive welding bench and walked to the wall of eyes, so to speak. Laughing to myself, I picked up a couple of aircraft instrument panel gauges from this wooden bin. I saw the radium dial. I showed some to Hoff and our immediate fright somewhat subsided. We were totally relieved at this point. Now to make things really laughable, I was totally responsible for placing all those instruments in this bin as one of many duties delivering parts to incoming and outgoing benches in the shop. All my work had been accomplished in daylight hours, so the radium dials were not visible, but this was the first night I had spent in here. At this time I told Hoffman about a scene in an old movie where the night has a thousand eyes. Well this night certainly played havoc on our nervous systems.

Often I was asked over the years, "Weren't you guys terrified that night?" My answer is always the same, "No! But we were scared like hell!"

We were so relieved, we crawled to our mattress and, exhausted from one hellish day of carnage and disaster, we entered snooze land while fires and minor explosions of ruptured water and gas lines could be heard. The flames and smoke continued to pollute our Hawaiian skies to a point where it would choke a healthy horse.

This early-rising twenty-year-old farm boy awoke well ahead of Hoff, and I was thinking to myself, at this hour in Kansas, I would be clad in a heavy overcoat, ear flap cap, gloves and buckled overshoes with a kerosene lantern, stumbling around in snow banks searching for our milk cows.

Now being without electrical power was no big concern of mine, as I never knew of such luxuries in my eighteen years as a farm boy. Hoff is now awake and we ask each other if all of this was a nightmare or was it for real. By this time, the mess cooks were frantically hustling about their devastating areas in search of food for breakfast. I usually had a box or two tin cans of chlorinated swimming pool water. We considered we had a very yummy breakfast.

People all over were now stirring about, working on various work details for this massive aftermath cleanup. Tapping sounds were heard coming from some of the sunken ships and were immediately reported to our expert divers with underwater cutting torches and pumps. What kept many alive during their entombed hours was enough air supply was filtering through a ventilator shaft aboard ship. Many others weren't this lucky nor was this twenty-one-year-old dark haired Navy diver. While his crew lowered him down, somehow his attached cable became unhooked and he sank to the floor. In a frantic state the crew fumbled for what seemed an eternity with grappling hooks before they finally latched on to this poor sailor and brought him up topside. His air supply was still attached when they removed the heavy steel from his head. They discovered a gruesome sight never believed possible. With a Navy doctor standing by, some fainted when they saw this snow-haired man in the suit, with deep wrinkles all over his face. It was enough to scare anyone.

He had a frightful fixed stare and was rushed off to a nearby hospital. The doctor on the scene told all of the crew, "Today I examined the body of a eighty-year-old man." Just try to picture yourself in this position lying in the mud on the Pearl Harbor floor knowing your diver's suit will be your coffin. I never did learn where that poor soul wound up. Other divers had horror stories of survivors whose shipmates perished under horrifying conditions. Those undersized portholes aboard our ships at that time in our history were far too small. We would have more Pearl

Harbor survivors today if they had been larger fifty-eight years ago. Evidence was discovered aboard one ship survivors remained alive up to a day before Christmas Eve.

Ensign Forgay, aboard the cruiser *New Orleans,* was in charge of the ammunition department that morning when some lifting device failed. He shouted out, "Praise the lord and pass the ammunition," and the rest is history. I recall some of the words:

> Praise the lord and pass the ammunition
> We can't afford to sit around a-wishin
> Praise the lord and pass the ammunition
> and we'll all stay free.
> The sky pilot said it,
> We've got to give 'em credit
> For a son of a gunner was he.

Hoffman and I were assigned to a clean-up and rescue detail. As a welder and metalsmith, I mounted some wooden tines on the bow of one of our small motor launches to gather dismembered seamen from the oily channel and wrap them in burlap and bed sheets for burial at the Punch Bowl Cemetery in Honolulu. This wasn't the most pleasant task, seeing all those rating badges and hashmarks on those waterlogged remains. I spotted a diary floating among the tons of debris. I grabbed it and showed it to Hoff. Identification and what ship was blotted and oil stained, but whoever owned it did make his last entry on December 6, 1941. He wrote, "Today was a peaceful day, and tomorrow morning I get to sleep in."

Oh, the stories that were swapped among the crews of their experiences and the strafing of civilians on the runway, etc. Some incendiary and larger bombs fell over Honolulu, mainly in the sections of Japanese ancestry, which leveled several skid row type shacks. I have a photo of this event.

All four of the huge sound clocks on the Aloha Tower in the Honolulu Harbor, were stopped simultaneously from the jolt of a Japanese bomb nearby. The Chamber of Commerce of Honolulu decided to leave them undisrupted as a reminder to the rest of the world of Hirohito's dastardly attack on December 7. They were still silent when I left for the States in May 1944. I still have a picture of a Nippon plane we fished from the channel with the pilot strapped in and totally bullet-riddled. He wore a class ring from one of our West Coast universities and he also had a flask of Kentucky whiskey in a small pocket. His plane was visibly shod with Goodyear tires, and on his instrument panel, most of the gauges looked very similar to the radium dialed ones I showed to Hoffman a few hours before. All these instruments were made at a plant in El Segundo, California.

We took that plane into my repair shop and, being an aviation metalsmith, I snipped a small piece of aluminum from one of the wings as a souvenir, along with that charred U.S. quarter from the *Arizona*. The Japanese pilot was given full military honors by our Navy for his burial service. I've often wondered, had the situation been reversed and an American pilot crashed into Tokyo Bay, what honors he would have received.

Crews were busy everywhere on Ford Island. Word was passed to paint all the windows in our shop and hangars solid black. The order also included the headlights and taillights of all vehicles. All flashlights had to go to supply to have blue cellophane paper inserted between the lens and bulb. Our top brass decided that the blue light was more difficult to spot from the air.

Blackouts were immediately mandatory throughout the area. Early morning commuters from Honolulu to Ford Island and various bases had far fewer accidents on the roadways with their painted headlights. Most traveled at a snail's pace.

Around the clock work schedules were immediately effective and all those Japanese civilian men and women workers were employed in our shops throughout. That sneaky scheme didn't cut ice with our top brass. Many of these Orientals had access to records and pertinent data in various departments. Two days following the attack a sailor walked into my small office in the A&R shop, with a copy of Sunday's Honolulu newspaper, to show me an ad that was placed by a Honolulu jeweler.

It depicted a harbor with pearls and jewelry with a bright sun rising over the hill and all the wristwatches setting at the exact same time of the attack. It has bothered me ever since.

Speaking of jewelry, all the Honolulu and Waikiki jewelers became avid souvenir collectors to a point of greed.

U.S. Naval shipboard supplies were in big demand, especially the stainless steel tableware and mess trays with USN stamped on them. Two sailors in my shop concocted the idea of making a few bucks instantly. They swiped numerous forks, knives, spoons, mess trays, etc., from the base mess hall and brought them to the shop. With the aid of an acetylene torch and a few tongs and hammers, they heated these objects and twisted them into various shapes with a few holes punched in to resemble bullet holes, etc. The black smoke from the torch gave them the finishing touch. They thought the greedy jewelers would be easily fooled.

Carrying gas masks by all became law immediately following the slaughter at Pearl. Now for sure all our welding and metal departments became busy with all the demand and bullet riddled panels everywhere. We formed an around the clock schedule with work four hours and sleep four hours. Hoffman and I watched the *Oklahoma* being erected with over four hundred entombed seaman aboard.

Twenty-one cable winches were mounted on Ford Island and was each driven by huge diesel engines connected to low ratio gearboxes. Crews on the *Oklahoma* welded twenty-one lifting lugs to attach the large and heavy steel cables, spanning across the channel. Two sailors lost their lives as one cable snapped and added two more deaths to the Pearl Harbor tragedy.

Five Japanese mini subs at Pearl were shortlived and very ineffective. I have a photo of one.

Aboard a Dutch Indies ship, the *Doeschfontein*, I sailed out of the Honolulu Harbor in May 1944 and staring at those clocks on the Aloha Tower brought back unforgotten memories. Seasickness again plagued this Kansas boy.

Chapter 16

Schofield Barracks

In 1872, Maj. Gen. John M. Schofield, commander of the Pacific Division, visited the Hawaiian Islands to determine the defense capabilities of its ports. The general determined that a harbor could be formed at the mouth of Pearl River and easily defended.

After the annexation of Hawaii to the United States in 1898, army troops were deployed to the island's coast. Capt. Joseph C. Castner, a part of the deployment, made plans and started the development of today's Schofield Barracks. Although the area was known as Castner Village, in 1909 the War Department named it Schofield Barracks after Maj. Gen. Schofield.

In 1911, the Secretary of War approved plans for construction of and troop buildup at Schofield Barracks. The plan called for five infantry regiments, and one each of cavalry and field artillery. Those plans were later altered but permanent quarters were needed for the four regiments already on post. The first permanent structures, which still exist today, were the quadrangle barracks.

When all of Schofield's troops were called to war in 1917, the Hawaiian National Guard moved in and began beautifying the post. Many of the large trees on the post, including the Norfolk pines, were planted by the National Guard. In the 1920s, an extension of the Oahu Railway and Land Company Railroad was built to pass in front of the quads.

In the 1930s construction continued with round-edge art decor. Many of the streets were named to commemorate military leaders such as generals Henry Butner and Harry Bishop.

On December 7, 1941, the 24th and 25th Divisions were at Schofield Barracks when the Japanese attacked. The two divisions were deployed to defend the northern and southern shores against further attacks.

During the Korean War, the base was underutilized, but in 1954 the 25th Infantry returned to Hawaii and the additional population required more of a demand for expansion.

During the Vietnam conflict, it was underutilized again, and as a result, was remodeled with semi-private rooms. In the 1970s, all the facilities were upgraded to include childcare and restaurant facilities. The post stockade was closed in 1977 but was still used as a correctional custody facility until 1990.

Today Schofield Barracks is the largest post operated outside the continental United States.

SERGEANT ALPHONSE SIENCHIO
U.S. Army

SCHOFIELD BARRACKS

In August 1941, we picked up six 268 radars at Fort Shafter. Radar was so secret that from the time the radars were picked up, we were under the command of the Hawaiian Department–Diamond Head. No one could enter our site without a special pass from headquarters. Our sites were secured by barbed wire. Men on guard carried live ammunition. We were a gypsy outfit setting up radar sites throughout the Islands. Looking for high ground. Then the range of 268 radars was 10,000 yards. We had sites at Barbers Point, Kaena Point, Wahiawa, Kahuku Point, Kaneohe, and Waimea.

Radar 268 Kaena Point North Shore. Our tracking was cut to one hour at dawn and one hour at dusk. Told to conserve fuel power to our radars supplied from Leroi Motors 100% octane gasoline was used. Radar tracking transmitted 105 meg cycle. If our radar hit a target or bogie (enemy plane) it would echo a return called a blip. Peaks were the return signals from the planes we tracked. We had antennas that received the information and transferred it to gun sights, who in turn could track the incoming planes and fire at them if they were enemy planes.

We had been on alert since August 1941 every other day and on weekends. On the morning of December 7, 1941, we began tracking at 7 A.M. Our range was limited to between 10 and 20 miles. Suddenly we picked up a large group of planes incoming. They were in the formation of an arrow.

I was sent to the second radar unit just outside Wheeler Field to check with the radar units there. The planes came over and were so low that you could see the pilots. We had no ammunition. When the attack started they knocked out all of our communications. For hours we didn't know what was going on other than we had been attacked by the Japanese.

Our radar units were not camouflaged, just sitting out in the open. After the attack started we tried to cover the equipment the best we could. A few hours later we received ammunition, but by then the attack was over.

That night we moved our radar to the other side of the island. Army units were set up along the shores for the defense of the island. Rumors ran wild: the Japanese were going to land with troops or the Japanese had landed on the beaches of Oahu. It was tense throughout the night.

The next morning I returned to Schofield. I helped secure a general store named Hasbe's. Hasbe was arrested by the Army intelligence agents as a spy. He had been under surveillance for months. His rank in the Japanese [Navy] was commander. His store and bar catered to soldiers all over the area, ranging from Schofield to Kolokdo and the firing range. The bar was a stop for drinks, plus there was the general store where food was sold. Hasbe was the only store for miles around. He developed film in the store and had access to most photos taken from Army installations plus he heard all loose talk, as the soldiers after a few drinks would talk. When he was arrested, boxloads of film and photos were taken and used against him.

After securing the store I helped build some barriers with barbed wire and assisted in making some roadblocks. After that I went back to my radar unit.

THE WAR CONTINUES

As the war continued radar equipment improved. Al Sienchio received more training in radar school. He participated in the Battle of Midway and Tarawa. In 1945, after 49 months overseas, Al returned to the United States.

POINTS OF INTEREST

Haleiwa Field

Haleiwa Field is a small airstrip about eight miles north of Wahiawa, Schofield Barracks, and Wheeler Field. The 47th Pursuit Squadron were at the field after an all-night poker game when the attack started. Second Lieutenants George Welch and Ken Taylor, pilots for the 47th Squadron, sped to the airfield and, still in their tuxedos, engaged a flight of twelve Japanese planes over Barbers Point. Between them, the two pilots shot down five planes. The fight continued and the pilots ended with eight Japanese planes shot down.

Bellow Field

Bellow Field is only a few miles south and east of Kaneohe Naval Air Station. The small base was home of the 86th Observation Squadron.

At the time of the attack, there were six P–47s and two P–49s at the base and one squadron of P–40s.

At 0900, nine planes attacked Bellow Field. One man was wounded, a gasoline tank truck set afire, and one P–49 and one P–47 damaged. One pilot, Lt. Whiteman of the 44th Squadron of P–40s, was shot down after taking off. Lt. Hans C. Christensen was killed getting into his plane, and Lt. Samuel W. Bishop was airborne when the Japanese, right behind him, shot him down.

SERGEANT WALTER W. TRIPP
U.S. Army Air Forces

SCHOFIELD BARRACKS

On Saturday, December 6, 1941, I was on duty and woke about 6 A.M. Lt. Johnson was the officer of the day and both of us went on duty at 12 noon and I was to be off duty at 12 noon Sunday December 7. At about 6:15 A.M. on Sunday morning we went to breakfast and left about 30 minutes later. Lt. Johnson went to his quarters and I went back to the office.

About 7:55 A.M. I happened to look out the window at Wheeler Field and I noticed smoke rising on the airfield. I walked to the window and looked out for a closer look. I could see planes diving at the airfield. The Navy had practice attacks on the airfield and when Lt. Johnson came to the office he said that the Navy was really putting on a show. He went to battalion headquarters to check it out. From the east I could see a plane approaching and I went outside to check it out. When the plane came over battalion headquarters I could see the Rising Sun on the wing. He tipped his wing and turned. He was so low I could see his face. It took a minute, but then I realized that it was Japanese and this was no practice. About that time Lt. Johnson came running out of headquarters and told me that the Japanese were attacking Pearl Harbor. By this time several of our troops started arriving. We mustered and were the first unit to Hickam Field. There was so much confusion nobody knew what to do. After several planes were blown up and burning on the runways we were ordered to try to clear the airfield from burning planes. We had gone into a hangar for some equipment when one of the Japanese planes was hit and crashed into the hangar. I had just left the building when the explosion hit. It killed all the men inside and I got hit by a small piece of metal. The rest of the squad was working a machine gun. One of the men saw blood on the back of my shirt and called for a medic. The medic came over and pulled the metal out of my back. He put a pressure bandage on it and gave me some pills for pain. But, at the time, my back was numb. I felt no pain. I returned to the airfield and helped clear wreckage from the runway. We worked all day in what seemed a never-ending situation.

I was stationed at Schofield Barracks until December 28, 1941. After a short combat training period we boarded a ship at Pearl Harbor and headed for Bakers Island.

POINT OF INTEREST

Wheeler Field

Soldiers from Schofield Barracks began clearing an area to make a landing strip in February 1922. The airfield was named on November 11, 1922, in honor of Maj. Shelton H. Wheeler. Maj. Wheeler, former commander of Luke Field on Ford Island, died when his plane crashed during a demonstration on July 13, 1921. Wheeler Field became a separate military post on August 31, 1939. The first commander of the field was Maj. George E. Straterneyer, later to be Chief of the Army Air Corps in World War II. Wheeler, a former U.S. Air Force base, was returned to the Department of the Army on November 1, 1991. The base comprises 1,389 acres of land adjacent to Schofield Barracks.

Chapter 17

Kaneohe Bay

Marine Corps base Kaneohe Bay is located on the windward side of Oahu, on Mokapu Peninsula, approximately 12 miles northeast of Honolulu. The base consists of 2,951 acres of land.

In 1918, Fort Hase became commissioned and was known as the Kuwaahoe Military Reservation. In 1939, the Navy constructed a small seaplane base there and called it the Kaneohe Bay Naval Air Station. Its role was soon expanded to include the administration of the Kaneohe Bay Naval Defense Sea Area. On December 7, 1941, the first blow by the Japanese attack was directed at Kaneohe Bay Naval Air Station. One sailor there was cited for his heroic actions and later became one of the first Medal of Honor recipients in World War II. After the war, the operations at the base were limited.

In 1951, the air station was proposed as an ideal site for a combined air-ground team. The Marines assumed control of its activities when naval aviation moved to Barbers Point Naval Air Station, and in 1952, Kaneohe was commissioned.

In April 1994, the Marine Corps consolidated the Support Facility, Manana Family Housing Area, Puuloa Range and the Pearl City Warehouse Annex to form a new command, Marine Corps Base Hawaii, headquartered at MCBH Kaneohe Bay, which is home to more than 15,000 Marines, sailors, family members, and civilian employees.

A shot of Kaneohe Bay from the air.

AVIATION ORDNANCE FIRST CLASS ALFRED D. PERUCCI
U.S. Navy

NAVAL AIR STATION KANEOHE BAY, OAHU

I was attached to Patrol Squadron Fourteen (VP–14) stationed at the Naval Air Station at Kaneohe Bay, Oahu. Based at the Naval Air Station Kaneohe Bay were three Navy seaplanes patrol squadrons, VP–14, VP–11, and VP–12, totaling 36 planes. I was a first class petty officer, aviation ordnance. I functioned as an ordnance crew leader and duty section leader. On December 7, 1941, I was the duty section leader, waiting to be relieved by the oncoming duty section leader. At approximately 0745, as I was walking toward the hangar I heard aircraft noise. I looked up and noticed three planes flying in a westerly direction toward the Pali. I also noticed the marking under the wings, a red ball or circle. I said to myself these are Japanese planes. Then in a matter of seconds, the planes made a 180 degree turn and began heading back toward our hangars and planes. The Japanese planes plummeted towards the hangars and began strafing our hangars and planes. This happened at approximately 0750. After the initial shock of the enemy attack, a matter of a few seconds, I immediately ran toward the duty barracks located close to the hangar area and alerted the duty section crew that we were under attack. Immediate action was taken. The armory was located next to the duty barracks. I began issuing rifles, machine guns and machine gun mounts. We went immediately to ready the ammunition locker. Not having a key, I removed the lock by shooting it off with my gun. I began issuing bandoleers for the rifles, belted ammunition for the machine guns and unbelted ammunition. I organized a belting crew and a crew to supply ammunition to the men manning the machine guns. Three machine guns were positioned outside the hangar facing the bay, two .50 caliber on either side of the hangar and a .30 caliber in between. The enemy continued to strafe the area while the machine guns were being positioned. To the best of my recollection the above took less than ten minutes. The actions we took made it possible to effectively return fire to the enemy planes. In the meantime, other planes appeared and commenced bombing and strafing the hangars, planes parked on the ramp, and planes anchored in the bay.

During the beginning of the first attack, I manned one of the .50 caliber machine guns and I believe Frank Tucci, AMM3, manned the other machine gun, and Glen Cummings, AM2, manned the .30 caliber machine gun. Knowing that I had to continue supervising the manpower and see to it that ample supplies of ammunition were being belted, and that the crews were supplying ammunition to personnel manning rifles and machine guns, I turned the machine gun over to one of the crew members of the duty section.

Through my initiative, skill and courage, I materially aided in making it possible to have ample supplies of ammunition available at the commencement of the second attack. What I have just stated could not have been accomplished without the assistance of the men in duty section 4.

I cannot recall how much time passed between the first attack and the second attack when the squadron personnel began reporting to the scene of action. The first person I recognized was Chief John Finn, who was the ordnance division chief, and my supervisor.

Sometime between the first and second attacks, I noticed the planes anchored in the bay were on fire. Knowing that plane guards and equipment

Kaneohe Bay after the Japanese attack.

such as machine guns and belted ammunition were on board, I hailed a coxswain in a whale boat positioned in the bay and with the assistance of Paul Van Nostrand, we picked up the plane guards and equipment and returned to shore. After unloading the guards and equipment, I spotted depth bombs loaded on the bomb trailers in the hangars. I immediately attached the bomb trailers to a truck that Chief Sullivan procured and we moved them to an area away from the hangar, planes, and personnel. While performing all of the above, we were constantly being bombed and strafed by the enemy. It was a miracle that we escaped with so few causalities; Laxton Newman, AMM3, was killed in action, Chief Finn was wounded while manning a machine gun and Earl L. Jones was also wounded. The attack on the Naval Air Station at Kaneohe Bay, Oahu, ceased at approximately 0900, December 7, 1941.

I learned later that the 40 Japanese planes that attacked the Naval Air Station at Kaneohe Bay at 0750, on December 7, 1941, were part of the main 300 warplanes assault group. The Japanese forces knew that our planes were fueled and were lined up on the ramp and anchored in the bay. Since our planes stationed at Kaneohe Bay could have been able to disrupt the enemy's attack, it is my belief that the Japanese first attacked Kaneohe Bay. The Japanese succeeded in destroying many aircraft and two hangars.

Appendix A

Ships Present at Pearl Harbor

U.S.S. *Allen* (DD-66)
U.S.S. *Antares* (AKS-3)
U.S.S. *Argonne* (AG-31)
U.S.S. *Arizona* (BB-39)
U.S.S. *Avocet* (AVP-4)
U.S.S. *Aylwin* (DD-355)
U.S.S. *Bagley* (DD-386)
U.S.S. *Blue* (DD-387)
U.S.S. *Bobolink* (AM-20)
U.S.S. *Breese* (DM-18)
U.S.S. *Cachalot* (SS-170)
U.S.S. *California* (BB-44)
U.S.S. *Case* (DD-370)
U.S.S. *Cassin* (DD-372)
U.S.S. *Castor* (AKS-1)
U.S.S. *Chew* (DD-106)
U.S.S. *Conyngham* (DD-371)
U.S.S. *Cummings* (DD-365)
U.S.S. *Curtis* (AV-A)

U.S.S. *Dale* (DD-353)
U.S.S. *Detroit* (CL-8)
U.S.S. *Dewey* (DD-349)
U.S.S. *Dobbin* (AD-3)
U.S.S. *Dolphin* (SS-169)
U.S.S. *Downes* (DD-375)
U.S.S. *Farragut* (DD-348)
U.S.S. *Gamble* (DM-15)
U.S.S. *Grebe* (AM-43)
U.S.S. *Helena* (CL-50)
U.S.S. *Helm* (DD-388)
U.S.S. *Henley* (DD-391
U.S.S. *Honolulu* (CL-48)
U.S.S. *Hulbert* (AVD-6)
U.S.S. *Hull* (DD-350)
U.S.S. *Jarvis* (DD-393)
U.S.S. *Keosanqua* (AT-38)
U.S.S. *MacDonough* (DD 351)
U.S.S. *Maryland* (BB-46)

U.S.S. *Medusa* (AR-1)
U.S.S. *Monaghan* (DD-354)
U.S.S. *Montgomery* (DM-17)
U.S.S. *Mugford* (DD-389)
U.S.S. *Narwhal* (SS-167)
U.S.S. *Neosho* (AO-23)
U.S.S. *Nevada* (BB-36)
U.S.S. *New Orleans* (CA-32)
U.S.S. *Oglala* (CM-4)
U.S.S. *Oklahoma* (BB-47)
U.S.S. *Ontario* (AT-13)
U.S.S. *Patterson* (DD-392)
U.S.S. *Pelias* (AS-14)
U.S.S. *Pennsylvania* (BB-38)
U.S.S. *Perry* (DMS-17)
U.S.S. *Phelps* (DD-360)
U.S.S. *Phoenix* (CL-46)
U.S.S. *Preble* (DM-20)
U.S.S. *Pruitt* (DM-22)
U.S.S. *Pyro* (AE-1)
U.S.S. *Rail* (AM-26)
U.S.S. *Raleigh* (CL-7)
U.S.S. *Ralph Tablot* (DD-390)
U.S.S. *Ramapo* (AO-12)
U.S.S. *Ramsay* (DM-16)
U.S.S. *Reid* (DD-369)
U.S.S. *Rigel* (AR-11)
U.S.S. *Sacramento* (PG-49)
U.S.S. *Schley* (DD-103)
U.S.S. *Selfridge* (DD-357)
U.S.S. *Shaw* (DD-373)
U.S.S. *Sicard* (DM-21)
U.S.S. *Solace* (AH-5)
U.S.S. *St. Louis* (CL-49)
U.S.S. *Summer* (-32)
U.S.S. *Sunnadin* (AT-28)
U.S.S. *Swan* (AVP-7)
U.S.S. *Tangier* (AV-8)
U.S.S. *Tautog* (SS-199)
U.S.S. *Tennessee* (B-43)
U.S.S. *Tern* (AM-31)

U.S.S. *Thornton* (AVD-11)
U.S.S. *Tracy* (DMS-16)
U.S.S. *Trever* (DMS-16)
U.S.S. *Tucker* (DD-374)
U.S.S. *Turkey* (AM-13)
U.S.S. *Utah* (AG-16)
U.S.S. *Vega* (AK-4)
U.S.S. *Vestal* (AR-4)
U.S.S. *Vireo* (AM-52)
U.S.S. *Ward* (DD-139)
U.S.S. *Wasmuth* (DMS-15)
U.S.S. *West Virginia* (BB-48)
U.S.S. *Whitley* (AD-4)
U.S.S. *Widgeon* (ASR-1)
U.S.S. *Worden* (DD-352)
U.S.S. *Zane* (DMS-14)

Service Craft

Ash (YN-2)
Cheng-Ho (IX-52)
Cinchona (YN-7)
Cockatoo (Amc-8)
Cockenoe (YN-47)
Condor (Amc-14)
Crossbill (Amc-9)
Hoga (YT-146)
Manuwai (YFB-16)
Marin (YN-53)
Nihoa (YFB817)
Nokomis (YT-142)
Osceola (YT-129)
PT-20
PT-21
PT-22
PT-23
PT-24
PT-25
PT-26
PT-27
PT-28
PT-29

PT-30
PT-42
Reedbird (AMC-30)
Sotoyomo (YT-9)
Wapello (YN-56)
YG-15
YG-17
YG-21
YMT-5
YN-10
Yng-17
YO-21
YO-28
YO-30
YO-43
YO-44
YP-109

YR-20
YR-22
YSD-19
YT-119
YT-130
YT-152
YT-153
YTT-3
YW-16

Coast Guard

USCG CG-8
USCG *Reliance* (PC-150)
USCG *Taney* (PG-37)
USCG *Tiger* (PC-152

Appendix B

President Roosevelt's Speech to Congress: "The Day of Infamy"

Yesterday, December 7, 1941—a date which will live in infamy—the United States of America was suddenly and deliberately attacked by Naval and Air Forces of the Empire of Japan.

The United States was at peace with that Nation and, at the solicitation of Japan, was still in conversation with its government and its Emperor looking toward the maintenance of peace in the Pacific. Indeed, one hour after the Japanese squadrons had commenced bombing Oahu, the Japanese Ambassador to the United States and his colleague delivered to the Secretary of State a formal reply to a recent American message. While this reply stated that it seemed useless to continue the existing diplomatic negotiations, it contained no threat or hint of war or armed attack.

It will be recorded that the distance of Hawaii from Japan makes it obvious that the attack was deliberately planned many days or even weeks ago. During the intervening time the Japanese Government had deliberately sought continued peace.

The attack yesterday on the Hawaiian Islands has caused severe damage to American Naval and Military forces. Very many American lives have been lost. In addition, American ships have been reported torpedoed on the high seas between San Francisco and Honolulu.

Yesterday the Japanese Government also launched an attack against Hawaii.

Last night Japanese forces attacked Hong Kong.

Last night Japanese forces attacked Guam.

Last night Japanese forces attacked the Philippine Islands.

Last night the Japanese attacked Wake Island.

This morning the Japanese attacked Midway Island.

Japan has, therefore, undertaken a surprise offensive extending throughout the Pacific area. The facts of yesterday speak for themselves. The people of the United States have already formed their opinions; and well understand the implications to the very life and safety of our nation.

As Commander-in-Chief of the Army and Navy I have directed that all measures be taken for our defense.

Always will we remember the character of the onslaught against us.

No matter how long it may take us to overcome this premeditated invasion, the American people in their righteous might will win through to absolute victory.

I believe I interpret the will of the Congress and of the people when I assert that we will not only defend ourselves to the uttermost but will make very certain that this form of treachery shall never endanger us again.

Hostilities exist. There is no blinking at the fact that our people, our territory, and our interests are in grave danger.

With confidence in our armed forces— with the unbounded determination of our people — we will gain the inevitable triumph — so help us God.

I ask that the Congress declare that since the unprovoked and dastardly attack by Japan on Sunday, December seventh, a state of war has existed between the United States and the Japanese Empire.

Appendix C

Casualties

This is a list of persons, both military and civilian, who died as a result of the Pearl Harbor attack or were killed later that day in the performance of their duties. The listing of servicemen is by branch of service and duty station. The list of civilians is by location. Sailors and Marines killed onboard the USS *Arizona* are identified in Appendix D.

THE FIRST CASUALTIES

In the first hours of America's Pacific war, the nation suffered among its worst wartime losses: 2,388 men, women, and children were killed in the attack on Hawaii. The targets were naval ships and military facilities throughout Oahu. The number of casualties suffered by each ship and facility is enumerated below.

Civilians

Various locations, 48

United States Army

Camp Malakole, 3
Fort Barrette, 1
Fort Kamehameha, 5

Fort Shafter, 1
Fort Weaver, 1
Schofield Barracks, 5

United States Army Air Forces

Bellows Field, 2
Hickam Field, 182
Wheeler Field, 33

United States Marine Corps

Ewa Marine Corps Air Station, 4
USS *Arizona*, 73
USS *California*, 4
USS *Helena*, 1
USS *Nevada*, 7
USS *Oklahoma*, 14
USS *Pennsylvania*, 6

United States Navy

Ford Island Naval Air Station, 1
Kaneohe Bay Naval Air Station,18
Pearl Harbor Naval Hospital, 1
Naval Mobile Hospital #2, 1
USS *Arizona*, 1,104
USS *California*, 98

USS *Chew*, 2
USS *Curtiss*, 21
USS *Dobbin*, 4
USS *Downes*, 12
USS *Enterprise*, 11
USS *Helena*, 33
USS *Maryland*, 4
USS *Nevada*, 50
USS *Oklahoma*, 415
USS *Pennsylvania*, 18
USS *Pruitt*, 1
USS *Shaw*, 24
USS *Sicard*, 1
USS *Tennessee*, 5
USS *Tracy*, 3
USS *Utah*, 58
USS *Vestal*, 7
USS *West Virginia*, 106

C I V I L I A N

Ewa

Yaeko Lillian Oda, 6
Francisco Tacderan, 34

Honolulu

John Kalauwae Adams, 18
Joseph Kanehoa Adams, 50
Nancy Masako Arakaki, 8
Patrick Kahamokupuni Chong, 30
Matilda Kaliko Faufata, 12
Emma Gonsalves, 34
Ai Harada, 54
Kisa Hatate, 41
Fred Masayoshi Higa, 21
Jackie Yoneto Hirasaki, 8
Jitsuo Hirasaki, 48
Robert Yoshito Hirasaki, 3
Shirley Kinue Hirasaki, 2
Paul S. Inamine, 19
Robert Seiko Izumi, 25
David Kahookele, 23
Edward Koichi Kondo, 19
Peter Souza Lopes, 33
George Jay Manganelli, 14

Joseph McCabe, Sr., 43
Masayoshi Nagamine, 27
Frank Ohashi, 29
Hayako Ohta, 19
Janet Yumiko Ohta, 3 months
Kiyoko Ohta, 21
Barbara June Ornellas, 8
Gertrude Ornellas, 16
James Takao Takefuji, aka Koba, 20
Yoshio Tokusato, 19
Hisao Uyeno, 20
Alice White, 42
Eunice Wilson, 7 months

John Rodgers Airport

Robert H. Tyce, 38

Kaneohe Bay Naval Air Station

Kamiko Kookano, 35
Isaac William Lee, 21

Pearl City

Rowena Kamohaulani Foster, 3

Wahiawa

Chip Soon Kim, 66
Richard Masaru Soma, 22

Waipahu

Tomoso Kimura, 19

Honolulu Fire Department
(Hickam Field)

John Carriera, 51
Thomas Samuel Macy, 59
Harry Tuck Lee Pang, 30

Federal Government Employees
(Hickam Field)

August Akina, 37
Philip Ward Eldred, 36

Pearl Harbor

Tai Chung Loo, 19

Red Hill

Daniel LaVerne, 25

MILITARY RANKS AND RATINGS KEY

U.S. Army and Marine Corps Ranks

1st Lt	First Lieutenant
2d Lt	Second Lieutenant
MSgt	Master Sergeant
1st Sgt	First Sergeant
TSgt	Technical Sergeant
SSgt	Staff Sergeant
Sgt	Sergeant
Cpl	Corporal
PFC	Private First Class
Pvt	Private

U.S. Navy Ranks and Rates

Commissioned Officers

Capt (CO)	Captain (Commanding Officer)
Lt. Comdr	Lieutenant Commader
Lt.	Lieutenant
Lt. (jg)	Lieutenant Junior Grade
Lt. (jg)(ChC)	Lieutenant Junior Grade, Chaplain Corps
Lt. (jg)(MC)	Lieutenant Junior Grade, Medical Corps
Ens	Ensign

Warrant Officers

Chf Bosn	Chief Boatswain
Chf Carp	Chief Carpenter
Chf Pay Clk	Chief Pay Clerk
Chf Radio Elec	Chief Radio Electrician
Mach	Machinist

Enlisted

1c	First Class
2c	Second Class
3c	Third Class
(AA)	Acting Appointment
(PA)	Permanent Appointment
AM	Aviation Machinist
AMM	Aviation Machinist's Mate
AOM	Aviation Ordnance Man
AS	Apprentice Seaman
Bgmstr	Buglemaster
Bkr	Baker
BM	Boatswain's Mate
Bmkr	Boilermaker
Bug	Bugler
CBM	Chief Boatswain's Mate
CBmstr	Chief Bandmaster
CCM	Chief Carpenter's Mate
CCStd	Chief Commissary Steward
CEM	Chief Electrician's Mate
CFC	Chief Fire Controlman
CGM	Chief Gunner's Mate
CM	Carpenter's Mate

CMM	Chief Machinist's Mate	MM	Machinist's Mate
CMsmth	Chief Metalsmith	Msmth	Metalsmith
Cox	Coxswain	Mus	Musician
CPhM	Chief Pharmacist's Mate	OC	Officer's Cook
CQM	Chief Quartermaster	OS	Officer's Steward
CRM	Chief Radioman	PhM	Pharmacist's Mate
CSF	Chief Shipfitter	Pmkr	Patternmaker
CSK	Chief Storekeeper	Prtr	Printer
CSM	Chief Signalman	Ptr	Painter
CTC	Chief Turret Captain	QM	Quartermaster
CWT	Chief Watertender	RM	Radioman
CY	Chief Yeoman	Sea	Seaman
EM	Electrician's Mate	SC	Ship's Cook
F	Fireman	SF	Shipfitter
FC	Fire Controlman	SK	Storekeeper
GM	Gunner's Mate	SM	Signalman
HA	Hospital Apprentice	TM	Torpedoman's Mate
MAtt	Mess Attendant	WT	Watertender
Mldr	Molder	Y	Yeoman

UNITED STATES ARMY

Camp Malakole

F Battery 251st
Coast Artillery (AA)

(These soldiers were shot down by Japanese planes over John Rodgers Airport while taking flying lessons.)

Henry C. Blackwell, Sgt
Clyde C. Brown, Cpl
Warren D. Rasmussen, Sgt

Fort Barrette

C Battery 15th Coast Artillery
Joseph A. Medlen, Spl

Fort Kamehameha

C Battery 41st Coast Artillery
Claude L. Bryant, Cpt
Eugene B. Bubb, Pvt
Oreste DaTorre, PFC
Donat G. Duquette, Jr., Pvt

C Battery 55th Coast Artillery
Edward F. Sullivan, Pvt

Fort Shafter

E Battery 64th
Coast Artillery (AA)
Arthur A. Favreau, PFC

Fort Weaver

97th Coast Artillery (AA)
William G. Sylvester, 1st Lt.

(Killed in a car while driving through Hickam Field.)

Schofield Barracks

L Company 21st Infantry
Paul J. Fadon, Sgt

(Killed in a truck accident 10 miles north of Schofield Barracks.)

HQ BTY 63rd Field Artillery
Theodore J. Lewis, Cpt

89th Field Artillery
Walter R. French, Pvt

A Battery 98th Field Artillery
Conrad Kujawa, PFC

(Killed in an accidental electrocution.)

D Company 298th Infantry
Torao Migita, Pvt

(Killed in downtown Honolulu by "friendly fire.")

UNITED STATES ARMY AIR FORCES

Bellows Field

44th Pursuit Squadron
Hans C. Christiansen, 2d Lt
George A. Whiteman, 2d Lt.

Hickam Field

4th Reconnaissance Squadron
Lawrence R. Carlson, Pvt
Donald F. Meahger, Cpl
Louis Schleifer, PFC

HQ Sqd 5th Bombardment Group
George P. Bolan, SSgt
Richard A. Dickerson, Cpl
Alfred Hays, Pvt
Richard E. Livingston, Pvt
George M. Martin, Jr., Sgt

7th Aircraft Squadron (Weather)
Harold W. Borgelt, Cpl
Daniel A. Dyer, Jr., TSgt
Sherman Levine, PFC
James M. Topalian, Cpl

HQ Sqd 11th Bombardment Group
Robert L. Avery, Cpl
Robert S. Brown, Pvt
Edward J. Cashman, TSgt
Donal V. Chapman, PFC
Monroe M. Clark, SSgt
Robert H. Gooding, Pvt

James A. Horner, PFC
George F. Howard, PFC
Lawrence P. Lyons, Jr., Pvt
Wallace R. Martin, 1st Sgt
William W. Merithew, PFC
George A. Moran, Pvt
Herman C. Reuss, TSgt
Robert M. Richey, 1st Lt
Harry E. Smith, Pvt
Edward F. Vernick, PFC
Marion H. Zaczkiewicz, PFC

HQ Sqd 17th Air Base Group
Jerry M. Angelich, Pvt
Malcolm J. Brummwell, 1st Lt
Jack A. Downs, Pvt
Paul R. Eichelberger, Pvt
Arnold E. Field, Pvt
Joseph Jedrysik, Pvt
Andrew J. Kinder, Pvt
Herbert E. McLaughlin, Pvt
Emmett E. Morris, Cpl
Joseph F. Nelles, PFC
Willard C. Orr, PFC
Halvor E. Rogness, Pvt
Leo H. Surrells, Pvt

18th Air Base Squadron
Joseph Bush, Pvt
John H. Couhig, Pvt
Harold C. Elyard, SSgt
Willard E. Fairchild, Pvt
Paul V. Fellman, SSgt
Homer E. Ferris, TSgt
Stuart H. Fiander, Pvt

James J. Gleason, PFC
Otto C. Klein, Pvt
Harry W. Lord, Jr., Pvt
Joseph Malatak, Pvt
Russell M. Penny, Pvt
Allen G. Rae, Pvt
George J. Smith, PFC
Elmer W. South, Pvt
Hermann K. Tibbets, Jr., Pvt
George W. Tuckerman, Pvt
Martin Vanderelli, Pvt
Walter H. Wardigo, Pvt
Lawton J. Woodworth, Pvt
Thomas M. Wright, Pvt
Virgil J. Young, Pvt

HQ Sqd 18th Bombardment Wing
Garland C. Anderson, Pvt
Manfred C. Anderson, Pvt
Gordon R. Bennett, Jr., Pvt
Frank G. Boswell, Pvt
Frank B. Cooper, Pvt
John E. Cruthirds, PFC
Robert C. Duff, Jr., Pvt
Lyle O. Edwards, Pvt
Russell E. Gallagher, Pvt
James E. Gossard, Jr., PFC
John S. Greene, 1st Lt
Earl A. Hood, Pvt
Theodore K. Joyner, Pvt
Edmund B. Lepper, Sgt
Durward A. Meadows, PFC
LaVerne J. Needham, Cpl
Paul L. Staton, Pvt
Anderson G. Tennison, PFC

19th Transport Squadron
William T. Anderson, Cpl
William B. Blakley, Pvt
Russell C. Defenbaugh, Pvt
Joseph H. Guttmann, Pvt
John J. Horan, Pvt
Carl A. Johnson, Pvt
Olaf A. Johnson, PFC
Doyle Kimmey, SSgt
James I. Lewis, PFC
William E. McAbee, PFC
Stanley A. McLeod, Sgt
Walter D. Zuckoff, Pvt

22nd Materiel Squadron
Arthur F. Boyle, Pvt

Billy O. Brandt, SSgt
Rennie V. Brower, Jr., Pvt
William J. Brownlee, Pvt
Brooks J. Brubaker, Pvt
Weldon C. Burlison, Pvt
Leroy R. Church, Pvt
Jack H. Feldman, Pvt
Leo E. A. Gagne, Pvt
Allen E. W. Goudy, Pvt
William E. Hasenfuss, Jr.,PFC
James R. Johnson, Pvt
Robert H. Johnson, Pvt
Marion E. King, Jr., Pvt
Roderick O. Klubertanz, Pvt
John H. Mann, SSgt
James J. McClintock, PFC
Horace A. Messam, PFC
Victor L. Meyers, Pvt
Edwin N. Mitchell, Cpl
Thomas F. Philipsky, PFC
William F. Shields, Pvt
Ralph S. Smith, PFC
John B. Sparks, PFC
Merton I. Staples, Pvt
Jerome J. Szematowicz, PFC
William F. Timmerman, Pvt
Ernest M. Walker, Jr., Pvt

23rd Bombardment Squadron
Lee I. Clendenning, PFC
Richard L. Coster, Pvt
Byron G. Elliott, Pvt
William Hislop, PFC
Howard N. Lusk, Pvt
Lionel J. Moorhead, PFC

23rd Materiel Squadron
Francis E. Campiglia, Pvt
Herbert B. Martin, 1Sgt
Joseph G. Moser, Pvt
Frank St. E. Posey, TSgt
Raymond E. Powell, TSgt
William T. Rhodes, PFC
Maurice J. St. Germain, Pvt
Strickland, James E., Jr., Pvt
Joseph S. Zappala, Pvt
Walter J. Zuschlag, SSgt

26th Bombardment Squadron
Felix Bonnie, SSgt
Clarence A. Conant, Pvt
Frank J. DePolis, SSgt

Patrick l. Finney, Cpl
Elwood R. Gummerson, SSgt
Vincent J. Kechner, Pvt
Robert H. Markley, 2d Lt
Jay E. Pietzsch, 2d Lt
Antonio S. Tafoya, Cpl
Robert H. Westbrook, Jr., Pvt

31st Bombardment Squadron
Jack W. Fox, PFC
Frank J. Lango, Pvt
William M. Northway, Pvt
Felix S. Wegrzyn, Pvt

38th Reconnaissance Squadron
William R. Schick, 1st Lt

42nd Bombardment Squadron
Leland V. Beasley, Pvt
William Coyne, Jr., PFC
Eugene B. Denson, PFC
Robert R. Garrett, Cpl
Charles l. Hrusecky, Pvt
Joseph N. Jencuis, Pvt
Robert R. Kelley, PFC
Hal H. Perry, Jr., Pvt
Carey K. Stockwell, Pvt

50th Reconnaissance Squadron
Ralph Alois, SSgt
Louis H. Dasenbrock, Pvt
John T. Haughey, Pvt.
Clarence E. Hoyt, PFC
Henry J. Humphrey, SSgt
Lester H. Libolt, Cpl
Harell K. Mattox, PFC
William H. Offutt, Cpl

72nd Bombardment Squadron
Edward R. Hughes, Pvt
John J. Kohl, PFC
George Price, Pvt

1st Photo Group, attached to Ferry Command
(These airmen, originally attached to the 44th Bomb Group, arrived in Hawaii two days prior to the attack to outfit their plane for a secret photo mission. They were killed on the ground and their B–24 was destroyed near Hangar 15.)

Louis G. Moslener, Jr., 2d Lt
Daniel J. Powloski, Pvt

Wheeler Field

46th Pursuit Squadron
Donald D. Plant, Pvt
Gordon H. Sterling, Jr., 2d Lt

47th Pursuit Squadron
John l. Dains, 2d Lt
(Shot down by "friendly fire.")

72nd Pursuit Squadron
Edward J. Burns, 1st Sgt
Malachy J. Cashen, Cpl
Dean W. Cebert, Pvt
William C. Creech, PFC
James Everett, SSgt
Paul B. Free, SSgt
Joseph E. Good, SSgt
James E. Guthrie, SSgt
Robert L. Hull, Pvt
George G. Leslie, Pvt
John A. Price, SSgt

73rd Pursuit Squadron
James M. Barksdale, SSgt

78th Pursuit Squadron
Vincent M. Horan, Cpl
Morris E. Stacey, Sgt

UNITED STATES MARINE CORPS

USS *California*
(BB-44, Battleship)

John A. Blount, Jr., PFC

Roy E. Lee, Jr., Pvt
Shelby C. Shook, Pvt
Earl D. Wallen, PFC

USS *Helena*
(CL-50, Light Cruiser)

George E. Johnson, PFC

USS *Nevada*
(BB-36, Battleship)

Thomas A. Britton, Cpl
Francis C. Heath, PFC
Orveil V. King, Jr., PFC
Jack L. Lunsford, PFC
Edward F. Morrissey, PFC
Keith V. Smith, Pvt
Richard I. Trujillo, PFC

USS *Oklahoma*
(BB-37, Battleship)

Marley R. Arthurholtz, PFC
Waldean Black, Pvt
Walter L. Collier, PFC
Alva J. Cremean, PFC
Elmer E. Drefahl, Cpl
Harry H. Gaver, Jr., 2d Lt
Ted Hall, Pvt
Otis W. Henry, Pvt
Robert K. Holmes, PFC
Vernon P. Keaton, Pvt

John F. Middleswart, PFC
Robert H. Peak, Pvt
Raymond Pennington, Pvt
Charles R. Taylor, PFC

USS *Pennsylvania*
(BB-38, Battleship)

Thomas N. Barron, Cpl
Morris E. Nations, Cpl
Floyd D. Stewart, PFC
Patrick P. Tobin, PFC
Jesse C. Vincent, Jr., Cpl
George H. Wade, Jr., PFC

Ewa Marine Corps Air Station

*Marine Aircraft Group
21 Headquarters and
Service Squadron 21*
William E. Lutschan, Jr., Sgt

Scouting-Bombing Squadron 231
William G. Turner, Pvt

Scouting-Bombing Squadron 232
Edward S. Lawrence, PFC

Utility Squadron 252
Carlo A. Micheletto, Sgt

UNITED STATES NAVY

USS *California*
(BB-44, Battleship)

Howard L. Adkins, F1c
Moses A. Allen, MAtt1c
Thomas B. Allen, GM2c
Wilbur H. Bailey, Sea1c
Glen Baker, Sea2c
James W. Ball, F2c
Harold W. Bandemer, Sea1c
Michael L. Bazetti, Sea1c
Albert Q. Beal, RM2c
Thomas S. Beckwith, SF3c
Henry W. Blankenship, PhM1c
Edward D. Bowden, F2c

Robert K. Bowers, Ens (VO-2)
Robert L. Brewer, Sea1c
Samuel J. Bush, MAtt1c
James W. Butler, F2c
Elmer L. Carpenter, BM1c
Cullen B. Clark, F1c
Francis E. Cole, Msmth2c
Kenneth J. Cooper, FC3c
Herbert S. Curtis, Jr., Sea2c
Lloyd H. Cutrer, Sea2c
Edward H. Davis, SK1c
John W. Deetz, GM3c
Marshall L. Dompier, SK2c
Norman W. Douglas, Sea1c
Guy Dugger, F1c

Billie J. Dukes, Sea1c
Thomas R. Durning, Jr., Sea2c
Robert W. Ernest, Sea2c
Alfred J. Farley, Sea2c
Marvin L. Ferguson, Jr., AS
Stanley C. Galaszewski, Sea2c
Robert S. Garcia, SK3c
Thomas J. Gary, Sea2c
George H. Gilbert, Ens
Tom Gilbert, Sea1c
Helmer A. Hanson, Sea2c
Gilbert A. Henderson, MAtt2c John
A. Hildebrand, Jr., F1c
Merle C. J. Hillman, PhM2c
Paul E. Holley, Sea1c
Richard F. Jacobs, SF3c
Ira W. Jeffrey, Ens
Melvin G. Johnson, RM3c
Ernest Jones, MAtt3c
Herbert C. Jones, Ens
Harry Kaufman, BM1c
Arlie G. Keener, SK3c
Harry W. Kramer, F1c
John T. Lancaster, PhM3c
Donald C. V. Larsen, RM3c
John E. Lewis SK1c
James E. London, SK1c
Howard E. Manges, FC3c
John W. Martin, F3c
George V. McGraw, F1c
Clyde C. McMeans, Sea1c
Aaron L. McMurtrey, Sea1c
James W. Milner, F1c
James D. Minter, Sea2c
Bernard J. Mirello, Sea1c
William A. Montgomery, GM3c
Marlyn W. Nelson, F2c
Wayne E. Newton, Sea1c
June W. Parker, QM3c
Kenneth M. Payne, Sea1c
George E. Pendarvis, F3c
Lewis W. Pitts, Jr., Sea2c
Alexander J. Przybysz, Prtr2c
Roy A. Pullen, Sea2c
Edward S. Racisz, Sea1c
Thomas J. Reeves, CRM (PA)
Joseph L. Richey, Ens (VO–2)
Edwin H. Ripley, Sea2c
Earl R. Roberts, Sea1c
Alfred A. Rosenthal, RM3c
Joe B. Ross, RM2c

Frank W. Royse, RM3c
Morris F. Saffell, F1c
Robert R. Scott, MM1c
Erwin L. Searle, GM3c
Russell K. Shelly, Jr., Mus2c
Frank L. Simmons, MAtt2c
Tceollyar Simmons, Sea2c
Lloyd G. Smith, Sea2c
Gordon W. Stafford, Sea2c
Leo Stapler, MAtt1c
Charles E. Sweany, EM1c
Edward F. Szurgot, SK3c
Frank P. Treanor, RM3c
Pete Turk, Sea2c
George V. Ulrich, F1c
George E. Vining, MAtt2c
David Walker, MAtt3c
Milton S. Wilson, F3c
Steven J. Wodarski, Sea1c
John C. Wydila, SF3c

USS *Chew*
(DD-106, Destroyer)

Mathew J. Agola, Sea2

Clarence A. Wise, F3c
(Killed on the Pennsylvania.*)*

USS *Curtiss*
(AV-4, Seaplane Tender)

Joseph I. Caro, F1c
Lee H. Duke, Sea2c
Clifton E. Edmonds, Sea1c
John W. Frazier, Cox
Nickolas S. Ganas, Sea2c
George H. Guy, Sea2c
Kenneth J. Hartley, F1c
Edward S. Haven, Jr., Sea1c
Anthony Hawkins, Jr., MAtt2c
Thomas Hembree, AS
Andrew King, AS
Robert S. Lowe, Sea2c
James E. Massey, AS
Maurice Mastrototaro, Sea1c
Jesse K. Milbourne, AS
Dean B. Orwick. RM2c
William J. Powell, MAtt2c
Wilson A. Rice, Sea1c
Howard A. Rosenau, Sea2c

Benjamin Schlect, RM2c
Joseph Sperling, SF1c

USS *Dobbin*
(AD-3, Destroyer Tender)

J. W. Baker, TM3c
Howard F. Carter, Cox
Roy A. Gross, F1c

Andrew M. Marze, GM1c
(Killed on the Pennsylvania.*)*

USS *Downes*
(DD-375, Destroyer)

James E. Bailey, RM3c
Benjamin L. Brown, Sea2c
Marvin J. Clapp, SC3c
Thomas W. Collins, F3c
Edward C. Daly, Cox
Albert J. Hitrik, F2c
George E. Jones, Rm3c
John A. Marshall, WT2c
Nolan E. Pummill, MM2c
William H. Silva, Sea2c
Perry W. Strickland, Sea1c
James Vinson, F3c

USS *Enterprise*
(CV-6, Aircraft Carrier)

(At the time of the attack the Enterprise *was at sea, about 200 miles due west of Oahu.)*

Scouting Squadron SIX

(These aviators arrived over Oahu during the attack and were shot down by the Japanese.)

Mitchell Cohn, RM3c
Fred J. Ducolon, Cox
Manuel Gonzalez, Ens
Leonard J. Kozelek, RM3c
William C. Miller, Rm1c
Signey Pierce, Rm3c
John H. L. Vogt, Jr., Ens
Walter M. Willis, Ens

Fighting Squadron SIX

(These aviators were shot down by "friendly fire" in an attempt to make a night landing at Ford Island NAS.)

Eric Allen, Jr., Lt. (jg)
Frederick F. Hebel, Lt. (jg)
Herbert H. Menges, Ens

USS *Helena*
(CL-50, Light Cruiser)

Salvatore J. Albanese, F2c
Thomas E. Aldridge, Sea2c
Robert A. Arnesen, F1c
Loren L. Beardsley, EM3c
Regis J. Bodecker, Y1c
William J. Carter, Sea2c
Luther E. Cisco, Sea2c
Allen A. Davis, F3c
Ernest B. Dickens, F2c
Richard H. Dobbins, EM2c
Robert N. Edling, RM3c
Leland E. Erbes, F2c
Robert J. Flannery, FC3c
Eugene D. Fuzi, FC3c
Arthur J. Gardner, WT2c
Robert D. Greenwald, Sea1c
Arvel C. Hines, Sea2c
Donald W. Johnson, Sea2c
Ernest G. Kuzee, Sea1c
Carl R. Love, Sea2c
Marvin W. Mayo, FC2c
Orville R. Minix, Sea1c
Edo Morincelli, MM2c
Hugh K. Naff, Sea2c
John C. Pensyl, GM2c
Joe O. Powers, SK3c
Ralph W. Thompson, F3c
Edward B. Uhlig, Sea2c
John J. Urban, MM2c
Benjamin F. Vassar, Sea2c
Hoge C. Venable, Jr., SK2c
Oswald C. Wohl, Sea2c
Michael C. Yugovich, EM2c

USS *Maryland*
(BB-46, Battleship)

Claire R. Brier, MM2c
Howard D. Crow, Ens
James B. Ginn, Lt.(jg)(VO-4)

Warren H. McCutcheon, Sea2c
(Killed in an air crash 10 miles west of Barbers Pt.)

USS *Nevada*
(BB-36, Battleship)

Arnold L. Anderson, Sea1c
Zoilo Aquino, MAtt1c
James R. Bingham, Sea2c
Herman Bledsoe, MAtt2c
Lyle L. Briggs, EM2c
Harold J. Christopher, Ens
Joseph W. Cook, GM3c
Leon J. Corbin, GM1c
Leo P. Cotner, Sea2c
Frederick C. Davis, Ens (VO-1)
Lonnie W. Dukes, Sea1c
Edward W. Echols, Cox
Harry L. Edwards, Sea1c
George L. Faddis, GM3c
Kay I. Fugate, Sea1c
Samuel M. Gantner, BM2c
Thomas R. Giles, EM3c
Herman A. Goetsch, Sea1c
Arthur K. Gullachson, Sea2c
Johnie W. Hallmark, Sea1c
Charles W. Harker, FC3c
Gerald L. Heim, Sea2c
Edwin J. Hill, Chf Bosn
Edgar E. Hubner, Sea1c
Robert C. Irish, Sea2c
Flavous B. M. Johnson, GM3c
Kenneth T. Lamons, BM2c
Wilbur T. Lipe, Sea2c
John K. Luntta, Sea1c
Andres F. Mafnas, MAtt1c
Dale L. Martin, SC1c
Frazier Mayfield, MAtt1c
Lester F. McGhee, Sea1c
Edward L. McGuckin, Sea1c
William F. Neuendorf, Jr., Sea1c
Alwyn B. Norvelle, CSK (AA)
Elmer M. Patterson, OC2c
Eugene E. Peck, Sea2c
Mark C. Robison, MAtt1c
Emil O. Ronning, Cox
Harvey G. Rushford, Sea2c
Herbert C. Schwarting, Sea1c
Donald R. Shaum, Sea1c
Adolfo Solar, BM1c
Herman A. Spear, Sea1c
Delbert J. Spencer, Sea1c
George J. Stembrosky, Sea1c
Charles E. Strickland, Sea1c

Lee V. Thunhorst, Sea2c
Ivan I. Walton, Cox

USS *Oklahoma*
(BB-37, Battleship)

Marvin B. Adkins, GM3c
Willard H. Aldridge, Sea1c
Hugh R. Alexander, Lt. Comdr
Stanley W. Allen, Ens (VO-1)
Hal J. Allison, F2c
Leon Arickx, Sea1c
Kenneth B. Armstrong, Mldr1c
Daryle E. Artley, QM2c
John C. Auld, Sea2c
John A. Austin, Chf Carp
Walter H. Backman, RM2c
Gerald J. Bailey, Sea1c
Robert E. Bailey, SF3c
Wilbur F. Ballance, Sea1c
Layton T. Banks, Cox
Leroy K. Barber, F1c
Malcolm J. Barber, F1c
Randolph H. Barber, F2c
Cecil E. Barncord, EM3c
Wilber C. Barrett, Sea2c
Harold E. Bates, F1c
Ralph C. Battles, F2c
Earl P. Baum, Sea1c
Howard W. Bean, RM3c
Walter S. Belt, Jr., F1c
Robert J. Bennett, F3c
Harding C. Blackburn, Y3c
William E. Blanchard, Bmkr1c
Clarence A. Blaylock, F3c
Leo Blitz, MM2c
Rudolph Blitz, F1c
John G. Bock Jr., Sea2c
Paul L. Boemer, Cox
James B. Booe, Cbmster
James B. Boring, F2c
Ralph M. Boudreaux, MAtt1c
Lawrence A. Boxrucker, F2c
Raymond D. Boynton, Sea2c
Carl M. Bradley, F2c
Orix V. Brandt, Sea1c
Jack A. Breedlove, FC3c
Randall W. Brewer, MAtt1c
William Brooks, Sea1c
Wesley J. Brown, F1c
William G. Bruesewitz, Sea1c

James R. Buchanan, MM2c

Earl G. Burch, Bkr3c

Oliver K. Burger, WT1c

Millard Burk, Jr., Sea1c

Rodger C. Butts, SC1c

Archie Callahan, Jr., MAtt2c

Raymond R. Camery, F1c

William V. Campbell, Sea2c

Murry R. Cargile, Sea1c

Harold F. Carney, MM1c

Joseph W. Carroll, F2c

Edward E. Casinger, F2c

Biacio Casola, Sea1c

Carles R. Casto, F1c

Richard E. Casto, F2c

James T. Chesire, CPhM(PA)

Patrick L. Chess, SF3c

David Clark, Jr., Sea2c

Gerald L. Clayton, SK2c

Hubert P. Clement, FC1c

Floyd F. Clifford, Sea2c

George A. Coke, Sea1c

James E. Collins, Sea1c

John G. Connolly, Chf Pay Clk

Keefe R. Connolly, HA1c

Edward L. Conway, EM1c

Grant C. Cook, Jr., F1c

Robert L. Corn, FFC1c

Beoin H. Corzatt, F1c

John W. Craig, SK1c

Warren H. Crim, F3c

Samuel W. Crowder, F1c

William M. Curry, EM1c

Glenn G. Cyriack, SK2c

Marshall E. Darby, Jr., Ens

James W. Davenport, Jr., F1c

Francis D. Day, CWT (PA)

Leslie P. Delles, EM3c

Ralph A. Derrington, CMM (PA)

Francis E. Dick, Mus2c

Leaman R. Dill, EM2c

Kenneth E. Doernenburg, F1c

John M. Donald, SF3c

Carl D. Dorr, F2c

Bernard V. Doyle, Sea2c

Stanislaw F. Drwall, Pmkr1c

Cyril I. Dusset, MAtt1c

Buford H. Dyer, Sea1c

Wallace E. Eakes, SK3c

Eugene K. Eberhardt, MM1c

David B. Edmonston, Sea2c

Earl M. Ellis, RM3c

Bruce H. Ellison, RM3c

Julius Ellsberry, MAtt1c

John C. England, Ens

Ignacio C. Farfan, MAtt1c

Luther J. Farmer, MM1c

Lawrence H. Fecho, F1c

Charlton H. Ferguson, Mus2c

Robert A. Fields, EM3c

William M. Finnegan, Ens

Francis C. Flaherty, Ens

James M. Flanagan, Sea2c

Felicismo Florese, OS2c

Walter C. Foley, Sea1c

George P. Foote, SK3c

George C. Ford, F2c

Joy C. French, Sea2c

Tedd M. Furr, CCM (AA)

Michael Galajdik, F1c

Martin A. Gara, F2c

Jesus F. Garcia, MAtt2c

Eugene Garris, MAtt2c

Paul H. Gebser, MM1c

Leonard R. Geller, F1c

George T. George, Sea2c

George H. Gibson, EM3c

George E. Giesa, F2c

Quentin J. Gifford, RM3c

George Gilbert, FC2c

Warren C. Gillette, Sea1c

Benjamin E. Gilliard, MAtt1c

Arthur Glenn, MM1c

Daryl H. Goggin, Mach

Jack R. Goldwater, RM3c

Charles C. Gomez, Jr., Sea2c

George M. Gooch, EM3c

Clifford G. Goodwin, Sea1c

Robert Goodwin, SC3c

Duff Gordon, CMsmth

Claude O. Gowey, F1c

Wesley E. Graham, Sea1c

Arthur M. Grand Pre, F1c

Thomas E. Griffith, RM3c

Edgar D. Gross, WT2c

Vernon N. Grow, Sea2c

Daniel L. Guisinger, Jr., Sea1c

William I. Gurganus, CEM (AA)

William F. Gusie, FC3c

Hubert P. Hall, Sea2c

Robert E. Halterman, Sea1c

Harold W. Ham, MM2c

Dale R. Hamlin, GM3c
Eugene P. Hann, GM3c
Francis L. Hannon, SF3c
George Hanson, MM1c
Robert J. Harr, F1c
Charles H. Harris, EM3c
Daniel F. Harris, CFC (PA)
Louis E. Harris, Jr., Mus2c
Albert E. Hayden, CEM (PA)
Harold L. Head, Sea2c
Robert W. Headington, Sea1c
William F. Hellstern, GM2c
Floyd D. Helton, Sea2c
Jimmie L. Henrichsen, Sea2c
William E. Henson, Jr., Sea2c
Harvey C. Herber, EM1c
George Herbert, GM1c
Austin H. Hesler, SM3c
Denis H. Hiskett, F1c
Joseph P. Hittorff, Jr., Ens
Frank S. Hoag, Jr., RM3c
Herbert J. Hoard, CSK (PA)
Joseph W. Hoffman, Mus1c
Kenneth L. Holm, F3c
Harry R. Holmes, F3c
James W. Holzhauer, Sea1c
Edwin C. Hopkins, F3c
Chester G. Hord, SK3c
Frank A. Hryniewicz, Sea1c
Charles E. Hudson, WT1c
Lorentz E. Hultgren, MM2c
Robert M. Hunter, Ens
Claydon I. C. Iverson, F3c
Willie Jackson, OC1c
Herbert B. Jacobson, F3c
Challis R. James, Sea2c
George W. Jarding, F3c
Kenneth L. Jayne, F3c
Theodore Q. Jensen, RM3c
Jesse B. Jenson, GM3c
Charles H. Johannes, Sea2c
Billy J. Johnson, F1c
Edward D. Johnson, F1c
Joseph M. Johnson, Sea1c
Jim H. Johnston, F1c
Charles A. Jones, Sea2c
Fred M. Jones, MM1c
Jerry Jones, MAtt3c
Julian B. Jordan, Lt.
Wesley V. Jordan, Sea1c
Thomas V. Jurashen, Sea2c

Albert U. Kane, F1c
John A. Karli, Sea1c
Howard V. Keffer, RM3c
Ralph H. Keil, Sea1c
Donald G. Keller, Sea1c
Joe M. Kelley, Sea2c
Warren J. Kempf, RM3c
Leo T. Keninger, F1c
William H. Kennedy, F1c
Elmer T. Kerestes, F1c
David L. Kesler, Bkr2c
William A. Klasing, EM3c
Verne F. Knipp, Cox
Hans C. Kvalnes, Sea2c
William L. Kvidera, CM3c
D. T. Kyser, Sea2c
Elliott D. Larsen, Mus1c
Johnnie C. Laurie, MAtt1c
Elmer P. Lawrence, Sea1c
Willard I. Lawson, F3c
Gerald G. Lehman, F3c
Myron K. Lehman, Sea2c
Lionel W. Lescault, Bgmstr2c
Harold W. Lindsey, Sea2c
John H. Lindsley, F3c
Alfred E. Livingston, F3c
Clarence M. Lockwood, WT2c
Adolph J. Loebach, FC3c
Vernon T. Luke, MM1c
Octavius Mabine, MAtt1c
Howard S. Magers, Sea2c
Michael Malek, Sea2c
Algeo V. Malfante, SF2c
Walter B. Manning, EM1c
Henri C. Mason, Mus1c
Joseph K. Maule, Sea1c
Edwin B. McCabe WT1c
Donald R. McCloud, FC2c
James O. McDonald, F1c
Bert E. McKeeman, F1c
Hale McKissack, Sea1c
Lloyd E. McLaughlin, Sea2c
Earl R. Melton, MM1c
Herbert F. Melton, BM2c
Archie T. Miles, MM2c
Wallace G. Mitchell, Sea1c
Charles A. Montgomery, RM3c
John M. Mulick, HA1c
Ray H. Myers, Sea2c
George E. Naegle, Sea1c
Elmer D. Nail, F1c

Paul A. Nash, FC1c
Don O. Neher, EM3c
Arthur C. Neuenschwander, GM1c
Sam D. Nevill, Y3c
Wilbur F. Newton, Sea1c
Carl Nichols, Sea2c
Harry E. Nichols, SK3c
Frank E. Nicoles, F1c
Arnold M. Nielsen, BM1c
Laverne A. Nigg, Sea2c
Joe R. Nightingale, Sea1c
Charles E. Nix, SM3c
Camillus M. O'Grady, Sea1c
Charles R. Ogle, F1c
Eli Olsen, SK3c
Jarvis G. Outland, F1c
Lawrence J. Overley, FC2c
Alphard S. Owsley, EM3c
Millard C. Pace, F1c
James Palides, Jr., Mus2c
Calvin H. Palmer, Sea2c
Wilferd D. Palmer, Sea2c
George L. Paradis, PhM3c
Isaac Parker, MAtt3c
Dale F. Pearce, Sea2c
Walter R. Pentico, Sea2c
Stephen Pepe, WT1c
Charles F. Perdue, SF1c
Wiley J. Perway, Bmkr2c
Milo E. Phillips, WT1c
James N. Phipps, Sea2c
Gerald H. Pirtle, F1c
Rudolph V. Piskuran, Sea2c
Herbert J. Poindexter, Jr., Sea1c
Brady O. Prewitt, Sea2c
Robert L. Pribble, FC3c
George F. Price, F1c
Lewis B. Pride, Jr., Ens
Jasper L. Pue, Jr., F3c
Paul S. Raimond, Sea1c
Eldon C. Ray, SK3c
Dan E. Reagan, F1c
Leo B. Regan, F1c
Irvin F. Rice, RM3c
Porter L. Rich, WT2c
Clyde Ridenour, Jr., RM3c
David J. Riley, Sea2c
Russell C. Roach, Sea1c
Joseph M. Robertson, Sea2c
Harold W. Roesch, Sea1c
Walter B. Rogers, F1c

Joseph C. Rouse, Sea1c
Charles L. Ruse, Mus2c
Edmund T. Ryan, Y3c
Roman W. Sadlowski, EM3c
Kenneth H. Sampson, Sea1c
Dean S. Sanders, CMM (PA)
Charles L. Saunders, Sea2c
Lyal J. Savage, Sea1c
John E. Savidge, Sea1c
Paul E. Saylor, F1c
Walter F. Schleiter, F1c
Herman Schmidt, GM3c
Aloysius H. Schmitt, Lt. (jg) (ChC)
Andrew J. Schmitz, F1c
John H. Schoonover, PhM1c
Bernard O. Scott, MAtt1c
Chester E. Seaton, F1c
Verdi D. Sederstrom, Ens
William L. Sellon, Sea2c
Everett I. Severinson, SF1c
William K. Shafer, F2c
William J. Shanahan, Jr., SM3c
Edward J. Shelden, FC1c
William G. Silva, GM1c
Eugene M. Skaggs, SM1c
Garold L. Skiles, Sea2c
Edward F. Slapikas, Sea1c
Leonard F. Smith, Msmth1c
Merle A. Smith, EM3c
Rowland H. Smith, Mus1c
Walter H. Sollie, WT1c
James C. Solomon, Sea1c
Maurice V. Spangler, Sea1c
Kirby R. Stapleton, Sea1c
Ulis C. Steely, MM1c
Walter C. Stein, Sea1c
Samuel C. Steiner, F1c
Charles M. Stern, Jr., Ens
Everett R. Stewart, MM2c
Lewis S. Stockdate, Ens
Donald A. Stott, Sea1c
Robert T. Stout, FC3c
James Stouten, CBM (AA)
Milton R. Surratt, Sea1c
Charles H. Swanson, MM1c
Edward E. Talbert, Sea1c
Rangner F. Tanner, Jr., Sea2c
Monroe Temple, Sea1c
Houston Temples, Sea1c
Benjamin C. Terhune, F2c
Arthur R. Thinnes, Sea2c

Charles W. Thompson, F1c
Clarence Thompson, SC1c
George A. Thompson, Sea2c
Irvin A. R. Thompson, Ens
William M. Thompson, Ens
Richard J. Thomson, Sea2c
Cecil H. Thornton, Sea2c
Robert L. Thrombley, Sea2c
David F. Tidball, Sea1c
Lloyd R. Timm, Sea2c
Lewis F. Tindall, F1c
Dante S. Tini, RM3c
Henry G. Tipton, Sea1c
Everett C. Titterington, F1c
Neal K. Todd, F1c
Natale I. Torti, Sea1c
Orval A. Tranbarger, Sea1c
Harold F. Trapp, FC2c
William H. Trapp, EM3c
Shelby Treadway, GM3c
William D. Tucker, F1c
Victor P. Tumlinson, FC3c
Billy Turner, Sea1c
Louis J. Tushla, F1c
Russell O. Ufford, Sea2c
Lowell E. Valley, F2c
Durrell Wade, AMM2c
Lewis L. Wagoner, Sea2c
Harry E. Walker, SK1c
Robert N. Walkowiak, F3c
Eugene A. Walpole, Sea2c
Charles E. Walters, Sea2c
James R. Ward, Sea1c
Edward Wasielewski, Sea1c
Richard L. Watson, Sea1c
James C. Webb, F1c
William E. Welch, Sea1c
Alfred F. Wells, MM1c
Ernest R. West, Sea1c
John D. Wheeler, F2c
Claude White, CWT (PA)
Jack D. White, Sea1
Alton W. Whitson, EM3c
Eugene W. Wicker, Sea1c
Lloyd P. Wiegand, Mus2c
George J. Wilcox, Jr., Sea2c
Albert l. Williams, Mus2c
James C. Williams, Sea1c
Wilbur S. Williams, OS3c
Bernard R. Wimmer, FC1c
Everett G. Windle, Sea2c

Starring B. Winfield, RM3c
Rex E. Wise, F1c
Frank Wood, Sea2c
Lawrence E. Woods, F1c
Winfred O. Woods, MM1c
Creighton H. Workman, F1c
John L. Wortham, GM2c
Paul R. Wright, CWT (PA)
Eldon P. Wyman, Ens
Martin D. Young, F2c
Robert V. Young, Sea1c
Joseph J. Yurko, WT1c
Thomas Zvansky, CSM (PA)

USS *Pennsylvania*
(BB-38, Battleship)

Robert E. Arnott, PhM2c
Henry E. Baker, Jr., Cox
Charles Braga, Jr., Y2c
Evan B. Brekken, Sea1c
Frederick A. Browne, GM3c
Harold K. Comstock, Sea1c
James E. Craig, Lt. Comdr
Clarence F. Haase, Sea1c
Dancil J. McIntosh, Sea2c
Joseph A. Huhofski, RM3c
James P. Owens, RM3c
Joseph W. Pace, RM3c
Damian M. Portillo, SC1c
Richard R. Rall, Lt. (jg) (MC)
William H. Rice, GM3c
Martin R. Slifer, GM1c
Payton L. Vanderpool, Jr., F2c
Claude B. Watson, Jr., Sea1c

USS *Pruitt*
(DM-22, Light Minelayer)

George R. Keith, RM3c
(Killed on the Pennsylvania.*)*

USS *Shaw*
(DD-373, Destroyer)

Frank J. Annunziato, Sea1c
Anthony Bilyi, SC3c
Albert J. Bolen, F1c
Guy W. Carroll, QM2c
Leon Egbert, MAtt2c

Fred Fugate, CCStd (PA)
Joseph L. B. Gaudrault, Sea1c
Paul G. Gosnell, GM1c
Rodney W. Jones, Sea2c
John S. McAllen, Sea2c
Robert C. McQuade, Sea1c
Clyde C. Moore, RM2c
Chester L. Parks, Sea1c
George A. Penuel, Jr., BM2c
Robert A. Petz, Sea1c
Daniel P. Platschorre, Sea2c
Edward J. Quirk, F1c
John T. Rainbolt, F1c
Benjamin N. Russell, AS
Johnnie H. Spaeth, Sea2c
Frank W. Stief, Jr., SC2c
Palmer L. Taylor, MAtt1c
James R. Westbrook, Sea1c
Clyde Williams, Sea1c

USS *Sicard*
(DM-21, Light Minelayer)

Warren P. Hickok, Sea2c
(Killed on the Pennsylvania.*)*

USS *Tennessee*
(BB-43, Battleship)

Jesse L. Adams, Sea1c
Alfred W. Hudgell, BM1c
J. B. Delane Miller, Cox
Eugene O. Roe, Sea1c
Gerald O. Smith, SK1c

USS *Tracy*
(DM-19, Light Minelayer)

John A. Bird, Sea1c
John W. Pence, RM3c
Laddie J. Zacek, Sea1c
(All three were killed on the Pennsylvania.*)*

USS *Utah*
(AG-16, Target/Gunnery Training Ship)

William D. Arbuckle, Sea2c
Joseph Barta, F3c
Rudolph P. Bielka, Lt. Comdr

Virgil C. Bigham, Sea1c
John E. Black, Lt. (jg)
John T. Blackburn, F1c
Pallas F. Brown, Sea2c
William F. Brunner, F3c

Feliciano T. Bugarin, OC2c
(Killed by "friendly fire" aboard Argonne.*)*

George V. Chestnutt, Jr., Sea2c
Lloyd D. Clippard, Sea2c
Joseph U. Conner, F1c
John R. Crain, F1c
David L. Crossett, Sea1c
Billy R. Davis, F2c
Leroy Dennis, Sea2c
Douglas R. Rieckhoff, SM1c
William H. Dosser, Sea2c
Vernon J. Eidsvig, Sea1c
Melvyn A. Gandre, QM1c
Kenneth M. Gift, BM2c
Charles N. Gregoire, Sea2c
Herold A. Harveson, Lt. (jg)
Clifford D. Hill, Sea2c
Emery L. Houde, Bkr2c
David W. Jackson, Ens
Leroy H. Jones, Sea1c
William A. Juedes, SC2c
John L. Kaelin, Y3c
Eric T. Kampmeyer, GM3c
Joseph N. Karabon, F1c
William H. Kent, Sea1c
George W. LaRue, GM3c
John G. Little III, Lt. (jg)
Kenneth L. Lynch, Sea2c
William E. Marshall, Jr., Sea2c
Rudolph M. Martinez, EM3c
Charles O. Michael, Lt. Comdr
Marvin E. Miller, Sea2c
Donald C. Norman, Sea2c
Orris N. Norman, F2c
Edwin N. Odgaard, EM2c
Elmer A. Parker, CSK (PA)
Forrest H. Perry, SC3c
James W. Phillips, Sea1c
Walter H. Ponder, MM1c
Frank E. Reed, SF3c
Ralph E. Scott, Sea1c
Henson T. Shouse, F1c
George R. Smith, Matt1c
Robert D. Smith, Sea1c
Joseph B. Sousley, Sea2c

Gerald V. Strinz, F3c
Peter Tomich, CWT (PA)
Elmer H. Ulrich, F3c
Michael W. Villa, F3c
Vernard O. Wetrich, FC1c
Glen A. White, F1c

USS *Vestal*
(AR-4, Repair Ship)

Harold R. Arneberg, F3c
William Duane, CBM (PA)
Lowell B. Jackson, Sea2c
Charles W. Jones, Msmth2c
Raymond J. Kerrigan, MM1c
Guy E. Long, Sea2c
William H. Reid, F1c

USS *West Virginia*
(BB-48, Battleship)

Welborn L. Ashby, F3c
Benjamin E. Bargerhuff, Jr., SF3c
William L. Barnett, F3c
Frank J. Bartek, Jr., F2c
Mervyn S. Bennion, Capt (CO)
Charlie V. Booton, Sea1c
Fred H. Boyer, F1c
George O. Branham, Mldr1c
Ennis E. Brooks, F1c
Charles D. Brown, EM3c
Riley M. Brown, F1c
John E. Burgess, Jr., Sea2c
William C. Campbell, Cox
William G. Christian, Bkr2c
Harold K. Costill, F3c
Louis A. Costin, F1c
Charles E. Cottier, F1c
Howard D. Cromwell, CM2c
Eugene V. Downing, Sea2c
Donald L. Drum, F2c
George S. Dunn, Jr., Sea2c
Edward N. Durkee, CMM (AA)
Clement E. Durr, Sea1c
Tommy Dye, F1c
Roland W. Edwards, F2c
Ronald B. Endicott, F3c
Richard B. England, MM2c
Woodrow W. Evans, GM3c
Jose S. N. Flores, Matt2c
Jack Foth, EM1c

Gilbert R. Fox, F1c
Neil D. Frye, Matt3c
Angelo M. Gabriele, F1c
Claude R. Garcia, SF2c
Bibian B. Gonzales, Sea1c
Myron E. Goodwin, Sea2c
Arthur Gould, RM3c
Harry J. Halvorsen, F1c
Hugh B. Harriss, HA1c
Hadley I. Heavin, F2c
Fred A. Hilt, MM1c
Howard D. Hodges, F1c
Joseph E. Hood, F1c
William D. Horton, Sea1c
Ira D. Hudson, F3c
William C. Jackson, EM3c
Carl S. Johnson, Sea1c
Sanford V. Kelley, Jr., GM3c
Chester F. Kleist, Cox
Milton J. Knight, Jr., F1c
William P. Kubinec, F2c
Henry E. LaCrosse, Jr., SK3c
Thomas F. Leary, F1c
Joseph S.L. Lemire, Sea1c
Eugene V. Lish, Mus1c
Royle B. Luker, F3c
Donald W. Lynch, F1c
Arnold E. Lyon, GM3c
Charles W. Mann, Sea1c
Jesus M. Mata, Matt1c
Donald J. Mathison, FC3c
Luther K. McBee, Sea1c
Thomas A. McClelland, Ens
Lawrence J. McCollom, MM2c
Clarence W. McComas, Sea1c
Quentin G. McKee, Sea2c
John A. Meglis, F1c
John R. Melton, Sea1c
Enrique C. Mendiola, Matt1c
Joe E. Mister, Matt1c
Wallace A. Montgomery, MM2c
William F. Morris, F1c
Albin J. Mrace, WT2c
Clair C. Myers, Sea1c
Earl T. Nermoe, Sea1c
Paul E. Newton, Sea1c
Emile S. Noce, EM2c
Maurice M.O'Connor, MM1c
Clifford N. Olds, F1c
Arnold J. Owsley, Sea1c
Walter J. Paciga, Sea2c

James A. Paolucci, Sea2c
Andrew A. Pinko, EM3c
Jack A. Pitcher, Sea1c
Roy W. Powers, SF2c
George B. Reid, SF1c
Albert Renner, F2c
Leonard C. Richter, MM1c
Ernest C. Rose, SC1c
Glenn D. Sahl, F3c
Theodore H. Saulsbury, OC2c
Richard M. Schuon, Jr., Sea1c
George W. Scott, SK2c
Gordon E. Smith, SK2c
Ernest E. Speicher, EM2c
Otis D. Sterling, Matt1c
George E. Taber, MM2c
Ernie E. Tibbs, CMM (PA)
Keith W. Tipsword, MM1c
Albert P. VanderGoore, F1c
Joseph Vogelgesang, Jr., F2c
Thomas G. Wagner, Sea1c
Bethel E. Walters, F1c
Harold Wilbur, CM3c
Clyde R. Wilson, Sea1c
Lester F. Zobeck, Sea1c

Ford Island

Patrol Squadron 21
Theodore W. Croft, AOM1c

Kaneohe Naval Air Station

Headquarters, Naval Air Station
Stanley D. Dosick, Sea1c

Patrol Squadron 11
John D. Buckley, AOM3c
Clarence M. Formoe, AMM1c
Rodney S. Foss, Ens
Milburn A. Manning, AMM3c
James H. Robinson, Sea2c
Joseph G. Smartt, Ens
Luther D. Weaver, Sea1c

Patrol Squadron 12
Walter S. Brown, AMM2c
Lee Fox, Jr., Ens
Daniel T. Griffin, AMM1c
George W. Ingram, Sea2c
Charles Lawrence, AMM2c
Carl W. Otterstetter, Sea2c
Robert K. Porterfield, AMM3c
Robert W. Uhlmann, Ens
Raphael A. Watson, AMM1c

Patrol Squadron 14
Laxton G. Newman, AMM3c

Pearl Harbor Naval Hospital

Arthur W. Russett, PhM1c

Naval Mobile Hospital #2

John H. Thuman, PhM3c

Appendix D

U.S.S. *Arizona*
Casualty List[*]

These are the 1,177 sailors and Marines killed on the battleship USS *Arizona* on December 7, 1941.

Name	Rank	Service	Home
AARON, Hubert Charles Titus	F2c	USN	Arkansas
ABERCROMBIE, Samuel Adolphus	S1c	USN	Texas
ADAMS, Robert Franklin	S1c	USN	Alabama
ADKISON, James Dillion	S1c	USN	Texas
AGUIRRE, Reyner Aceves	S2c	USN	
AGUON, Gregorio San N.	MATT1c	USN	Guam
AHERN, Richard James	F1c	USN	California
ALBEROVSKY, Francis Severin	BMKR1c	USN	California
ALBRIGHT, Galen Winston	S1c	USN	Indiana
ALEXANDER, Elvis Author	S2c	USN	Arkansas
ALLEN, Robert Lee	SF3c	USN	Texas
ALLEN, William Clayborn	EM1c	USN	California
ALLEN, William Lewis	SK2c	USNR	Texas
ALLEY, Jay Edgar	GM1c	USN	
ALLISON, Andrew K.	F1c	USN	Missouri

*USS Arizona *casualty list provided courtesy of the U.S.S.* Arizona *Memorial, U.S. Department of the Interior, National Park Service, No. 1, Arizona Memorial Place, Honolulu, Hawaii 96818.*

Name	Rank	Service	Home
ALLISON, J. T.	F1c	USN	
ALTEN, Ernest Mathew	S2c	USN	California
AMON, Frederick Purdy	S1c	USN	
AMUNDSON, Leo DeVere	PVT	USMC	
ANDERSON, Charles Titus	CM2c	USN	California
ANDERSON, Delbert Jake	BM2c	USN	Minnesota
ANDERSON, Donald William	SM3c	USN	
ANDERSON, Harry	S1c	USN	California
ANDERSON, Howard Taisey	F1c	USN	Maryland
ANDERSON, James Pickins Jr.	S1c	USN	
ANDERSON, Lawrence Donald	ENS	USNR	
ANDERSON, Robert Adair	GM3c	USN	Missouri
ANDREWS, Brainerd Wells	CCMP	USN	Vermont
ANGLE, Earnest Hersea	F2c	USN	West Virginia
ANTHONY, Glenn Samuel	S1c	USN	California
APLIN, James Raymond	CWTP	USN	California
APPLE, Robert William	F1c	USN	Illinois
APREA, Frank Anthony	COX	USN	
ARLEDGE, Eston	SM2c	USN	Louisiana
ARNAUD, Achilles	F3c	USN	Louisiana
ARNEBERG, William Robert	F2c	USN	
ARNOLD, Claude Duran Jr.	F3c	USN	Louisiana
ARNOLD, Thell	SC1c	USN	Arkansas
ARRANT, John Anderson	MM1c	USN	Florida
ARVIDSON, Carl Harry	CMMP	USN	Washington
ASHMORE, Wilburn James	S2c	USN	Louisiana
ATCHISON, John Calvin	PVT	USMC	Missouri
ATKINS, Gerald Arthur	HA1c	USN	Nebraska
AUSTIN, Laverne Alfred	S1c	USN	New York
AUTRY, Eligah T. Jr.	COX	USN	Arkansas
AVES, Willard Charles	F2c	USN	
AYDELL, Miller Xavier	WT2c	USN	Louisiana
AYERS, Dee Cumpie	S2c	USN	
BADILLA, Manuel Domonic	F1c	USN	
BAILEY, George Richmond	PFC	USMC	California
BAIRD, Billy Bryon	S1c	USN	Indiana
BAJORIMS, Joseph	S1c	USN	Illinois
BAKER, Robert Dewey	CMM	USN	
BALL, William V.	S1c	USN	
BANDY, Wayne Lynn	MUS2c	USN	Missouri
BANGERT, John Henry	FC1c	USN	
BARAGA, Joseph	SGT	USMC	Michigan
BARDON, Charles Thomas	S2c	USN	Oklahoma
BARKER, Loren Joe	COX	USN	Iowa
BARNER, Walter Ray	S2c	USN	Texas
BARNES, Charles Edward	Y3c	USN	Missouri
BARNES, Delmar Hayes	LTJG	USNR	California
BARNETT, William Thermon	S2c	USN	Arkansas
BARTLETT, David William	CPL	USMC	California

Name	Rank	Service	Home
BARTLETT, Paul Clement	MM1c	USN	Texas
BATES, Edward Munroe Jr.	ENS	USNR	New York
BATES, Tobert Alvin	PHM3c	USN	Texas
BATOR, Edward	F1c	USN	New York
BAUER, Harold Walter	RM3c	USN	Kansas
BEATON, Freddie	PVT	USMC	California
BEAUMONT, James Ammon	S2c	USN	Texas
BECK, George Richard	S1c	USN	California
BECKER, Marvin Otto	GM3c	USN	Kansas
BECKER, Wesley Paulson	S1c	USN	Kansas
BEDFORD, Purdy Renaker	F1c	USN	Kentucky
BEERMAN, Henry Carl	CM3c	USN	Washington
BEGGS, Harold Eugene	F1c	USN	Missouri
BELL, Hershel Homer	FC2c	USN	Illinois
BELL, Richard Leroy	S2c	USN	California
BELLAMY, James Curtis	OS3c	USN	California
BELT, Everett Ray Jr.	PFC	USMC	Missouri
BENFORD, Sam Austin	BKR2c	USN	Minnesota
BENNETT, William Edmond Jr.	Y3c	USN	Illinois
BENSON, James Thomas	S1c	USN	Alabama
BERGIN, Roger Joseph	F2c	USN	Canada
BERKANSKI, Albert Charles	COX	USN	Pennsylvania
BERNARD, Frank Peter	SF2c	USN	
BERRY, Gordon Eugene	F2c	USN	Colorado
BERRY, James Winford	F2c	USN	California
BERTIE, George Allan Jr.	S2c	USN	Arizona
BIBBY, Charles Henry	F2c	USN	Alabama
BICKEL, Kenneth Robert	F1c	USN	Nebraska
BICKNELL, Dale Deen	S1c	USN	Washington
BIRCHER, Frederick Robert	RM3c	USN	Pennsylvania
BIRDSELL, Rayon Delois	F2c	USN	Missouri
BIRGE, George Albert	S1c	USN	New York
BISHOP, Grover Barron	MM1c	USN	Texas
BISHOP, Millard Charles	F3c	USN	Alabama
BISHOP, Wesley Horner Jr.	RM3c	USNR	New York
BLACK, James Theron	PVT	USMC	Alabama
BLAIS, Albert Edward	RM3c	USNR	New York
BLAKE, James Monroe	F2c	USN	Missouri
BLANCHARD, Albert Richard	COX	USN	Minnesota
BLANKENSHIP, Theron A.	S1c	USN	Alabama
BLANTON, Atticus Lee	SF3c	USN	Florida
BLIEFFERT, Richmond Frederick	S1c	USN	Washington
BLOCK, Ivan Lee	PHM2c	USN	New Mexico
BLOUNT, Wayman Boney	S1c	USN	Texas
BOGGESS, Roy Eugene	SF2c	USN	California
BOHLENDER, Sam	GM2c	USN	Colorado
BOLLING, Gerald Revese	S1c	USN	Arkansas
BOLLING, Walter Karr	F3c	USN	Kentucky
BOND, Burnis Leroy	CPL	USMC	Missouri

Name	Rank	Service	Home
BONEBRAKE, Buford Earl	F2c	USN	Kansas
BONFIGLIO, William John	EM1c	USN	New York
BOOTH, Robert Sinclair Jr.	ENS	USNR	
BOOZE, Asbury Legare,	BM1c	USN	Georgia
BORGER, Richard	CMMA	USN	California
BOROVICH, Joseph John	S1c	USN	California
BORUSKY, Edwin Charles	CPL	USMC	North Dakota
BOSLEY, Kenneth Leroy	EM3c	USN	Missouri
BOVIALL, Walter Robert	AMM2c	USN	Wisconsin
BOWMAN, Howard Alton	S2c	USN	Iowa
BOYD, Charles Andrew	CM3c	USN	Alabama
BOYDSTUN, Don Jasper	S2c	USN	Texas
BOYDSTUN, R. L.	S2c	USN	Texas
BRABBZSON, Oran Merrill	MUS2c	USN	New York
BRADLEY, Bruce Dean	S2c	USN	Illinois
BRAKKE, Kenneth Gay	F3c	USN	Washington
BRICKLEY, Eugene	PVT	USMC	Indiana
BRIDGES, James Leon	S1c	USN	Tennessee
BRIDGES, Paul Hyatt	S1c	USN	Arkansas
BRIDIE, Robert Maurice	F1c	USN	
BRIGNOLE, Erminio Joseph	S2c	USN	California
BRITTAN, Charles Edward	S2c	USN	Claifornia
BROADHEAD, Johnnie Cecil	F2c	USN	Alabama
BROCK, Walter Pershing	S1c	USN	Kentucky
BROMLEY, George Edward	SM3c	USN	Washington
BROMLEY, Jimmie	S1c	USN	
BROOKS, Robert Neal	ENS	USNR	Washington
BROOME, Loy Raymond	SM3c	USN	Oklahoma
BROONER, Allen Ottis	S1c	USN	Indiana
BROPHY, Myron Alonzo	F2c	USN	Vermont
BROWN, Charles Martin	S2c	USN	California
BROWN, Elwyn Leroy	EM3c	USN	Kansas
BROWN, Frank George	QM3c	USN	Oregon
BROWN, Richard Corbett	S1c	USN	California
BROWN, William Howard	S2c	USN	Oregon
BROWNE, Harry Lamont	CMMA	USN	California
BROWNING, Tilmon David	S1c	USN	West Virginia
BRUNE, James William	RM3c	USNR	Missouri
BRYAN, Leland Howard	S1c	USN	Texas
BRYANT, Lloyd Glenn	BM2c	USN	California
BUCKLEY, Jack C.	FC3c	USN	Kentucky
BUDD, Robert Emile	F2c	USN	Michigan
BUHR, Clarence Edward	S1c	USN	New Mexico
BURDEN, Ralph Leon	RM3c	USN	Ohio
BURDETTE, Ralph Warren	MUS2c	USN	New Jersey
BURKE, Frank Edmond Jr.	SK2c	USN	Tennessee
BURNETT, Charlie Leroy	S2c	USN	
BURNS, John Edward	F1c	USN	Pennsylvania
BUSICK, Dewey Olney	F3c	USN	Ohio

Name	*Rank*	*Service*	*Home*
BUTCHER, David Adrian	F2c	USN	Washington
BUTLER, John Dabney	F1c	USN	Texas
BYRD, Charles Dewitt	S1c	USN	Tennessee
CABAY, Louis Clarence	S1c	USN	Illinois
CADE, Richard Esh	S2c	USN	Washington
CALDWELL, Charles Jr.	F3c	USN	Missouri
CALLAGHAN, James Thomas	BM2c	USN	Colorado
CAMDEN, Raymond Edward	S2c	USN	Oklahoma
CAMM, William Fielden	Y2c	USN	Arkansas
CAMPA, Ralph	S1c	USN	California
CAMPBELL, Burdette Charles	S1c	USN	California
CAPLINGER, Donald William	SC3c	USN	Ohio
CAREY, Francis Lloyd	SK3c	USN	New York
CARLISLE, Robert Wayne	S1c	USNR	Texas
CARLSON, Harry Ludwig	SK3c	USN	Connecticut
CARMACK, Harold Milton	F2c	USN	Colorado
CARPENTER, Robert Nelson	MATT1c	USN	Virginia
CARROLL, Robert Lewis	S1c	USN	
CARTER, Burton Lowell	S2c	USN	California
CARTER, Paxton Turner	WO (PYCLK)	USN	California
CASEY, James Warren	S1c	USN	
CASILAN, Epifanio Miranda	OS3c	USN	New York
CASKEY, Clarence Merton	S1c	USN	Washington
CASTLEBERRY, Claude W. Jr.	S1c	USN	Texas
CATSOS, George	F1c	USN	California
CHACE, Raymond Vincent	CSKP	USN	California
CHADWICK, Charles Bruce	MM2c	USN	Mississippi
CHADWICK, Harold	MATT1c	USN	California
CHANDLER, Donald Ross	PVT	USMC	Alabama
CHAPMAN, Naaman N.	S1c	USN	Nebraska
CHARLTON, Charles Nicholas	WT1c	USNR	California
CHERNUCHA, Harry Gregory	MUS2c	USN	New York
CHESTER, Edward	S1c	USN	Kansas
CHRISTENSEN, Elmer Emil	MM2c	USN	Wyoming
CHRISTENSEN, Lloyd Raymond	F1c	USN	Nebraska
CHRISTIANSEN, Edward Lee	BKR3c	USN	Wyoming
CIHLAR, Lawrence John	PHM3c	USN	Minnesota
CLARK, George Francis	GM3c	USN	Illinois
CLARK, John Crawford Todd	F3c	USN	California
CLARK, Malcolm	BKR3c	USN	Louisiana
CLARK, Robert William Jr.	FC3c	USN	Pennsylvania
CLARKE, Robert Eugene	S1c	USN	Kansas
CLASH, Donald	F2c	USN	Michigan
CLAYTON, Robert Roland	COX	USN	Missouri
CLEMMENS, Claude Albert	S1c	USN	Oklahoma
CLIFT, Ray Emerson	COX	USN	Missouri
CLOUES, Edward Blanchard	ENS	USN	New Hampshire
CLOUGH, Edward Hay	GM1c	USN	Nebraska
COBB, Ballard Burgher	S1c	USN	Texas

Name	Rank	Service	Home
COBURN, Walter Overton	S1c	USN	Oklahoma
COCKRUM, Kenneth Earl	MM1c	USN	Indiana
COFFIN, Robert	SF3c	USN	Washington
COFFMAN, Marshall Herman	GMec	USN	Indiana
COLE, Charles Warren	SGT	USMC	Washington
COLE, David Lester	ENS	USNR	California
COLEGROVE, Willett S. Jr.	S2c	USN	Washington
COLLIER, John	F2c	USN	Oregon
COLLIER, Linald Long Jr.	BKR3c	USN	Texas
COLLINS, Austin	SF3c	USN	
COLLINS, Billy Murl	S1c	USN	California
CONLIN, Bernard Eugene	S2c	USN	Illinois
CONLIN, James Leo	F2c	USN	Illinois
CONNELLY, Richard Earl	CQMA	USN	California
CONRAD, Homer Milton Jr.	S1c	USN	Ohio
CONRAD, Robert Frank	S2c	USN	California
CONRAD, Walter Ralph	QM2c	USN	
COOPER, Clarence Eugene	F2c	USN	
COOPER, Kenneth Erven	F2c	USN	
CORCORAN, Gerard John	S1c	USN	New York
COREY, Ernest Eugene	PHM3c	USN	Washington
CORNELIUS, P. W.	SC3c	USN	
CORNING, Russell Dale	RM3c	USN	
COULTER, Arthur Lee	S1c	USN	Oklahoma
COWAN, William	COX	USN	Missouri
COWDEN, Joel Beman	S2c	USN	Oregon
COX, Gerald Blinton	MUS2c	USN	Illinois
COX, William Milford	S1c	USN	Kentucky
CRAFT, Harley Wade	CM3c	USN	Oregon
CRAWLEY, Wallace Dewight	COX	USN	Indiana
CREMEENS, Louis Edward	S1c	USN	Arizona
CRISCUOLO, Michael	Y2c	USN	California
CRISWELL, Wilfred John	S1c	USN	Indiana
CROWE, Cecil Thomas	GM2c	USN	Kentucky
CROWLEY, Thomas Ewing	LCDR(DC)	USN	California
CURRY, William Joseph	WT2c	USN	Oregon
CURTIS, Lloyd B.	S1c	USN	Missouri
CURTIS, Lyle Carl	RM2c	USN	Wisconsin
CYBULSKI, Harold Bernard	S1c	USN	
CYCHOSZ, Francis Anton	S1c	USN	Michigan
CZARNECKI, Stanley	F1c	USN	Michigan
CZEKAJSKI, Theophil	SM3c	USNR	Michigan
DAHLHEIMER, Richard Norbert	S1c	USN	Minnesota
DANIEL, Lloyd Naxton	Y1c	USN	Montana
DANIK, Andrew Joseph	S2c	USN	Ohio
DARCH, Phillip Zane	S1c	USN	Massachusetts
DAUGHERTY, Paul Eugene	Em3c	USN	Ohio
DAVIS, John Quitman	S1c	USN	Louisiana
DAVIS, Milton Henry	S1c	USN	Kansas

Name	Rank	Service	Home
DAVIS, Murle Melvin	RM2c	USN	Ohio
DAVIS, Myrle Clarence	F3c	USNR	Iowa
DAVIS, Thomas Ray	SF1c	USN	California
DAVIS, Virgil Denton	PVT	USMC	Missouri
DAVIS, Walter Mindred	F2c	USN	Missouri
DAWSON, James Berkley	PVT	USMC	Kentucky
DAY, William John	S2c	USN	Washington
DE ARMOUN, Donald Edwin	GM3c	USN	California
DE CASTRO, Vicente	OS3c	USN	
DEAN, Lyle Bernard	COX	USN	
DELONG, Frederick Eugene	CPL	USMC	Ohio
DERITIS, Russell Edwin	S1c	USN	
DEWITT, John James	COX	USN	
DIAL, John Buchanan	S1c	USN	
DICK, Ralph R.	GM1c	USN	California
DINE, John George	F2c	USN	California
DINEEN, Robert Joseph	S1c	USN	Pennsylvania
DOBEY, Milton Paul Jr.	S1c	USN	Texas
DOHERTY, George Walter	S2c	USN	California
DOHERTY, John Albert	MM2c	USN	California
DONOHUE, Ned Burton	F1c	USN	
DORITY, John Monroe	S1c	USN	California
DOUGHERTY, Ralph McClearn	FC1c	USN	Massachusetts
DOYLE, Wand B.	COX	USN	Kentucky
DREESBACH, Herbert Allen	PFC	USMC	Illinois
DRIVER, Bill Lester	RM3c	USN	California
DUCREST, Louis Felix	S1c	USN	Louisiana
DUKE, Robert Edward	CCSTDA	USN	California
DULLUM, Jerald Fraser	EM3c	USN	Montana
DUNAWAY, Kenneth Leroy	EM3c	USN	Oklahoma
DUNHAM, Elmer Marvin	S1c	USN	
DUNNAM, Robert Wesley	PVT	USMCR	Texas
DUPREE, Arthur Joseph	F2c	USN	Missouri
DURHAM, William Teasdale	S1c	USN	North Carolina
DURIO, Russell	PFC	USMC	Louisiana
DUVEENE, John	1SGT	USMC	California
DVORAK, Alvin Albert	BM2c	USN	Minnesota
EATON, Emory Lowell	F3c	USN	Oklahoma
EBEL, Walter Charles	CTCP	USN	California
EBERHART, Vincent Henry	COX	USN	Minnesota
ECHOLS, Charles Louis Jr.	EM3c	USN	Tennessee
ECHTERNKAMP, Henry Clarence	S1c	USN	Michigan
EDMUNDS, Bruce Roosevelt	Y2c	USN	New Hampshire
EERNISSE, William Frederick	PTR1c	USN	California
EGNEW, Robert Ross	S1c	USN	Illinois
EHLERT, Casper	SM3c	USN	Wisconsin
EHRMANTRAUT, Frank Jr.	S1c	USN	Indiana
ELLIS, Francis Arnold Jr.	EM3c	USN	Canada
ELLIS, Richard Everrett	S2c	USN	Nebraska

Name	*Rank*	*Service*	*Home*
ELLIS, Wilbur Danner	RM2c	USN	California
ELWELL, Royal	S1c	USN	Texas
EMBREY, Bill Eugene	F3c	USN	California
EMERY, Jack Marvin	ENS	USN	California
EMERY, John Marvin	GM3c	USN	North Dakota
EMERY, Wesley Vernon	SK2c	USN	Indiana
ENGER, Stanley Gordon	GM3c	USN	Minnesota
ERICKSON, Robert	S1c	USN	
ERSKINE, Robert Charles	PFC	USMC	Illinois
ERWIN, Stanley Joe	MM1c	USN	Texas
ERWIN, Walton Aluard	S1c	USN	Texas
ESTEP, Carl James	S1c	USN	Texas
ESTES, Carl Edwen	S1c	USN	Texas
ESTES, Forrest Jesse	F1c	USN	California
ETCHASON, Leslie Edgar	S1c	USN	Illinois
EULBERG, Richard Henry	FC2c	USN	Iowa
EVANS, David Delton	PVT	USMC	Louisiana
EVANS, Evan Frederick	ENS	USNR	California
EVANS, Mickey Edward	S1c	USN	Missouri
EVANS, Paul Anthony	S1c	USN	Illinois
EVANS, William Orville	S2c	USN	Idaho
EWELL, Alfred Adam	WT1c	USN	
EYED, George	SK3c	USN	Indiana
FALLIS, Alvin E.	PHM2c	USN	California
FANSLER, Edgar Arthur	S1c	USN	Oklahoma
FARMER, John Wilson	COX	USN	Tennessee
FEGURGUR, Nicolas San Nicolas	MATT2c	USN	Guam
FESS, John Junior	F1c	USN	California
FIELDS, Bernard	RM3c	USNR	
FIELDS, Reliford	MATT2c	USN	Florida
FIFE, Ralph Elmer	S1c	USN	California
FILKINS, George Arthur	COX	USN	Minnesota
FINCHER, Allen Brady	ACK	USMC	Texas
FINCHER, Dexter Wilson	SGT	USMC	Oregon
FINLEY, Woodrow Wilson	PFC	USMC	Tennessee
FIRTH, Henry Amis	F3c	USN	
FISCHER, Leslie Henry	S1c	USN	Washington
FISHER, Delbert Ray	S1c	USN	Wyoming
FISHER, James Anderson	MATT1c	USN	Virginia
FISHER, Robert Ray	S2c	USN	California
FISK, Charles Porter III	Y1c	USN	California
FITCH, Simon	MATT1c	USN	Texas
FITZGERALD, Kent Blake	PVT	USMC	Utah
FITZSIMMONS, Eugene James	F3c	USN	Illinois
FLANNERY, James Lowell	SK3c	USN	Ohio
FLEETWOOD, Donald Eugene	PFC	USMC	Iowa
FLOEGE, Frank Norman	MUS2c	USN	Illinois
FLORY, Max Edward	S2c	USN	Indiana
FONES, George Everett	FC3c	USN	Washington

Name	Rank	Service	Home
FORD, Jack C.	S1c	USN	California
FORD, William Walker	EM3c	USN	Kentucky
FOREMAN, Elmer Lee	F2c	USN	Indiana
FORTENBERRY, Alvie Charles	COX	USN	Mississippi
FOWLER, George Parten	S2c	USN	Texas
FOX, Daniel Russell	LTCOL	USMC	California
FRANK, Leroy George	S1c	USN	Arkansas
FREDERICK, Charles Donald	EM2c	USN	Louisiana
FREE, Thomas Augusta	MM1c	USN	Texas
FREE, William Thomas	S2c	USN	Texas
FRENCH, John Edmund	LCDR	USN	Washington, D.C.
FRIZZELL, Robert Niven	S2c	USN	Alabama
FULTON, Robert Wilson	AMSMTH1c	USN	Missouri
FUNK, Frank Francis	BM2c	USN	Missouri
FUNK, Lawrence Henry	S1c	USN	Wisconsin
GAGER, Roy Arthur	S2c	USN	Kansas
GARGARO, Ernest Russell	S2c	USN	
GARLINGTON, Raymond Wesley	S1c	USN	California
GARRETT, Orville Wilmer	SF2c	USN	Missouri
GARTIN, Gerald Ernest	S1c	USN	California
GAUDETTE, William Frank	S1c	USN	Washington
GAULTNEY, Ralph Martin	Em3c	USN	Illinois
GAZECKI, Philip Robert	ENS	USNR	Wisconsin
GEBHARDT, Kenneth Edward	S1c	USN	North Dakota
GEER, Kenneth Floyd	S2c	USN	California
GEISE, Marvin Frederick	S1c	USN	Wisconsin
GEMIENHARDT, Samuel Henry Jr.	MM2c	USN	Ohio
GHOLSTON, Roscoe	Y2c	USN	Texas
GIBSON, Billy Edwin	S1c	USN	West Virginia
GIESEN, Karl Anthony	Y2c	USN	Iowa
GILL, Richard Eugene	S1c	USN	Nevada
GIOVENAZZO, Michael James	WT2c	USN	Illinois
GIVENS, Harold Reuben	Y3c	USN	
GOBBIN, Angelo	SC1c	USN	California
GOFF, Wiley Coy	S2c	USN	Oklahoma
GOMEZ, Edward Jr.	S1c	USN	Colorado
GOOD, Leland	S2c	USN	Illinois
GOODWIN, William Arthur	S2c	USN	Colorado
GORDON, Peter Charles Jr.	F1c	USN	Colorado
GOSSELIN, Edward Webb	ENS	USNR	Illinois
GOSSELIN, Joseph Adjutor	RM1c	USN	Massachuttes
GOULD, Harry Lee	S1c	USN	Illinois
GOVE, Rupert Clair	S1c	USN	California
GRANGER, Raymond Edward	F3c	USN	Iowa
GRANT, Lawrence Everett	Y3c	USN	Missouri
GRAY, Albert James	S1c	USN	Washington
GRAY, Lawrence Moore	F1c	USN	Missouri
GRAY, William James Jr.	S1c	USN	California
GREEN, Glen Hubert	S1c	USN	Mississippi

Name	Rank	Service	Home
GREENFIELD, Carroll Gale	S1c	USN	Oregon
GRIFFIN, Lawrence J.	PFC	USMC	Louisiana
GRIFFIN, Reese Olin	EM3c	USN	Texas
GRIFFITHS, Robert Alfred	EM3c	USN	California
GRISSINGER, Robert Beryle	S2c	USN	Illinois
GROSNICKLE, Warren Wilbert	EM2c	USN	Iowa
GROSS, Milton Henry	CSKA	USN	California
GRUNDSTROM, Richard Gunner	S2c	USN	Iowa
GURLEY, Jesse Herbert	SK3c	USN	Illinois
HAAS, Curtis Junior	MUS2c	USN	Missouri
HADEN, Samuel William	COX	USN	Kansas
HAFFNER, Floyd Bates	F1c	USN	Illinois
HAINES, Robert Wesley	S2c	USN	California
HALL, John Rudolph	CBMP	USN	Arkansas
HALLORAN, William Ignatius	ENS	USNR	Ohio
HAMEL, Don Edgar	FLDMUS	USMCR	Illinois
HAMILTON, Clarence James	MM1c	USN	Washington
HAMILTON, Edwin Carrell	S1c	USN	
HAMILTON, William Holman	GM3c	USN	Oklahoma
HAMMERUD, George Winston	S1c	USN	North Dakota
HAMPTON, "J" "D"	F1c	USN	Kansas
HAMPTON, Ted "W" Jr.	S1c	USN	Oklahoma
HAMPTON, Walter Lewis	BM2c	USN	Pennsylvania
HANNA, David Darling	EM3c	USN	Texas
HANSEN, Carlyle B.	MM2c	USN	
HANSEN, Harvey Ralph	S1c	USN	Wisconsin
HANZEL, Edward Joseph	WT1c	USN	Michigan
HARDIN, Charles Eugene	S1c	USN	Missouri
HARGRAVES, Kenneth William	S2c	USN	Washington
HARMON, William D.	PFC	USMC	Oregon
HARRINGTON, Keith Homer	S1c	USN	Missouri
HARRIS, George Ellsworth	MM1c	USN	Illinois
HARRIS, Hiram Dennis	S1c	USN	Georgia
HARRIS, James William	F1c	USN	Michigan
HARRIS, Noble Burnice	COX	USN	Missouri
HARRIS, Peter John	COX	USN	Nebraska
HARTLEY, Alvin	GM3c	USN	Oklahoma
HARTSOE, Max June	GM3c	USN	Missouri
HARTSON, Lonnie Moss	SM3c	USN	Texas
HASL, James Thomas	F1c	USN	Nebraska
HAVERFIELD, James Wallace	ENS	USNR	Ohio
HAVINS, Harvey Linfille	S1c	USN	
HAWKINS, Russell Dean	SM3c	USN	Illinois
HAYES, John Doran	BM1c	USN	California
HAYES, Kenneth Merle	F1c	USN	California
HAYNES, Curtis James	QM2c	USN	Idaho
HAYS, William Henry	SK3c	USN	Kansas
HAZDOVAC, Jack Claudius	S1c	USN	California
HEAD, Frank Bernard	CYA	USN	California

Name	Rank	Service	Home
HEATER, Verrell Roy	S1c	USN	Oregon
HEATH, Alfred Grant	S1c	USN	Wisconsin
HEBEL, Robert Lee	SM3c	USNR	Illinois
HECKENDORN, Warren Guy	S1c	USN	
HEDGER, Jess Laxton	S1c	USN	California
HEDRICK, Paul Henry	BM1c	USN	California
HEELY, Leo Shinn	S2c	USN	Colorado
HEIDT, Edward Joseph	F1c	USN	California
HEIDT, Wesley John	MM2c	USN	California
HELM, Merritt Cameron	;S1c	USN	Minnesota
HENDERSON, William Walter	S2c	USN	
HENDRICKSEN, Frank	F2c	USN	Michigan
HERRICK, Paul Edward	PVT	USMC	Wisconsin
HERRING, James Junior	SM3c	USN	Iowa
HERRIOTT, Robert Asher Jr.	S1c	USN	Texas
HESS, Darrel Miller	FC1c	USN	Utah
HESSDORFER, Anthony Joseph	MM2c	USN	Washington
HIBBARD, Robert Arnold	BKR2c	USN	
HICKMAN, Arthur Lee	SM3c	USN	
HICKS, Elmer Orville	GM3c	USN	Washington
HICKS, Ralph Dueard	PTR2c	USNR	Missouri
HILL, Bartley Talor	AOM3c	USN	California
HILTON, Wilson Woodrow	GM1c	USN	
HINDMAN, Frank Weaver	S1c	USN	Alabama
HODGES, Garris Vada	F2c	USN	Texas
HOELSCHER, Lester John	HA1c	USN	Nebraska
HOLLAND, Claude Herbert Jr.	S2c	USN	Alabama
HOLLENBACH, Paul Zepp	S1c	USN	New York
HOLLIS, Ralph	LTJG	USNR	California
HOLLOWELL, George Sanford	COX	USN	Arizona
HOLMES, Lowell D.	F3c	USN	Alabama
HOLZWORTH, Walter	MGYSGT	USMC	New Jersey
HOMER, Henry Vernon	S1c	USN	Michigan
HOPE, Harold W.	PVT	USMC	Illinois
HOPKINS, Homer David	S1c	USN	Michigan
HORN, Melvin Freeland	F3c	USN	Ohio
HORRELL, Harvey Howard	SM1c	USN	
HORROCKS, James William	CGMP	USN	Arizona
HOSLER, John Emmet	S1c	USN	Ohio
HOUSE, Clem Raymond	CWTP	USN	California
HOUSEL, John James	SK1c	USN	Missouri
HOWARD, Elmo	S1c	USN	Kentucky
HOWARD, Rolan George	GM3c	USN	Minnesota
HOWE, Darrell Robert	S2c	USN	Oregon
HOWELL, Leroy	COX	USN	Indiana
HUBBARD, Haywood Jr.	MATT2c	USN	Virginia
HUDNALL, Robert Chilton	PFC	USMC	Texas
HUFF, Robert Glenn	PVT	USMC	Texas
HUFFMAN, Clyde Franklin	F1c	USN	Ohio

Name	Rank	Service	Home
HUGHES, Bernard Thomas	MUS2c	USN	Pennsylvania
HUGHES, Lewis Burton Jr.	S1c	USN	Alabama
HUGHES, Marvin Austin	PVT	USMCR	Texas
HUGHEY, James Clynton	S1c	USN	
HUIE, Doyne Conley	HA1c	USN	Missouri
HULTMAN, Donald Standly	PFC	USMC	Minnesota
HUNTER, Robert Fredrick	S1c	USN	Ohio
HUNTINGTON, Henry Louis	S2c	USN	California
HURD, Willard Hardy	MATT2c	USN	Tennessee
HURLEY, Wendell Ray	MUS2c	USN	Indiana
HUVAL, Ivan Joseph	S1c	USN	Louisiana
HUX, Leslie Creade	PFC	USMC	Louisiana
HUYS, Arthur Albert	S1c	USN	Indiana
HYDE, William Hughes	COX	USN	Missouri
IAK, Joseph Claude	Y3c	USN	
IBBOTSON, Howard Burt	F1c	USN	California
INGALLS, Richard Fitch	SC3c	USN	New York
INGALLS, Theodore "A"	SC3c	USN	New York
INGRAHAM, David Archie	FC3c	USN	
ISHAM, Orville Adalbert	CGMA	USN	Hawaii
ISOM, Luther James	S1c	USN	Alabama
IVERSEN, Earl Henry	S2c	USN	California
IVERSEN, Norman Kenneth	S2c	USN	California
IVEY, Charles Andrew Jr.	S2c	USN	California
JACKSON, David Paul Jr.	S1c	USN	Texas
JACKSON, Robert Woods	Y3c	USN	Iowa
JAMES, John Burditt	S1c	USN	Texas
JANTE, Edwin Earl	Y3c	USN	
JANZ, Clifford Thurston	LT	USN	California
JASTRZEMSKI, Edwin Charles	S1c	USN	Michigan
JEANS, Victor Lawrence	WT2c	USN	Oregon
JEFFRIES, Keith	COX	USN	Pennsylvania
JENKINS, Robert Henry Dawson	S2c	USN	Texas
JENSEN, Keith Marlow	EM3c	USN	Utah
JERRISON, Donald D.	CPL	USMC	California
JOHANN, Paul Frederick	GM3c	USN	Iowa
JOHNSON, David Andrew Jr.	OC2c	USN	Virginia
JOHNSON, Edmund Russell	MM1c	USN	California
JOHNSON, John Russell	RM3c	USN	Massachuttes
JOHNSON, Samuel Earle	CDR(MC)	USN	Alabama
JOHNSON, Sterling Conrad	COX	USN	Washington
JOLLEY, Berry Stanley	S2c	USNR	Idaho
JONES, Daniel Pugh	S2c	USN	Alabama
JONES, Edmon Ethmer	S1c	USN	Colorado
JONES, Floyd Baxter	MATT2c	USN	
JONES, Harry Cecil	GM3c	USN	Kansas
JONES, Henry Jr.	MATT1c	USN	California
JONES, Homer Lloyd	S1c	USN	Colorado
JONES, Hugh Junior	S2c	USN	California

Name	Rank	Service	Home
JONES, Leland	S1c	USN	Tennessee
JONES, Quincy Eugene	PFC	USMC	Texas
JONES, Thomas Raymond	ENS	USNR	Louisiana
JONES, Warren Allen	Y3c	USN	Nebraska
JONES, Willard Worth	S1c	USN	Tennessee
JONES, Woodrow Wilson	S2c	USN	Alabama
JOYCE, Calvin Wilbur	F2c	USN	Ohio
JUDD, Albert John	COX	USN	Michigan
KAGARICE, Harold Lee	CSKA	USN	California
KAISER, Robert Oscar	F1c	USN	Missouri
KALINOWSKI, Henry	PVT	USMCR	Texas
KATT, Eugene Louis	S2c	USN	California
KEEN, Billy Mack	PVT	USMC	Texas
KELLER, Paul Daniel	MLDR2c	USN	Michigan
KELLEY, James Dennis	SF3c	USN	Oklahoma
KELLOGG, Wilbur Leroy	F1c	USN	Iowa
KELLY, Robert Lee	CEMA	USN	California
KENISTON, Donald Lee	S2c	USN	Ohio
KENISTON, Kenneth Howard	F3c	USN	Ohio
KENNARD, Kenneth Frank	GM3c	USN	Idaho
KENNINGTON, Charles Cecil	S1c	USN	Tennessee
KENNINGTON, Milton Homer	S1c	USN	Tennessee
KENT, Texas Thomas Jr.	S2c	USN	Arkansas
KIDD, Isaac Campbell	RADM	USN	
KIEHN, Ronald William	MM2c	USN	California
KIESELBACH, Charles Ermin	CM1c	USN	California
KING, Gordon Blane	S1c	USN	Tennessee
KING, Leander Cleaveland	S1c	USN	Texas
KING, Lewis Meyer	F1c	USN	
KING, Robert Nicholas Jr.	ENS	USNR	New York
KINNEY, Frederick William	MUS1c	USN	Washington
KINNEY, Gilbert Livingston	QM2c	USN	California
KIRCHHOFF, Wilbur Albert	S1c	USN	Missouri
KIRKPATRICK, Thomas Larcy	CAPT(CHC)	USN	Missouri
KLANN, Edward	SC1c	USN	Michigan
KLINE, Robert Edwin	GM2c	USN	New York
KLOPP, Francis Lawrence	GM3c	USN	Ohio
KNIGHT, Robert Wagner	EM3c	USN	Ohio
KNUBEL, William Jr.	S1c	USN	Missouri
KOCH, Walter Ernest	S1c	USN	Minnesota
KOENEKAMP, Clarence D.	F1c	USN	Washington
KOEPPE, Herman Oliver	SC3c	USN	Illinois
KOLAJAJCK, Brosig	S1c	USN	Texas
KONNICK, Albert Joseph	CM3c	USN	Pennsylvania
KOSEC, John Anthony	BM2c	USN	California
KOVAR, Robert	S1c	USN	Illinois
KRAHN, James Albert	PFC	USMC	North Dakota
KRAMB, James Henry	S1c	USN	New York
KRAMB, John David	MSMTH1c	USN	New York

Name	Rank	Service	Home
KRAMER, Robert Rudolph	GM2c	USN	Indiana
KRAUSE, Fred Joseph	S1c	USN	Minnesota
KRISSMAN, Max Sam	S2c	USN	California
KRUGER, Richard Warren	QM2c	USN	California
KRUPPA, Adolph Louis	S1c	USN	Texas
KUKUK, Howard Helgi	S1c	USN	New York
KULA, Stanley	SC3c	USN	Nebraska
KUSIE, Donald Joseph	RM3c	USN	New York
LA FRANCEA, William Richard	S1c	USN	Michigan
LA MAR, Ralph "B"	FC3c	USN	California
LA SALLE, Willard Dale	S1c	USN	Washington
LADERACH, Robert Paul	FC2c	USN	West Virginia
LAKE, John Ervin Jr.	WO(PYCLK)	USN	California
LAKIN, Donald Lapier	S1c	USN	California
LAKIN, Joseph Jordan	S1c	USN	California
LAMB, George Samuel	CSFA	USN	California
LANDMAN, Henry	AM2c	USN	Michigan
LANDRY, James Joseph Jr.	BKR2c	USN	Massachusetts
LANE, Edward Wallace	COX	USN	
LANE, Mancel Curtis	S1c	USN	Oklahoma
LANGE, Richard Charles	S1c	USN	California
LANGENWALTER, Orville J.	SK2c	USN	Iowa
LANOUETTE, Henry John	COX	USN	Connecticut
LARSON, Leonard Carl	F3c	USN	Washington
LATTIN, Bleecker	RM3c	USN	
LEE, Carroll Volney Jr.	S1c	USN	Texas
LEE, Henry Lloyd	S1c	USN	South Carolina
LEEDY, David Alonzo	FC2c	USN	Iowa
LEGGETT, John Goldie	BM2c	USN	Washington
LEGROS, Joseph McNeil	S1c	USN	Louisiana
LEIGH, Malcolm Hedrick	GM3c	USN	North Carolina
LEIGHT, James Webster	S2c	USN	California
LEOPOLD, Robert Lawrence	ENS	USNR	Kentucky
LESMEISTER, Steve Louie	EM3c	USN	North Dakota
LEVAR, Frnak	CWTP	USNR	Washington
LEWIS, Wayne Alman	CM3c	USN	South Carolina
LEWISON, Neil Stanley	FC3c	USN	Wisconsin
LIGHTFOOT, Worth Ross	GM3c	USN	
LINBO, Gordon Ellsworth	GM1c	USN	Washington
LINCOLN, John William	F1c	USN	Iowa
LINDSAY, James E.	PFC	USMC	California
LINDSAY, James Mitchell	SF2c	USN	Colorado
LINTON, George Edward	F2c	USN	
LIPKE, Clarence William	F2c	USN	Michigan
LIPPLE, John Anthony	SF1c	USN	Iowa
LISENBY, Daniel Edward	S1c	USN	
LIVERS, Raymond Edward	S1c	USN	New Mexico
LIVERS, Wayne Nicholas	F1c	USN	New Mexico
LOCK, Douglas A.	S1c	USN	New York

Name	Rank	Service	Home
LOHMAN, Earl Wynne	S1c	USN	
LOMAX, Frank Stuart	ENS	USN	Nebraska
LOMIBAO, Marciano	OS1c	USN	Philipines
LONG, Benjamin Franklin	CYP	USN	North Carolina
LOUNSBURY, Thomas William	S2c	USN	Illinois
LOUSTANAU, Charles Bernard	S1c	USN	Iowa
LOVELAND, Frank Crook	S2c	USN	Idaho
LOVSHIN, William Joseph	PFC	USMC	Minnesota
LUCEY, Neil Jermiah	S1c	USN	New Jersey
LUNA, James Edward	S2c	USN	Oklahoma
LUZIER, Ernest Burton	MM2c	USN	
LYNCH, Emmett Isaac	MUS2c	USN	Washington
LYNCH, James Robert Jr.	GM3c	USN	Texas
LYNCH, William Joseph Jr.	S1c	USN	Texas
MADDOX, Raymond Dudley	CEMP	USN	California
MADRID, Arthur John	S2c	USN	California
MAFNAS, Francisco Reyes	MATT2c	USN	Guam
MAGEE, Gerald James	SK3c	USN	New York
MALECKI, Frank Edward	CYP	USN	California
MALINOWSKI, John Stanley	SM3c	USNR	Michigan
MALSON, Harry Lynn	SK3c	USN	Indiana
MANION, Edward Paul	S2c	USN	Illinois
MANLOVE, Arthur Cleon	WO(ELEC)	USN	California
MANN, William Edward	GM3c	USN	Washington
MANNING, Leroy	S2c	USN	Kentucky
MANSKE, Robert Francis	Y2c	USN	Iowa
MARINICH, Steve Matt	COX	USN	Utah
MARIS, Elwood Henry	S1c	USN	
MARLING, Joseph Henry	S2c	USN	Montana
MARLOW, Urban Herschel	COX	USN	Missouri
MARSH, Benjamin Raymond Jr.	ENS	USNR	Michigan
MARSH, William Arthur	S1c	USN	
MARSHALL, Thomas Donald	S2c	USN	California
MARTIN, Hugh Lee	Y3c	USN	Utah
MARTIN, James Albert	BM1c	USN	Texas
MARTIN, James Orrwell	S2c	USN	California
MARTIN, Luster Lee	F3c	USN	Arkansas
MASON, Byron Dalley	S2c	USN	Idaho
MASTEL, Clyde Harold	S2c	USN	California
MASTERS, Dayton Monroe	GM3c	USN	Texas
MASTERSON, Cleburne E. Carl	PHM1c	USN	California
MATHEIN, Harold Richard	BMKR2c	USN	Illinois
MATHISON, Charles Harris	S1c	USN	Wisconsin
MATNEY, Vernon Merferd	F1c	USN	Wisconsin
MATTOX, James Durant	AM3c	USN	Florida
MAY, Louis Eugene	SC2c	USN	Kansas
MAYBEE, George Frederick	RM2c	USNR	California
MAYFIELD, Lester Ellsworth	F1c	USN	Colorado
MAYO, Rex Haywood	EM2c	USN	Florida

Name	Rank	Service	Home
MEANS, Louis	MATT1c	USN	Texas
MEARES, John Morgan	S2c	USN	South Carolina
MENEFEE, James Austin	S1c	USN	Mississippi
MENO, Vicente Gogue	MATT2c	USN	
MENZENSKI, Stanley Paul	COX	USN	
MERRILL, Howard Deal	ENS	USN	Utah
MILES, Oscar Wright	S1c	USN	Arkansas
MILLER, Chester John	F2c	USN	Michigan
MILLER, Doyle Allen	COX	USN	Arkansas
MILLER, Forrest Newton	CEMP	USN	California
MILLER, George Stanley	S1c	USN	Ohio
MILLER, Jessie Zimmer	S1c	USN	Ohio
MILLER, John David	S1c	USN	
MILLER, William Oscar	SM3c	USN	Illinois
MILLIGAN, Weldon Hawvey	S1c	USN	Texas
MIMS, Robert Lang	S1c	USN	Georgia
MINEAR, Richard J. Jr.	PFC	USMC	
MLINAR, Joseph	COX	USN	Pennsylvania
MOLPUS, Richard Preston	CMSMTHP	USN	California
MONROE, Donald	MATT2c	USN	Missouri
MONTGOMERY, Robert E.	S2c	USN	California
MOODY, Robert Edward	S1c	USN	Mississippi
MOORE, Douglas Carlton	S1c	USN	South Carolina
MOORE, Fred Kenneth	S1c	USN	Texas
MOORE, James Carlton	SF3c	USN	South Carolina
MOORHOUSE, William Starks	MUS2c	USN	Kansas
MOORMAN, Russell Lee	S2c	USN	California
MORGAN, Wayne	S1c	USN	California
MORGAREIDGE, James Orries	F2c	USN	Wyoming
MORLEY, Eugene Elvis	F2c	USN	Illinois
MORRIS, Owen Newton	S1c	USN	Alabama
MORRISON, Earl Leroy	S1c	USN	Montana
MORSE, Edward Charles	S2c	USN	Michigan
MORSE, Francis Jerome	BM1c	USN	California
MORSE, George Robert	S2c	USN	Montana
MORSE, Norman Roi	WT2c	USN	Virginia
MOSS, Tommy Lee	MATT2c	USN	Kentucky
MOSTEK, Francis Clayton	PFC	USMC	Idaho
MOULTON, Gordon Eddy	F1c	USN	California
MUNCY, Claude	MM2c	USN	California
MURDOCK, Charles Luther	WT1c	USN	Alabama
MURDOCK, Melvin Elijah	WT2c	USN	Alabama
MURPHY, James Joseph	S1c	USN	Arizona
MURPHY, James Palmer	F3c	USN	Ohio
MURPHY, Jessie Huell	S1c	USN	Louisiana
MURPHY, Thomas J. Jr.	SK1c	USN	Virginia
MYERS, James Gernie	SK1c	USN	Missouri
McCARRENS, James Francis	CPL	USMC	Illinois
McCARY, William Moore	S2c	USN	Alabama

Name	Rank	Service	Home
McCLAFFERTY, John Charles	BM2c	USN	Ohio
McCLUNG, Harvey Manford	ENS	USNR	Pennsylvania
McFADDIN, Lawrence James	Y2c	USN	California
McGLASSON, Joe Otis	GM3c	USN	Illinois
McGRADY, Samme Willie Genes	MATT1c	USN	Alabama
McGUIRE, Francis Raymond	SK2c	USN	Michigan
McHUGHES, John Breckenridge	CWTA	USN	Washington
McINTOSH, Harry George	S1c	USN	Virginia
McKINNIE, Russell	MATT2c	USN	
McKOSKY, Michael Martin	S1c	USN	Oklahoma
McPHERSON, John Blair	S1c	USN	Tennessee
NAASZ, Erwin H.	SF2c	USN	Kansas
NADEL, Alexander Joseph	MUS2c	USN	New York
NATIONS, James Garland	FC2c	USN	South Carolina
NAYLOR, "J" "D"	SM2c	USN	Louisiana
NEAL, Tom Dick	S1c	USN	Texas
NECESSARY, Charles Raymond	S1c	USN	Missouri
NEIPP, Paul	S2c	USN	California
NELSEN, George	SC2c	USN	Washington
NELSON, Harl Coplin	S1c	USN	Arkansas
NELSON, Henry Clarence	BM1c	USN	Minnesota
NELSON, Lawrence Adolphus	CTCP	USN	California
NELSON, Richard Eugene	F3c	USN	North Dakota
NICHOLS, Alfred Rose	S1c	USN	Alabama
NICHOLS, Bethel Allan	S1c	USN	Washington
NICHOLS, Clifford Leroy	TC1c	USN	
NICHOLS, Louis Duffie	S2c	USN	Alabama
NICHOLSON, Glen Eldon	EM3c	USN	North Dakota
NICHOLSON, Hancel Grant	S1c	USN	
NIDES, Thomas James	EM1c	USN	California
NIELSEN, Floyd Theadore	CM3c	USN	Utah
NOLATUBBY, Henry Ellis	PFC	USMC	California
NOONAN, Robert Harold	S1c	USN	Michigan
NOWOSACKI, Theodore Lucian	ENS	USNR	New York
NUSSER, Raymond Alfred	GM3c	USN	
NYE, Frank Erskine	S1c	USN	California
O'BRIEN, Joseph Bernard	PFC	USMC	Illinois
O'BRYAN, George David	FC3c	USN	Massachusetts
O'BRYAN, Joseph Benjamin	FC3c	USN	Massachusetts
O'NEALL, Rex Eugene	S1c	USN	Colorado
O'NEILL, William Thomas Jr.	ENS	USNR	Connecticut
OCHOSKI, Henry Francis	GM2c	USN	Washington
OFF, Virgil Simon	S1c	USN	Colorado
OGLE, Victor Willard	S2c	USN	Oklahoma
OGLESBY, Lonnie Harris	S2c	USN	Mississippi
OLIVER, Raymond Brown	S1c	USN	California
OLSEN, Edward Kern	ENS	USNR	Kansas
OLSON, Glen Martin	S2c	USN	Washington
ORR, Dwight Jerome	S1c	USN	California

Name	Rank	Service	Home
ORZECH, Stanislaus Joseph	S2c	USN	Connecticut
OSBORNE, Mervin Eugene	F1c	USN	Kentucky
OSTRANDER, Leland Grimstead	PHM3c	USN	Minnesota
OTT, Peter Dean	S1c	USN	Ohio
OWEN, Fredrick Halden	S2c	USN	Texas
OWENS, Richard Allen	SK2c	USN	Colorado
OWSLEY, Thomas Lea	SC2c	USN	Idaho
PACE, Amos Paul	BM1c	USN	California
PARKES, Harry Edward	BM1c	USN	California
PAROLI, Peter John	BKR3c	USN	California
PATTERSON, Clarence Rankin	PFC	USMC	
PATTERSON, Harold Lemuel	S1c	USN	Texas
PATTERSON, Richard Jr.	SF3c	USN	Connecticut
PAULMAND, Hilery	OS2c	USN	Philippines
PAVINI, Bruno	S1c	USN	California
PAWLOWSKI, Raymond Paul	S1c	USN	New York
PEARCE, Alonzo Jr.	S1c	USN	
PEARSON, Norman Cecil	S2c	USN	California
PEARSON, Robert Stanley	F3c	USN	Montana
PEAVEY, William Howard	QM2c	USN	Iowa
PECKHAM, Howard William	F2c	USN	Missouri
PEDROTTI, Francis James	PVT	USMC	Missouri
PEERY, Max Valdyne	S2c	USN	California
PELESCHAK, Michael	S1c	USN	Alabama
PELTIER, John Arthur	EM3c	USN	Ohio
PENTON, Howard Lee	S1c	USN	Alabama
PERKINS, George Ernest	F1c	USN	Rhode Island
PETERSON, Albert H. Jr.	FC3c	USN	New Jersey
PETERSON, Elroy Vernon	FC2c	USN	California
PETERSON, Hardy Wilbur	FC3c	USN	Washington
PETERSON, Roscoe Earl	S2c	USN	California
PETTIT, Charles Ross	CRMP	USN	California
PETYAK, John Joseph	S1c	USN	Tennessee
PHELPS, George Edward	S1c	USN	New York
PHILBIN, James Richard	S1c	USN	Colorado
PIASECKI, Alexander Louis	CPL	USMC	
PIKE, Harvey Lee	EM3c	USN	Georgia
PIKE, Lewis Jackson	S1c	USN	Georgia
PINKHAM, Albert Wesley	S2c	USN	North Carolina
PITCHER, Walter Giles	GM1c	USN	California
POOL, Elmer Leo	S1c	USN	Indiana
POOLE, Ralph Ernest	S1c	USN	Ohio
POST, Darrell Albert	CMMA	USN	California
POVESKO, George	S1c	USN	Connecticut
POWELL, Jack Speed	PFC	USMC	California
POWELL, Thomas George	S1c	USN	Illinois
POWER, Abner Franklin	PVT	USMC	
PRESSON, Wayne Harold	S1c	USN	Ohio
PRICE, Arland Earl	RM2c	USN	Oregon

Name	Rank	Service	Home
PRITCHETT, Robert Leo Jr.	S1c	USN	Louisiana
PUCKETT, Edwin Lester	SK3c	USN	Kentucky
PUGH, John Jr.	SF3c	USN	California
PUTNAM, Avis Boyd	SC3c	USN	Alabama
PUZIO, Edward	S1c	USN	Pennsylvania
QUARTO, Mike Joseph	S1c	USN	Connecticut
QUINATA, Jose Sanchez	MATT2c	USN	Guam
RADFORD, Neal Jason	MUS2c	USN	Nebraska
RASMUSSEN, Arthur Severin	CM1c	USN	California
RASMUSSON, George Vernon	F3c	USN	Minnesota
RATKOVICH, William	WT1c	USN	California
RAWHOUSER, Glen Donald	F3c	USN	Oregon
RAWSON, Clyde Jackson	BM1c	USN	Maryland
RAY, Harry Joseph	BM2c	USN	California
REAVES, Casbie	S1c	USN	Arkansas
RECTOR, Clay Cooper	SK3c	USN	Kentucky
REECE, John Jeffris	S2c	USN	Oklahoma
REED, James Buchanan Jr.	SK1c	USN	California
REED, Ray Ellison	S2c	USN	Oklahoma
REGISTER, Paul James	LCDR	USN	North Dakota
REINHOLD, Rudolph Herbert	PVT	USMC	Utah
RESTIVO, Jack Martin	Y2c	USN	Maryland
REYNOLDS, Earl Arthur	S2c	USN	Colorado
REYNOLDS, Jack Franklyn	S1c	USN	
RHODES, Birb Richard	F2c	USN	Tennessee
RHODES, Mark Alexander	S1c	USN	North Carolina
RICE, William Albert	S2c	USN	Washington
RICH, Claude Edward	S1c	USN	Florida
RICHAR, Raymond Lyle	S1c	USN	
RICHARDSON, Warren John	COX	USN	Pennsylvania
RICHISON, Fred Louis	GM3c	USN	California
RICHTER, Albert Wallace	COX	USN	
RICO, Guadalupe Augustine	S1c	USN	California
RIDDEL, Eugene Edward	S1c	USN	Michigan
RIGANTI, Fred	SF3c	USN	California
RIGGINS, Gerald Herald	S1c	USN	California
RIVERA, Francisco Unpingoo	MATT2c	USN	Guam
ROBERTS, Dwight Fisk	F1c	USN	Kansas
ROBERTS, Kenneth Franklin	BM2c	USN	
ROBERTS, McClellan Taylor	CPHMP	USN	California
ROBERTS, Walter Scott Jr.	RM1c	USN	Missouri
ROBERTS, Wilburn Carle	BKR3c	USN	Louisiana
ROBERTS, William Francis	S2c	USN	
ROBERTSON, Edgar Jr.	MATT3c	USN	Virginia
ROBERTSON, James Milton	MM1c	USN	Tennessee
ROBINSON, Harold Thomas	S2c	USN	California
ROBINSON, James William	S2c	USN	California
ROBINSON, John James	EM1c	USN	Oregon
ROBINSON, Robert Warren	PHM3c	USN	West Virginia

Name	Rank	Service	Home
ROBY, Raymond Arthur	S1c	USN	California
RODGERS, John Dayton	S1c	USN	Pennsylvania
ROEHM, Harry Turner	MM2c	USN	Illinois
ROGERS, Thomas Spurgeon	CWTP	USN	Alabama
ROMANO, Simon	OC1c	USN	Virginia
ROMBALSKI, Donald Roger	S2c	USN	Washington
ROMERO, Vladimir M.	S1c	USN	Virginia
ROOT, Melvin Lenord	S1c	USN	Ohio
ROSE, Chester Clay	BM1c	USN	Kentucky
ROSENBERY, Orval Robert	SF2c	USN	Illinois
ROSS, Deane Lundy	S2c	USN	New York
ROSS, William Fraser	GM3c	USN	New York
ROWE, Eugene Joseph	S1c	USN	New Jersey
ROWELL, Frank Malcom	S2c	USN	Texas
ROYALS, William Nicholas	F1c	USN	Virginia
ROYER, Howard Dale	GM3c	USN	Ohio
ROZAR, John Frank	WT2c	USN	California
ROZMUS, Joseph Stanley	S1c	USN	New Hampshire
RUDDOCK, Cecil Roy	S1c	USN	
RUGGERIO, William	FC3c	USN	
RUNCKEL, Robert Gleason	BUG1c	USN	
RUNIAK, Nicholas	S1c	USN	New Jersey
RUSH, Richard Perry	S1c	USN	Texas
RUSHER, Orville Lester	MM1c	USN	Missouri
RUSKEY, Joseph John	CBMP	USN	California
RUTKOWSKI, John Peter	S1c	USN	New York
RUTTAN, Dale Andrew	EM3c	USN	Florida
SAMPSON, Sherley Rolland	RM3c	USN	Minnesota
SANDALL, Merrill Deith	SF3c	USN	Illinois
SANDERS, Eugene Thomas	ENS	USN	New York
SANDERSON, James Harvey	MUS2c	USN	California
SANFORD, Thomas Steger	F3c	USN	
SANTOS, Filomeno	OC2c	USN	California
SATHER, William Ford	PMKR1c	USN	California
SAVAGE, Walter Samuel Jr.	ENS	USNR	Louisiana
SAVIN, Tom	RM2c	USN	Nebraska
SAVINSKI, Michael	S1c	USN	Pennsylvania
SCHDOWSKI, Joseph	S1c	USN	
SCHEUERLEIN, George Albert	GM3c	USN	Pennsylvania
SCHILLER, Ernest	S2c	USN	Texas
SCHLUND, Elmer Pershing	MM1c	USN	Nebraska
SCHMIDT, Vernon Joseph	S1c	USN	Minnesota
SCHNEIDER, William Jacob	PFC	USMC	
SCHRANK, Harold Arthur	BKR1c	USN	Texas
SCHROEDER, Henry	BM1c	USN	New Jersey
SCHUMAN, Herman Lincoln	SK1c	USN	California
SCHURR, John	EM2c	USN	Kansas
SCILLEY, Harold Hugh	SF2c	USN	Montana
SCOTT, A. J.	S2c	USN	

Name	Rank	Service	Home
SCOTT, Crawford Edward	PFC	USMC	
SCOTT, George Harrison	PFC	USMC	
SCRUGGS, Jack Leo	MUS2c	USN	California
SEAMAN, Russell Otto	F1c	USN	Iowa
SEELEY, William Eugene	S1c	USN	Connecticut
SEVIER, Charles Clifton	S1c	USN	California
SHANNON, William Alfred	S1c	USN	Idaho
SHARBAUGH, Harry Robert	GM3c	USN	Pennsylvania
SHARON, Lewis Purdie	MM2c	USN	California
SHAW, Clyde Donald	S1c	USN	Ohio
SHAW, Robert K.	MUS2c	USN	Texas
SHEFFER, George Robert	S1c	USN	Indiana
SHERRILL, Warren Joseph	Y2c	USN	Texas
SHERVEN, Richard Stanton	EM3c	USN	North Dakota
SHIFFMAN, Harold Ely	RM3c	USN	Michigan
SHILEY, Paul Eugene	S1c	USN	Pennsylvania
SHIMER, Melvin Irvin	S1c	USN	
SHIVE, Gordon Eshom	PFC	USMC	California
SHIVE, Malcolm Holman	RM3c	USNR	California
SHIVELY, Benjamin Franklin	F1c	USN	Michigan
SHORES, Irland Jr.	S1c	USN	Alabama
SHUGART, Marvin John	S1c	USN	Colorado
SIBLEY, Delmar Dale	S1c	USN	New York
SIDDERS, Russell Lewis	S1c	USN	Ohio
SIDELL, John Henry	GM2c	USN	Illinois
SILVEY, Jesse	MM2c	USN	Texas
SIMENSEN, Carleton Elliott	2LT	USMC	
SIMON, Walter Hamilton	S1c	USN	New Jersey
SIMPSON, Albert Eugene	S1c	USN	
SKEEN, Harvey Leroy	S2c	USN	Arizona
SKILES, Charley Jackson Jr.	S2c	USN	Virginia
SKILES, Eugene	S2c	USN	
SLETTO, Earl Clifton	MM1c	USN	Minnesota
SMALLEY, Jack G.	S1c	USN	Ohio
SMART, George David	COX	USN	Montana
SMESTAD, Halge Hojem	RM2c	USN	Minnesota
SMITH, Albert Joseph	LTJG	USN	Virginia
SMITH, Earl Jr.	S1c	USN	Missouri
SMITH, Earl Walter	FC3c	USN	Florida
SMITH, Edward	GM3c	USN	Illinois
SMITH, Harry	S2c	USNR	California
SMITH, John A.	SF3c	USN	Ohio
SMITH, John Edward	S1c	USN	California
SMITH, Luther Kent	S1c	USN	Tennessee
SMITH, Mack Lawrence	S1c	USN	Arkansas
SMITH, Marvin Ray	S1c	USN	Texas
SMITH, Orville Stanley	ENS	USN	Oklahoma
SMITH, Walter Tharnel	MATT2c	USN	Mississippi
SNIFF, Jack Bertrand	CPL	USMC	

Name	Rank	Service	Home
SOENS, Harold Mathias	SC1c	USN	California
SOOTER, James Fredrick	RM3c	USN	
SORENSEN, Holger Earl	S1c	USN	New Mexico
SOUTH, Charles Braxton	S1c	USN	Alabama
SPENCE, Merle Joe	S1c	USN	Tennessee
SPOTZ, Maurice Edwin	F1c	USN	Illinois
SPREEMAN, Robert Lawrence	GM3c	USN	Michigan
SPRINGER, Charles Harold	S2c	USN	California
STALLINGS, Kermit Braxton	F1c	USN	North Carolina
STARKOVICH, Charles	EM3c	USN	Washington
STARKOVICH, Joseph Jr.	F2c	USN	Washington
STAUDT, Alfred Parker	F3c	USN	Washington
STEFFAN, Joseph Philip	BM2c	USN	Illinois
STEIGLEDER, Lester Leroy	COX	USN	Ohio
STEINHOFF, Lloyd Delroy	S1c	USN	California
STEPHENS, Woodrow Wilson	EM1c	USN	Washington
STEPHENSON, Hugh Donald	S1c	USN	New York
STEVENS, Jack Hazelip	S1c	USN	Texas
STEVENS, Theodore R.	AMM2c	USN	California
STEVENSON, Frank Jake	PFC	USMC	New York
STEWART, Thomas Lester	SC3c	USN	Arkansas
STILLINGS, Gerald Fay	F2c	USN	
STOCKMAN, Harold William	FC3c	USN	Idaho
STOCKTON, Louis Alton	S2c	USN	California
STODDARD, William Edison	S1c	USN	Louisiana
STOPYRA, Julian John	RM3c	USN	Massachusetts
STORM, Laun Lee	Y1c	USN	California
STOVALL, Richard Patt	PFC	USMC	
STRANGE, Charles Orval	F2c	USN	
STRATTON, John Raymond	S1c	USN	Indiana
SUGGS, William Alfred	S1c	USN	Florida
SULSER, Frederick Franklin	GM3c	USN	Ohio
SUMMERS, Glen Allen	Y1c	USN	Washington
SUMMERS, Harold Edgar	SM2c	USN	Ohio
SUMNER, Oren	S2c	USN	New Mexico
SUTTON, Clyde Westly	CCSTDP	USN	California
SUTTON, George Woodrow	SK1c	USN	Kentucky
SWIONTEK, Stanley Stephen	FLDCK	USN	Illinois
SWISHER, Charles Elijah	S1c	USN	California
SYMONETTE, Henry	OC1c	USN	California
SZABO, Theodore Stephen	PVT	USMCR	
TAMBOLLEO, Victor Charles	SF3c	USN	Maryland
TANNER, Russell Allen	GM3c	USN	Washington
TAPIE, Edward Casamiro	MM2c	USN	California
TAPP, Lambert Ray	GM3c	USN	Kentucky
TARG, John	CWTP	USN	California
TAYLOR, Aaron Gust	MATT1c	USN	California
TAYLOR, Charles Benton	EM3c	USN	Illinois
TAYLOR, Harry Theodore	GM2c	USN	Indiana

Name	Rank	Service	Home
TAYLOR, Robert Denzil	COX	USN	Iowa
TEELING, Charles Madison	CPRTP	USNR	California
TEER, Allen Ray	EM1c	USN	California
TENNELL, Raymond Clifford	S1c	USN	Texas
TERRELL, John Raymond	F2c	USN	Arkansas
THEILLER, Rudolph	S1c	USN	California
THOMAS, Houston O'Neal	COX	USN	Texas
THOMAS, Randall James	S1c	USN	West Virginia
THOMAS, Stanley Horace	F3c	USN	
THOMAS, Vincent Duron	COX	USN	California
THOMPSON, Charles Leroy	S1c	USN	Illinois
THOMPSON, Irven Edgar	S1c	USN	Ohio
THOMPSON, Robert Gary	SC1c	USN	California
THORMAN, John Christopher	EM2c	USN	Iowa
THORNTON, George Hayward	GM3c	USN	Mississippi
TINER, Robert Reaves	F2c	USN	Texas
TISDALE, William Esley	CWTP	USN	California
TRIPLETT, Thomas Edgar	S1c	USN	California
TROVATO, Tom	S1c	USN	California
TUCKER, Raymond Edward	COX	USN	Indiana
TUNTLAND, Earl Eugene	S1c	USN	North Dakota
TURNIPSEED, John Morgan	F3c	USN	Arkansas
TUSSEY, Lloyd Harold	EM3c	USN	North Carolina
TYSON, Robert	FC3c	USN	Louisiana
UHRENHOLDT, Andrew Curtis	ENS	USNR	Wisconsin
VALENTE, Richard Dominic	GM3c	USN	California
VAN ATTA, Garland Wade	MM1c	USN	California
VAN HORN, James Randolf	S2c	USN	Arizona
VAN VALKENBURGH, Franklin	CAPT(CO)	USN	Minnesota
VARCHOL, Brinley	GM2c	USN	Pennsylvania
VAUGHAN, William Frank	PHM2c	USN	
VEEDER, Gordon Elliott	S2c	USN	Idaho
VELIA, Galen Steve	SM3c	USN	Kansas
VIEIRA, Alvaro Everett	S2c	USN	Rhode Island
VOJTA, Walter Arnold	S1c	USN	Minnesota
VOSTI, Anthony August	GM3c	USN	California
WAGNER, Mearl James	SC2c	USN	California
WAINWRIGHT, Silas Alonzo	PHM1c	USN	New York
WAIT, Wayland Lemoyne	S1c	USN	
WALKER, Bill	S1c	USN	Texas
WALLACE, Houston Oliver	WT1c	USN	Arkansas
WALLACE, James Frank	S1c	USN	Wisconsin
WALLACE, Ralph Leroy	F3c	USN	Oregon
WALLENSTIEN, Richard Henry	S1c	USN	
WALTERS, Clarence Arthur	S2c	USN	California
WALTERS, William Spurgeon Jr.	FC3c	USN	New Mexico
WALTHER, Edward Alfred	FC3c	USN	
WALTON, Alva Dowding	Y3c	USN	Utah
WARD, Albert Lewis	S1c	USN	Oklahoma

Name	Rank	Service	Home
WARD, William E.	COX	USN	Illinois
WATKINS, Lenvil Leo	F2c	USN	Kentucky
WATSON, William Lafayette	F3c	USN	Florida
WATTS, Sherman Maurice	HA1c	USN	Arkansas
WATTS, Victor Ed	GM3c	USN	Texas
WEAVER, Richard Walter	S1c	USN	Nevada
WEBB, Carl Edward	PFC	USMC	
WEBSTER, Harold Dwayne	S2c	USN	Colorado
WEEDEN, Carl Alfred	ENS	USN	Colorado
WEIDELL, William Peter	S2c	USN	Minnesota
WEIER, Bernard Arthur	PVT	USMC	Illinois
WELLER, Ludwig Fredrick	CSKP	USN	California
WELLS, Floyd Arthur	RM2c	USN	
WELLS, Harvey Anthony	SF2c	USN	California
WELLS, Raymond Virgil Jr.	S1c	USN	Missouri
WELLS, William Bennett	S1c	USN	Missouri
WEST, Broadus Franklin	S1c	USN	South Carolina
WEST, Webster Paul	S1c	USN	Arkansas
WESTCOTT, William Percy Jr.	S1c	USN	Indiana
WESTERFIELD, Ivan Ayers	S1c	USN	California
WESTIN, Donald Vern	F3c	USN	Oregon
WESTLUND, Fred Edwin	BM2c	USN	California
WHISLER, Gilbert Henry	PFC	USMC	
WHITAKER, John William Jr.	S1c	USN	Louisiana
WHITCOMB, Cecil Eugene	EM3c	USN	Michigan
WHITE, Charles William	MUS2c	USN	
WHITE, James Clifton	F1c	USN	Texas
WHITE, Vernon Russell	S1c	USN	South Carolina
WHITE, Volmer Dowin	S1c	USN	Mississippi
WHITEHEAD, Ulmont Irving Jr.	ENS	USN	Conneticut
WHITLOCK, Paul Morgan	S2c	USN	Texas
WHITSON, Ernest Hubert Jr.	MUS2c	USN	California
WHITT, William Byron	GM3c	USN	Kentucky
WHITTEMORE, Andrew Tiny	MATT2c	USN	Tennessee
WICK, Everett Morris	FC3c	USN	Oregon
WICKLUND, John Joseph	S1c	USN	Minnesota
WILCOX, Arnold Alfred	QM2c	USN	Iowa
WILL, Joseph William	S2c	USN	Colorado
WILLETTE, Laddie James	S2c	USN	Michigan
WILLIAMS, Adrian Delton	S1c	USN	Louisiana
WILLIAMS, Clyde Richard	MUS2c	USN	Oklahoma
WILLIAMS, George Washington	S1c	USN	Virginia
WILLIAMS, Jack Herman	RM3c	USNR	South Carolina
WILLIAMS, Laurence "A"	ENS(AV)	USNR	Ohio
WILLIAMSON, Randolph Jr.	MATT2c	USN	
WILLIAMSON, William Dean	RM2c	USNR	California
WILLIS, Robert Kenneth Jr.	S1c	USN	Louisiana
WILSON, Bernard Martin	RM3c	USNR	New York
WILSON, Comer A.	CBMP	USN	Alabama

Name	Rank	Service	Home
WILSON, Hurschel Woodrow	F2c	USN	Ohio
WILSON, John James	S1c	USN	California
WILSON, Neil Mataweny	CWO(MACH)	USN	California
WILSON, Ray Milo	RM3c	USNR	Iowa
WIMBERLY, Paul Edwin	GM3c	USN	Tennessee
WINDISH, Robert James	PVT	USMC	Missouri
WINDLE, Robert England	PFC	USMC	Illinois
WINTER, Edward	WO(MACH)	USNR	Washington
WITTENBERG, Russell Duane	PVT	USMC	
WOJTKIEWICZ, Frank Peter	CMMP	USN	California
WOLF, George Alexanderson Jr.	ENS	USNR	Pennsylvania
WOOD, Harold Baker	BM2c	USN	Colorado
WOOD, Horace Van	S1c	USN	Texas
WOOD, Roy Eugene	F1c	USN	Arizona
WOODS, Vernon Wesley	S1c	USN	Texas
WOODS, William Anthony	S2c	USN	New York
WOODWARD, Ardenne Allen	MM2c	USN	California
WOODY, Harlan Fred	S2c	USN	
WOOLF, Norman Bragg	CWTP	USN	Alabama
WRIGHT, Edward Henry	S2c	USN	Illinois
WYCKOFF, Robert Leroy	F1c	USN	New Jersey
YATES, Elmer Elias	SC3c	USN	Nebraska
YEATS, Charles Jr.	COX	USN	Illinois
YOMINE, Frank Peter	F2c	USN	Illinois
YOUNG, Eric Reed	ENS	USN	Colorado
YOUNG, Glendale Rex	S1c	USN	
YOUNG, Jay Wesley	S1c	USN	Utah
YOUNG, Vivan Louis	WT1c	USN	Virginia
ZEILER, John Virgel	S1c	USN	Colorado
ZIEMBRICKE, Steve A.	S1c	USN	New York
ZIMMERMAN, Fred	Cox	USN	North Dakota
ZIMMERMAN, Lloyd McDonald	S2c	USN	Missouri
ZWARUN, Michael Jr.	S1c(S2c)	USN	New Jersey

Index

197